EPRP

EPRP:
BETWEEN A ROCK AND A HARD PLACE, 1975-2008

❖

Solomon Ejigu Gebreselassie

THE RED SEA PRESS
Trenton | London | New Delhi | Cape Town | Nairobi | Addis Ababa | Asmara | Ibadan

THE RED SEA PRESS
541 West Ingham Avenue | Suite B
Trenton, New Jersey 08638

Copyright © 2014 Solomon Ejigu Gebreselassie

All rights reserved. No part of this publication may be reproduced, stored in a retrieval system or transmitted in any form or by any means electronic, mechanical, photocopying, recording or otherwise without the prior written permission of the publisher.

Book design: WibTaye Publishers
Cover design: Dapo Ojo-Ade

Library of Congress Cataloging-in-Publication Data

Solomon Gebreselassie, author.
  EPRP : between a rock and a hard place, 1975-2008 / Solomon Gebreselassie.
    pages cm
  Includes bibliographical references and index.
  ISBN 978-1-56902-382-2 (hard cover) -- ISBN 978-1-56902-383-9 (pbk.) 1. Ethiopian Peoples' Revolutionary Party--History. 2. Political parties--Ethiopia. 3. Ethiopia--Politics and government--1974-1991. 4. Ethiopia--Politics and government--1991- I. Title.
  JQ3769.A558S35 2013
  324.263075--dc23
                  2013039081

Dedication

Recently many books have been rightly dedicated to those who perished during the Red Terror scourge. The patriots of the 1970s-80s died and passed the baton in the relay race for Ethiopian democratization and prosperity. The baton is now in the hands of the patriotic elements of the current generation. Some of its members are in jail, others struggling in constraining conditions inside Ethiopia, and still others forced to flee their country and screaming for its well-being from afar. This book is dedicated to them on whose backs history has now put a big load. It is my staying hope that they will learn from the follies of my generation and avoid them on one hand, and on the other, be inspired by its unparalleled commitment to a cause. May they be able to accomplish the national goals and humbly say they were able to do it on the shoulders of giants.

Table of Contents

Acknowledgment xi
List of Acronyms xiii
Preface xv
Introduction xxi
Chapter One: The End Game 1
  The Urban Setting 1
  The Youth League - EPRP's Engine 5
  The Forced Confessions 10
  Relation with TPLF 11
  The Final Nail in the Coffin: The Fourth EPRP CC Plenum..... 21
  Internal Turmoil and the Aftermath of the 4th Plenum's
  Document 26
  UDW -Structure and Operations 32
  UDW Activities versus EPRP Ethical Standards 34
  The Cause: The Import of Unresolved Issues? 40
  Relation with the Eritrean Fronts 48
  EPRP in the Eyes of Foreign Writers 54
  Why a Radical Movement, and Not a Reformist One? 59
  The Marxist-Leninist Ideology Influence 64
Chapter Two: Licking the Wounds 77
  EPRA's Retreat into Eritrea to Relaunch and Re-Create Itself.. 77
  Bertya 79
  The Tragedy in Armachiho 82
Chapter Three: Eihapa Aleme Dur Aderech Lamei 85

The Background 85
Women's Specific Oppression 87
The Religious Divide 89
Fighting Against Peasant False Beliefs and Bad Practices 90
Why the People Have Good Memories About Eihapa Aleme?. 91
Chapter Four: Returning to the Golden Years 93
Quarra 93
The Second Party Congress 95
The Signature Accomplishments of the 2nd Congress 96
EDU: A Distraction during the Golden Age 102
Development and War: The Twin Sisters 105
Chapter Five: The Sun Sets On EPRP's Golden Age 113
The TPLF War on EPRA -Round 3 113
Falling in Enemy Hands 121
The Fate of the Armed Struggle 127
The Kiddnaping in Ghedariff 131
Gayyim 134
Chapter Six: The Role of Major Defections in EPRP/A 139
Pre-Quarra Defections 139
The Defections in Quarra: Mistrust and Instability 141
Chapter Seven: Notable Foreign Relations 147
Relations with China 147
Sudan 150
Chapter Eight: How Democratic Was EPRP? 157
Background 157
The Case of "Ha" and "Le" 159
Re-Evaluating Berhanemeskel Redda 162
The Sojourn in Merhabete/Menz 164
In the Army 167
Chapter Nine: The Woman Question 175
The Early Days 175
Women, EPRP, and the Yekatit Revolution 182

TABLE OF CONTENTS

Chapter Ten: EPRP in the Diaspora: the Fulcrum of United
Fronts in the Era of Multy-Partyism 189
  COEDF: Preparation, Formation and Activities 189
  What was Paris 1? 194
  The Scene at Bole and Going to Jail 196
  Paris 2 200
  EPRP's 25th Anniversary Symposium 202
  EPRP Political Work in Europe 204
  Ethiopian Patriotic Front/Army 205
  UEDF 209
  Alliance for Freedom and Democracy (AFD) 216
Epilogue 223
Selected Bibiography 227
Index 231

Acknowledgment

Several people have opened up themselves and told me the stories they were part of, or about other heroes whose stories they believed had to be told. These include Aklilu Kebede, Kinfe Adefrsew, Wosenyelesh Debela, Genet Tarekegne, Mohammed Ahimed Jemil, Mersha Yosef, Tafere Abera, Mesfin Tefera, Beyene Gura'a, Abebech Bekele, and Solomon Workneh. I thank them for their time and being a part of the immense history of EPRP. Others have facilitated for me to complete the book in various ways: Shaleka (Berhanu) has been wonderful in setting me up with key people, Nigussie and Fikrte provided accommodations and friendship while I was in DC in May 2012 to do some interviews, Asmamaw Hailu set a good example for me in writing his book on EPRA, and provided valuable documents. Others who gave me documents for which I am grateful include Mesfin Medhinie, Yosef Asferi and Aklilu Kebede.

I am also profoundly grateful to the following people whom I asked to review the draft and provided me with valuable input within the time limit I imposed on them: Dr. Ghelawdewos Araya, Kiflu Tadesse, Mehari Gebre Egziabher, Abune Biru, Tariku Debretsion, Mohammed Ahimed Jemil, and my friend since our high school days, Abdukie Keffene, who emphasized the roles of EPRP and *Meison* to be viewed in the context of being the first political parties ever in the country. One critic, who wanted to remain anonymous and who was with EPRA to the bitter end in Quarra, was not happy that I have not included every detail. Although I understand his frustration, such a task is simply too difficult for a single author. Others have to fill in the gaps. Others, whom I asked to critique the book draft, could not get to it due to time constraints. While the author is in a privileged position to cherry pick and selectively accept the comments he/she receives, I have done my best to accept and incorporate those comments that critically add value and fairness to the book. A few of my reviewers are subjects of criticism in my book, and I especially thank them not to let our disagreements color their view about the book.

I also would like to thank the following for providing me with some of the pictures in the book: Takele Tsega, Mohammed Ahimed Jemil, Zeleke Alemu and Fassika Belete.

Last but not least, I would like to thank my wife Marta Mengistu who took care of the household chores, and still soldiers on, while I kept myself busy with the work that resulted in this book.

List of Acronyms

AA	Addis Ababa
AALC	African American Labor Center
AAU	Addis Ababa University
AFD	Alliance For Democracy
AFL/CIO	American Federation of Labor/Congress of Industrial Organizations
ALF	Afar Liberation Front
ANC	African National Congress
ANDM	Amhara National Liberation Movement
APOG	Armed Propaganda and Organizing Group
ARDUF	Afar Revolutionary Democratic United Front
CAFPDE	Council of Alternative Forces of Peoples for Democratic Ethiopia
CC	Central Committee
CELU	Confederation of Ethiopian Labor Unions
CIA	Central Intelligence Agency
CID	Central Intelligence Department
COEDF	Coalition of Ethiopian Democratic Forces
CPUSA	Communist Party of United States America
CUD	Coalition for Unity and Democracy
DCD	Dirgue Campaign Department
DMTP	Democratic Movement of Tigrean People
DSF	Dirgue Special Forces
ECP	Ethiopian Communist Party
EDP	Ethiopian Democratic Party
EDU	Ethiopian Democratic Union
ELAMA	EPRP's labor wing (Amharic acronym)
ELF	Eritrean Liberation Front
EMALEDH	Union of Ethiopian Marxist Organizations

ENC	Ethiopian National Congress
ENLF	Ethiopian National Liberation Front
EPDA	Ethiopian People's Democratic Alliance
EPF	Ethiopian Patriotic Front
EPLF	Eritrean Peoples Liberation Front
EPLO	Ethiopian People's Liberation Organization
EPRDF	Peoples Revolutionary Democratic Front
EPRA	Ethiopian People's Revolutionary Army
EPRP	Ethiopian People's Revolutionary Party
EPRPYL	EPRP's Youth League
ESANA	Ethiopian Students Association in NAmerica
ESUE	Ethiopian Students Union in Europe
ESUNA	Ethiopian Students Union in N. America
ETA	Ethiopian Teachers Association
EWP	Ethiopian Workers' Party
ICFTU	International Conference For Trade Unions
ILO	International Labor Organization
IZ	Inter-Zone
ML	Marxism-Leninism
MSPS	Ministry of State and Public Security
NGO	Non-Governmental Organizations
OATUU	Organization of African Trade Unions
OLF	Oromo Liberation Front
ONC	Oromo National Congress
ONLF	Oromo National Liberation Front
ORA	Oromo Relief Association
PB	Polit-Bureau
POMOA	Provisional Organization for Mass Organizations
POW	Prisoner Of War
REST	Rehabilitation Society of Tigray
ROFE	Relief Organization For Ethiopia
SLF	Sidama Liberation Front
TPLF	Tigrean People's Liberation Front
UAW	Urban Armed Wing
UDW	Urban Defense Wing
UEDF	Union of Ethiopian Democratic Forces
UF	United Front
UNHCR	United Nations High Commissioner for Refugees
UN	United Nations
WWESF	World Wide Ethiopian Students Federation

Preface

In the last decade or so, we are thankfully witnessing the publication of books about EPRP/A. From regional EPRP/A accounts, such as Sidamo's party work by Hareka Hareyo (*from Nairobi to the Jubilee Palace*), Abdi Abdulahi's book about the Negelle party work (*Yaltadelew Tiwulid*)- a book that was one of the earliest to come out, Dr. Chanyalew Kassa's book, *Kedemmelash Meqabir Afaf*, about the party's work in and around Debre Marqos to a historical fiction about the Addis Abeba urban political work by Konjit Berhan(*Mirqogna*), a book of short stories by Beljig Ali titled "*Kelebetein Situat*", Girmay Abraha's and Berhanu Sertsu's narration of the prison conditions under the Dirgue (*Yemiyanebu Egroch* and *Yederg Esir Betoch Tarik*, respectively), and Hiwot Teffera's "*Tower in the Sky*" . Real insiders like Kiflu Tadesse (*The Generation, I and II*) and Babile Tola (*To Kill a Generation*) have also documented the party's comprehensive history, the latter focusing on the Red Terror. In the last few years, EPRA's history has been documented by Asmamaw Hailu (*EPRA*); Mekonnen Araya (*Negotiating a Lion's Share of Freedom*), and Kahsay Abrha (*YeAssimba Fiqr*). Also of late, electronic libraries are springing up storing documents related to EPRP in general, and the Red Terror in particular. The websites "*yatiwuld tequam*" and Ethiopian Red Terror Documentation Center, are examples.

All these works add up to provide at once glimpses and wider views of the experiences of the first nationwide political party. The documentation, while valuable as a record of the martyrdom and accomplishments of a generation, also serves as the school from which lessons may be drawn by this and future generations. The fact that we need such lessons is an understatement. As Ethiopia continues to languish under dictatorship, new and existing political parties need to come up with a strategy of organization and struggle. To do that, carefully studying the experience of EPRP is a task that can't be overlooked or postponed. The lessons help those in the democratic struggle not to repeat the mistakes for which a generation dearly paid; and they also help those currently in the trenches to pay attention to the worthy accomplishments and the exceptional commitment of EPRP's members.

This is a reflective book: Its main currents are two: on one hand, unlike most books heretofore published on EPRP, this book provides a critical assessment of the party. Valid criticisms of the party in the eyes of the author are the mainstay of the book. To that effect, the author believes nothing shows better the fact than the two major challenges that tripped the party, thus epitomizing the squeeze between a rock and a hard place: the challenges were:

1. The inability of the party, roughly from 1976 to 1978, to pull out its forces to the countryside for a protracted war, rather than continually engaging the massively armed Dirgue in urban areas at a huge cost (although the subtitle of the book says 1975-2008, 1978 is used as a capstone for all events that preceded that year, and those crucial events ending in 1978 in urban Ethiopia, take a third of the book).

2. The confrontation and the back and forth with TPLF/Sudan/EPLF, 11 years later in Quarra, instead of a strategy of avoidance of confrontation and/or withdrawing into the hinterlands and the deployment of its cadres in incremental steps back to its urban roots.

The second current in this book is the presentation of "first time" facts about the Quarra deployment of the party, and the Round 3 wars with TPLF. As far as the author knows, this is the first, full and public account of the issue. The author used internal party documents for the material covered, mostly in chapters 4 and 5 of the book.

I also used a style that combines both written and oral history. The chapters with citations are part of the written history, and those without any citations are based on oral records, and the persons supplying the information are mentioned. One of the unfortunate criticisms leveled at EPRP, mainly by some ethno-nationalists, is the party was an Amhara ethnic-based party. Nothing could be further from the truth. And those who engage in this disinformation have most likely an axe to grind. To dispel that nonsense, I have provided

PERFACE

examples of leading members that came from the various ethnicities of Ethiopia. I did not find it helpful to list those hailing from Amhara ethnicity, or those with mixed ethnicity heritage.

Efforts have been made not to belabor subjects other authors have sufficiently documented. Only passing reference has been made on such subjects. So, it is not for lack of interest, or an underestimation of the importance of the subject matter, but it is because I thought the issue had been enough documented that I don't delve into it deeper here.

After the internal turmoil, the squeeze by both the Dirgue and the TPLF, EPRP has almost arisen from the dead like Lazarus. But this took place in the Diaspora, and not inside Ethiopia (chapter 10). In its latter reconstitution, the party heavily drew members from those who were ex-EPRAites. Even those who were in the rural areas with the army in civilian capacity as cadres and organizers did not come back in appreciable numbers. Calling out for explanation, those who were affiliated with the party around the student unions of ESUNA and ESUE also did not as much budge to re-embrace the party. Perhaps coming a distant second to ex-EPRAites were those who were in the urban structures, most of whom spent some jail time and, upon release, left the country legally or illegally. The staying away of their peers might be explained due to the psychological scars of the Red Terror which they witnessed first-hand, and later the confinement and abuse of the Dirgue's prison system.

This is the story of a party whose members average age at the party's founding was about 19 years old, and now even in their middle ages, the most persevering, still going strong despite all the complications and the challenges of marching on a winding, and uphill road.

In summary, in writing this book, what I tried to accomplish were: 1) to record the selfless sacrifices of a generation of young dreamers who rallied around EPRP/A at the various stops; 2) thus, to complete the history of the party and its accomplishments from where Kiflu left off (for those interested in chronology); 3) to give voices to dissident voices in the party and present their side of the story in as much as it was possible to 4) to reflect on what I thought were the critical failures of the party that prevented it from taking political power.

The Ethiopian left strode into history with a multitude of grievances, and with idealism for social equality. And yet, it conspicuously failed to have a larger-than-life leader to rally all the leftist and democratic forces under a single center; the potential candidates -Haile Fida, Tesfaye Debessay and Berhanemeskel Redda - seemed too bewitched with partisan politics to play that role. Thus the politics of the day acutely lacked a charismatic figure that could have obviated the inter-left, and intra-party schisms and divisions that contributed to a great degree to its demise, and most of the members alive today are carrying the scars of the Survivors' Remorse.

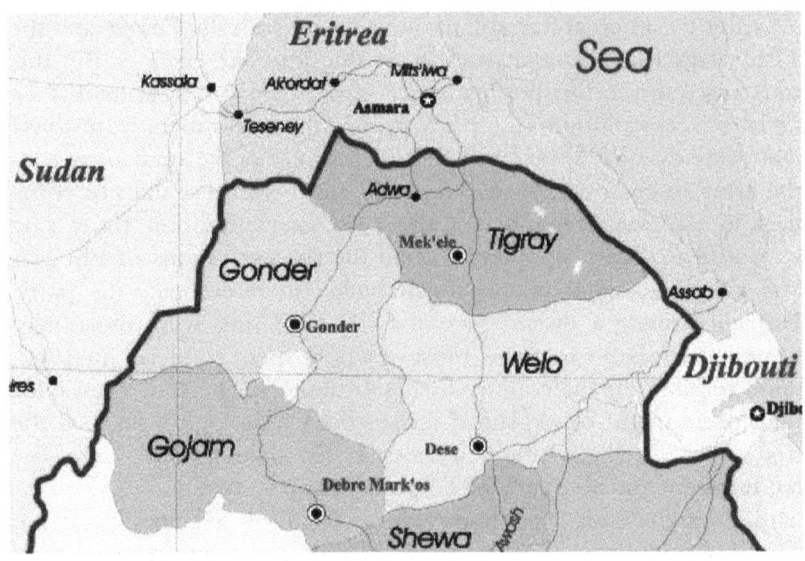

EPRP's Rural Operations and Areas Covered, 1975-1992

PERFACE

EPRP had urban structures organized into zones and interzones throughout the country, including in Eritrea on three separate levels: party, youth, and the labor organizations.

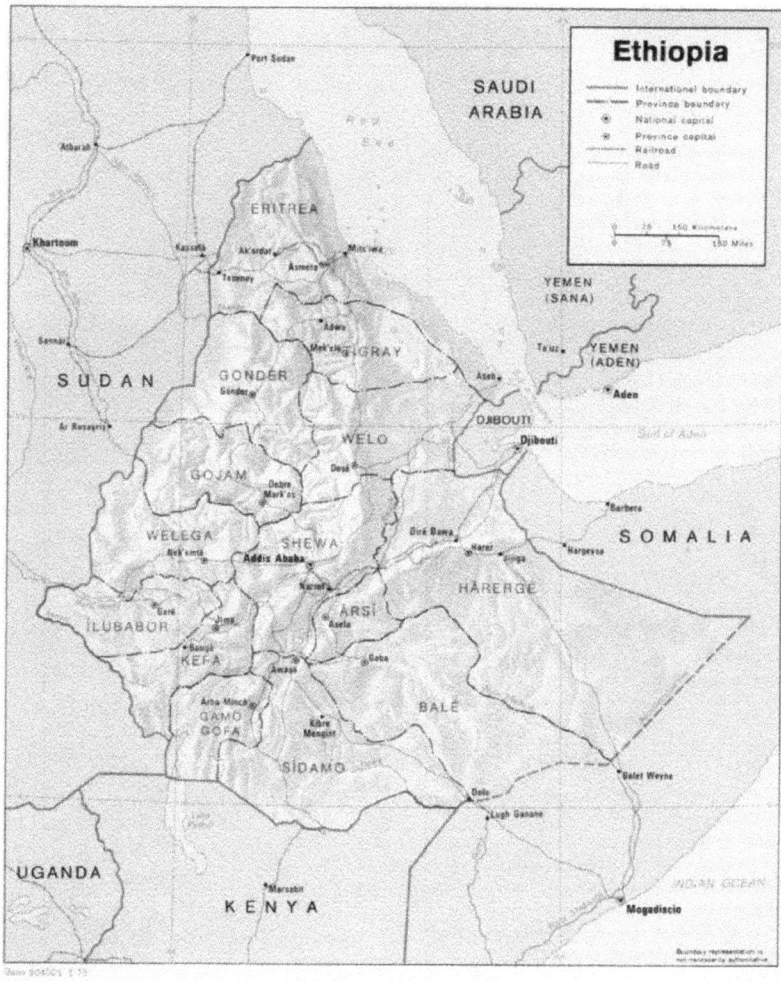

Introduction

The first and authoritative book on EPRP was written in 2 volumes in English with an Amharic translation some 15 years ago by Kiflu Tadesse. Kiflu has done a great service not only to the EPRP and those who passed through its struggles, but also for the larger Ethiopian society by leaving a written record of the first political party in Ethiopia. For the last 15 years, Kiflu's book has been cited by many writers and observers. Kiflu has inspired not only writers in the EPRP camp, but also others such as Meison, TPLF and the Dirgue, to name a few, to start to write their history (ies). The combined and aggregate history gives us some record to refelect on recent Ethiopian political history. In that regard, perhaps notable organizations from that era that have yet to write their history might be the OLF, the EPLF and the ELF.

Kiflu's style has been to provide narration and state the facts as he experienced them, or perceived them. He had a unique experience in that he was a member of the leadership of the party, and as such, he had direct experience in most of what he narrated. Mine is a bit different. For starters, I was not in a position to directly experience and to have a bird's eye view of the events. Secondly, my style in this book is radically different from Kiflu's. While he narrates, I try to interpret. I try to provide a critical assessment of the major facts and events. I understand that some people, within and inside the party, and some outside, might not agree with my interpretation. I have tried to be as fair and as objective in my interpretation (at least I can assure the reader she would not find in this book such cavalier and false statements found in Andargachew's and Tesfaye Mekonnen's book that accuse EPRP without a shred of evidence of killing Tselote). Still, that is no guarantee that a unanimity based on my interpretation would prevail. And it should not. What adds to our knowledge and enlivens our intellectual life is the multiple perspectives and the debates that ensue. For the younger generation born after the Ethiopian Revolution, this book will be another resource and another perspective that neither wholly demeans the party as some opponents had (Tesfaye Riste comes to mind), nor wholly endorses it. It is a critical assessment. In that regard, it is perhaps unique. It is an evaluation where party shortcomings are discussed as perceived, and party strengths are teased out for all to see. I have also gained, unlike Kiflu, from books and works that came out since Kiflu's publication of "the Generation". Most of these latter works are cited in this book.

EPRP was not only the first political party (I know Meison also makes a similar claim and there is enough room to allow both claims), but also the largest at the time. As a result, it is so difficult to record all its experiences in all areas and aspects. Besides, thousands of its members had been killed taking their history with them. Others have been silenced through the psychological scar of the Red Terror. Still others have simply walked away and gone onto other things never to reminisce on their past. As a result, in such areas as details of the various armed struggles the party attempted in Shoa, Harar, Sidamo and Keffa they will wait the hard work of other authors. Also, although I tried, I have not largely succeeded to hear from *anjas*, those accused of factional activities. The most I could do was use Hiwot Teffera's book *"Tower in the Sky"*, Berhanemeskel Redda's monograph *"On The Mass Line"*, and a document containing his forced confession.

The generation's dream has turned into a temporary (but so far long-lasting) setback. No one alive today dreamed the poverty facing our poorest would be so severe and pervasive. No one thought our sisters and mothers would be modern day slaves in the Middle East. No one thought Ethiopianity would be unacceptable by government officials for citizens who are forced to identify their ethnicity for voting and other rights. Our generation has been humbled and taught an expensive lesson in not to dream too much and too high. And for two decades and counting, history has conspired with fate in denying granting a second chance. Of those still active EPRP members, and for some not-so-active, a few would not want anyone to badmouth their party and they find it hard to admit that it is a party of humans

INTRODUCTION

destined to make mistakes. Some in their ranks might get offended at the revelation and interpretation of party mistakes.

The fact that the book is titled ' *EPRP: Between a Rock and a Hard Place*", does not mean that external factors only (Dirgue and TPLF) were the only responsible agencies for the party's misfortunes. The title locates the party's 30 + years of struggle in a historical, constraining context. It does not absolve the party from its own self-destruction moments, as narrated in Chapter 1.

One Ethiopian saying, *mut wokash,* which is frowned upon, needs to be modified perhaps to "*mut kesash*". In the latter case, suing the defenseless dead in court or in front of a panel, is worthless. But "mut *wokesa* and *mugesa"* is the domain of History. Without them, a society cannot bequeath any historical record to its progeny. All one must ask is that the "*wokesa"* be tempered and fair.

One puzzling issue, however, is the case of those who had the opportunity to be involved in the struggle, but chose not to. Instead, while radicals boycotted classes in the early 60's and early 70's- year after year- sacrificed limbs and lives in the mid 70's, this group quietly pursued their education and careers, and some even allied with the regimes in power. Now some have arrogated to themselves to mercilessly criticize the genuine mistakes of those who dared to struggle and sacrificed much on the way. What to make of this? On one hand, it is this group's fundamental right to express its views, a right for which the radicals sacrificed themselves. On the other, because this group decided to pursue their self-interests rather than the national interest, their criticisms often sound wanting.

Chapter One: The End Game

The Urban Setting

The year 1978 was in a way the fin-de-siècle for EPRP. It was the beginning of the slide to face more challenging times, and the time that signaled the push to leave the stage for other, anti-Ethiopian, opposition actors. The big stage that EPRP once filled and dominated was now creaking under its feet, and threatening to sink the party that only a few short years ago was almost in power. The last two remaining central committee members in Addis, Kiflu Tadesse and the late Samuel Alemayehu, had left town for the countryside. According to Kiflu, Samuel left Addis at the end of August, or the beginning of September 1977 and reached Tigrai in December, four months later. Kiflu himself followed suit soon after at the end of October 1977,"[1] two months after Samuel's departure.

What this meant was that the few urban structures still intact after resisting massive repression by the Dirgue were left to their own devices. Even when these two were there, the Addis Abeba Interzone (IZ), a hierarchy normally just below the Central Committee, had already started taking party bylaws into its own hands, and ignoring the 2-man CC team. Following the dissention of a faction some of whose members facilitated the Dirgue's attack against EPRP, The Addis Abeba IZ insisted on measures against the factional members. "After consulting the zones under their jurisdictions, the Addis Abeba IZ ignored the 2-man CC team and unilaterally decided to

---

1. Kiflu Tadesse: The Generation. Ethiopia: Transformation and Conflict. The History of the Ethiopian People's Revolutionary Party. University Press of America, inc., 1998,p.332

EPRP

take measures against suspected members of the faction. From mid-June 1977 on, the war declared by the faction was thus reciprocated"[2].

According to Kiflu, "members of the faction put out some leaflets and in some of them, they expressed opposition to the urban military actions of EPRP"[3]. Hence, it seems one may empathize for some of these factional elements who foresaw and saw the folly of EPRP's continued civil war with the government, while one has to resolutely condemn their cowardly and cruel alliance with the Dirgue. One such damage was the fact that the entire Central Intelligence Department (CID) that was under the influence of EPRP was compromised around July 1977 and the names of clandestine members given to the Dirgue by a Gezahegne Sime. As a result many members there were arrested, and a few went underground. Among the members and sympathizers were Gondarit, a civilian at the CID, Lieutenants Wassie Aman, Tafa Daba, Aklog Nigatu, Wondwossen, Tamene Galore and Mohammed Ali. Tamene was able to join the EPRA in Gondar where he sadly fell off a cliff and died. Gondarit, who was a high school classmate of MM, was about to leave Addis to join the army in Assimba, when on the day of departure, her safe house was surrounded and she was captured and killed[4].

Kiflu says "from May 1977 to the end of August [1977], the faction caused damage that surpassed that caused by POMOA in its entire existence[5]. However, he also states that Berhanemeskel, who had moved with his group to the Merhabete area around March 1977 (just 4 months before Samuel left Addis), probably could not have taken a direct role in factional activities in the Addis Abeba area[6], and Berhanemeskel had steadfastly denied his group's alliance with the Dirgue.

Beginning in the last weeks of November 1977 through January 1978, the EPRP underwent the most severe crisis in its history. When the Addis Abeba IZ secretary, Muhidin Mohammed, was arrested in January 1978, and disclosed all that he knew (members, party property, arms, etc.), there was no CC member in town to give

---

2. ibid.p.225
3. ibid., p.328
4. personal communication with MM
5. The Generation, Part ii, P.313
6. ibid., p.328

CHAPTER ONE: THE END GAME

guidance or repair the structure. The crisis that the Addis Abeba IZ (which was the center) faced was contagious to the other branches throughout the country. Structures and party-affiliated mass organizations were detached from the center and had to fend off for themselves.

EPRP was smarting from a propaganda barrage perpetrated against it by the Dirgue following the 1977 Ethio-Somali war. EPRP was portrayed to be a traitor and a fifth-column. Besides, the Soviets and the East Europeans, along with the Cubans were fully behind the Dirgue regime, and helping it with its war efforts and the suppression of the opposition. New technology was being used to tap telephones. All together, EPRP was subjected to at least four rounds of wars of annihilation and search and destroy repressions in what was commonly called "the Red Terror". The repression or the war of annihilation has many components and was very well designed by the leading Dirgue members and their civilian allies. Mass terror, mass confession, psychological war and isolation of the party from its base were part and parcel of the war strategy. The party lost tens of thousands of its hard core members and sympathizers as a result of the repression. The sacrifice was not just limited to rank and file members alone. The Addis Abeba IZ alone had to be reconstituted at least four times as one committee after another was being decimated. The EPRP leadership itself that numbered 18 central committee members in 1976 was reduced to 2 central committee members staying in Addis by mid-1977, and none in Addis at the start of 1978. The last Addis Abeba IZ, for the short duration of its life, had to operate without any CC member in Addis. For sure, some of the CC members, such as Tselote and Zeru were transferred to Tigrai by the CC's decision, but most others such as Tesfaye Debessay, Kiflu Tefera, Yohannes Berhane, Yosef Adane were martyred. While Birhanemeskel Redda and Getachew Maru were expelled from the party by this time, Iyassu Alemayehu was assigned abroad.

In light of the sacrifices the EPRP leadership paid losing most of its seasoned and senior members, how cruel to hear the shrill voices of critics who say that the party leadership has put the Ethiopian youth in the line of fire! No serious liberation of a country in any part of the world has taken place, whether from the clutches of European colonialism or domestic autocrats, without the sacrifice of those who cherish freedom. This was true yesterday, and is true today. If anything, the EPRP leadership might be faulted for *not* preserving itself to continue to provide leadership in urban areas past 1978, and not for the opposite.

Thus, by 1978, the urban problems that had plagued the party going back a few years developed in full and splashed across the stage: the internal problem of factions, the leadership crisis, the massive repression/and the fragmented offense-defense waged by the party, and the inability to cope with the complex issues of the revolution, such as the Ethio-Somali war and relations with the other leftist forces. <u>After holding 51 meetings from its formation in 1972 to March 1977[7], the EPRP leadership should be perhaps faulted for its total absorption in day-to-day issues to the total neglect of foreseeing the scope and meaning of the determined repression of the Dirgue</u>. Had that been the area of more focus, say starting in 1975-76, perhaps the party leadership could have shifted its seat from Addis to rural areas thus saving more CC members' lives to continue to provide leadership. Also, tens of thousands more members that eventually were lost could have been withdrawn to engage in a protracted rural war to the fledgling base areas in Tigrai and Gondar. The hope and calculation that the pro-EPRP wing of the Dirgue might prevail over Mengistu, and as a result the party might face less harsh times, may have played a role in underestimating the impending danger that proved fatal to the party. On a more fundamental level, the leadership's orientation of the strategies of the struggle (power through urban uprising versus through a protracted rural war) may not have been satisfactorily resolved. In fact, although it was launched with partial vigor, it was the start of the EPRA and the political cadre structure that helped EPRP to continue to carry the nation's hopes and aspirations for many years to come, thus avoiding the fate of its leftist rivals, whose demise in the urban areas meant the permanent end of their political lives. It is fair, however, to mention and appreciate the repeated unsuccessful efforts of the party to create rural base areas in Sidamo, Shoa, Keffa and Harer, plans that had they been successful, could have dramatically changed the direction and fate of EPRP. The gravity of the total immersion of the party in the urban confrontations and the resultant losses was going to infect like a virus all party and army work thereafter, and eventually to be a major cause for the party's loss of most of its members as we will see later.

---

7. ibid., p.206

CHAPTER ONE: THE END GAME

One case perhaps illustrates the problem very well. It was the case of one of the most intelligent and humorous CC members, Yohannes Berhane, or *"Arabu"* by his nickname. A geologist by training, he was a member of the *Democracia* editorial team until he was killed in March 1977. At the height of the revolution, he was exchanging letters with an Ethiopian woman friend of his who was studying art in London. They both used to teach at Kolfe High School before the lady left on a scholarship to London. They had a platonic relationship. The woman gave 4 of the letters he wrote to her while she was in London to an Ethiopian independent magazine called *Zega* that is no longer in publication. His letters were published in the Hamle/July 1995 Eth. calendar issue #7[8].

From the letters, one can see how the brilliant Yohannes reflects the feelings of the majority of us in opposition at that time: that we thought the Dirgue regime would fall in a short time; and that we overestimated the strength of the opposition and the support we had. His sense of humor is so magnificent that when his artist friend decided to draw his portrait, he joked that he would be the first Ethiopian for whom at his funeral mourners would cry over his portrait rather than the common studio photograph! Unfortunately, neither a portrait nor a photograph would be displayed for his and his generation's funeral. They were denied the simple luxury of a funeral as their corpses were either subjected to a mass burial, or in the worst cases, to rot in the fields to be eaten away by wild animals, only because they dared to idealize and fight for a better Ethiopia.

Compounding the problems, the EPRP was not destined to get any respite even in the remote corners of Assimba and Tigrai. Its members fleeing the Dirgue's repression were going to jump from the frying pan into the fire.

The Youth League - EPRP's Engine

Perhaps the first youth association in Ethiopia that was independently formed and that had the interests of the local community was formed in 1973 in Yohannes, around Ras Desta Hospital in Addis. During its 3-year existence, the association set a model for other youth associations and had spectacular accomplishments to show. The President of the association was

---

8. Zega, #7, Hamle/July 1995 (Eth.C.), PP. 21,22,23,24,36,37

Wosenyelesh Debela. Some of its major accomplishments included teaching literacy and numeracy, staging plays, awarding certificates to those who completed the literacy courses, hosting an exhibition of Ethiopia's products and services, and feeding the poor on holidays. It raised funds from the modest fees it collected staging plays, selling tea to customers and supporters, and hosting a table tennis game.

When the Ethiopian Revolution broke out in 1974, and as the nation was being politicized, the youth association was no exception. It hosted panel discussions. Other notables of the association were the late Alemayehu Egzeru from Medhanei Alem School and Zeudu Desta. One of the memorable panel discussions was its invitation to members of the Women Organizing Committee sometime in April 1976. The women invited were members or sympathizers of the two dominant leftist parties at the time. They included Fikrte Gebremariam, Selamawit Dawit, and Gerawork Gebreegziabher. Because EPRP had tremendous sympathy among the people, and the youth in particular, the association took extra caution to make sure that its non-EPRP guests were afforded equal time and treated with the same respect. Still, the youth and invited guests peppered Gerawork, a Meison member, with many questions. Later, she published a critical article of the youth association in an Ethiopian weekly, *Yezareitu Ethiopia*.

Within a month, in May 1976, the association celebrated its third year of founding. Its highlight was the invitations sent out to various government and private offices to showcase their products and services at the festival. The chairperson was assigned with her sister, the late Ejigayehu Debela who was murdered by the Dirgue, to invite the Milk Products Corporation. At the festival, over 20 corporations were represented. The late Markos Hagos, a victim of the Dirgue's Red Terror and a known labor leader who at the time was recently released from jail, agreed to award certificates to those who matriculated in literacy, but declined to make a speech in order not to provoke the Dirgue.

W/o Mulu Hadera (Mother) gave a speech on women's rights. Esatu Tessema's (an EPRP poet) titled "*Amtsalehu*" was read, and another poem, "*Tenagera*" composed by Wosenyelesh's husband, Chuchuye, was read by another youth association member, Tsigereda Tadelle. Other invited guests included two labor union leaders; Ato Tefera from Water and Sewage Department and Ato Michael Teferi representing banking services.

CHAPTER ONE: THE END GAME

In Yohannes, there used to be an area called "*Sar Sefer*", where poor and needy people that served and worked for a local feudal noble, Dejach Yigezu, lived in a squalor. They lived in leaking thatched roof huts. The youth association asked and got from Addis Abeba Municipality about 50 corrugated tin to use as roofing material. The members of the youth association all participated in various tasks and changed "Sar Sefer" into a *qorqoro bet sefer*. The famous Ethiopian artist, the late Gebrekristos Desta who used to live in Yohannes, agreed to draw "Sar Sefer" before it was demolished. When asked to sketch it, he said "how could I even say no when you youngsters are doing all these difficult manual work?" Gebrekristos used to give free art lessons at the youth association office.

Since the Dirgue came to power, the association's freedom of movement and operation was severely curtailed before it finally was crushed following the unsuccessful September 1977 labor strike. One of the association members and a labor union leader of the "*sebe-nek*" association, an association that had members ranging from prostitutes to daily laborers, Nigussie Tadesse, was the first victim who died of torture in the Dirgue's torture chambers. Then, Ejigayehu Debela, the sister of Wosenyelesh was shot and died of her wounds. She was athletic and very dynamic. She loved her neighborhood so much she said, "if I could embrace Yohannes like one would embrace a person, I would have embraced it". After she was shot, she got first aid at Ras Desta Hospital, and was then later taken to Paulos Hospital. From there, her sister and comrades helped her escape, but they did not have a place for the victim. Attempts by EPRP to get her a place were not immediately successful, costing her valuable time. Finally, she got a shelter, but sadly the comrades that sheltered her turned out to be members of a faction, and turned her in to the Dirgue who promptly and cruelly murdered her.

Wosenyelesh used to be invited by other youth associations, such as Kechenie's, to share her experience and help establish other associations throughout Addis Abeba. These associations, along with student associations were the breeding ground for EPRP Youth League membership[9].

EPRPYL had also its beginnings in the high school student movement that was highly organized in the summer of 1974. The key players of the high school student movement were Tito Hiruy,

---

9.   personal communication with Wosenyelesh Debela

Yishaq Teshome (a member of the faction later), Binyam Bogale (went to Assimba), the late Gezahegne, and Yifru. Tito's older brother, Aklilu (before the merger to form EPRP, belonged to the *Democracia* wing), and Alemayehu Egzeru (belonged to the *Abyot* wing) were instrumental in laying the structure of the youth movement. Study cells were established first around the Arat Kilo YMCA, then spreading out. Tito went to Agaro, Jimma for the *edget behibret campaign* which afforded him fertile ground for his organizational work. The campaign centers were effectively used by EPRP to recruit youth members. The Ethiopian Students Union had an underground paper called "*Dil Betigil*", and Gideon W/Ammanuel estimates its membership to range from 5,000 to 10,000[10].

The interaction and mobilization among students was not always peaceful. For instance at the Kokebe-Tsibah high school, amid a debate whether or not to go to the campaign, a supporter of the school principal's eye was injured. Similarly, a Meison supporter at Leul Mekonnen school in Merkato was thrown from a balcony. Later, a known Meison youth Gebreegziabher Hagos was killed by EPRP squads, and the mutual destruction was to continue.

As schools closed and EPRP showed its strength, the youth gradually found a home in EPRPYL. Along with the youth league, a Pioneers group for youngsters, and ululation committee for mothers were also established.

Finally, in 1976 Meskerem, a 5-day long meeting was held by 21 youth representatives from throughout Ethiopia (except Eritrea, Iluubabor and Wollo) in Akaki at Hana Mariam in a peasant's hut. Addis Abeba was divided into 4 youth zones. Among known individuals, Thomas Eskinder of Zone 4, Tito Hiruy, security and defense chief of Zone 3, Alemayehu Egzeru, chief of agit-prop, of Zone 1, Azeb Girma of Zone 1, chief of Women's affairs in the league as well as Dawit Tefera, and the late Meron Assefa of Zone 3. The only woman youth CC member was Saba Kidanemariam. Representing the CC of the party, Getachew Maru, Yohannes Berhane, and perhaps Berhannie Iyassu were present at the founding congress.

---

10. ed. Bahru Zewde , Documenting the Ethiopian Student Movement: An Exercise in Oral History, , Forum for Social Studies, reprinted 2010, Addis Abeba, "The High School Factor" by Gideon Wolde Ammanuel, p.131

CHAPTER ONE: THE END GAME

Zone 1 included the Merkato, Gulele and Tekle Haimanot areas. Zone 2 was Nefas Silk, Querra, and Sirak Tefera was the main guy there. Zone 3 included Bole, and Kazanchis, and Zone 4 was the 4 and 6 Kilo Areas up with Entoto. The basic structure started with a cell, then a sub-region, a region, subzone, zone, an interzone, and an EPRYL CC. The age range was 15-25. Young women held responsible positions in the EPRYL. In addition to Saba, Azeb and Meron at the top, others included Hiwot Teffera and Simegne Lemma as Zone 3 committee members along with others with the following code names: Nishan (Zone 2), Rahel (zone 2), and Yewubdar (sub-secretariat) (information based on torture-induced YL member confessions).

One of the amazing turnarounds influenced by EPRPYL's politics was its impact on city gangs. Known as "China Group", "Kinbibit Group", etc., they were notorious for molesting girls and beating up anyone who stood up to them. Once the youth league's politics spread, they were among the disciples, and steady forces of the revolution[11].

The main bone of contention between EPRP and Meison appears to be the control over the student/youth associations. As EPRP dominated and got accepted, it seemed Meison resented that and instead of working hard to work together sought the help of the Dirgue to stop the EPRP avalanche.

Sometime in September 1977, a Youth League CC meeting was called. Aklilu Hiruy, the Secretary was in detention and his brother Toto was elected to replace him, and chaired the meeting. A few weeks after that Tito and other Youth League CC members were arrested. By January 1978, the Youth League structure was in shambles, as the key leaders and members fell in the hands of the Dirgue. They were incessantly tortured to squeeze out of them any information about the organization, and to show the investigators where arms and money was hidden, and any unapprehended associates.

Most of them were forced to denounce EPRP in public. This gave fuel to the ongoing witch hunt of comrades, and the public scene of denunciation and self-denunciation that was gripping the nation.

---

11. personal communication with Aklilu Kebede

EPRP

The Forced Confessions

Between unspeakable tortures, the Dirgue's investigators, pen and paper in hand, forced the comrades to describe their organizational activities. The format of the questioning followed mostly the same line: it began by asking the victims what they or their parents lost in the revolution (whether or not houses or urban/ rural land was lost); then went to ask what the organizational responsibility of the victim was in their respective structures, and who they worked with- vertically and horizontally, then a question followed pressing the victim if he had killed any Dirgue/civilian allies of the Dirgue, and if so, to name them, and finally to name those they targeted for killing, but were unsuccessful.

Thus Ethiopia's best and brightest were subjugated to the most heinous crimes of torture and forced confessions, and the sadistic investigators were not usually satisfied after maiming their victims, and getting all the information they could. They still wanted more and kept torturing their almost-dead victims who had to be carried to their mattresses by newly-arrived comrades after each round of torture and investigation session.

It is so sad to read the investigative reports of these dim-witted and lumpen investigators forcing confessions out of these bright kids. More often, the reports were mangled, ascribing what "A" said under "B"s name, repeating the same aspects of confession in the same report just to embellish and produce a thick report, perhaps to impress their superiors, and using the same English words that have appropriate Amharic equivalents, such as "opposition", over and over again. It is not being elitist to highlight the incompetence of these goons who had no moral or aesthetic standing to be towering over these radical kids.

In the report, each victim was identified by name, age, school, residence, and date of capture. Then it details the forced confessions answering the lead questions described above. Giving a semblance of a regular court proceeding, the report makes a mockery of justice pretending to be a brief filed by a prosecutor when it is fully known that the action was extra-judicial.

The Youth League was a collection of self-less, bright and idealist young men and women who struggled to transform Ethiopian society by doing away with inequality and injustice. I knew some of the leaders at General Wingate School, fighters like Tito, Gezahegne,

CHAPTER ONE: THE END GAME

Habteselassie, and Gebeyehu. What I did not know then was that in the post-*zemecha* years, that they were going to play such a huge role, and sadly end up in death for dreaming a better Ethiopia.

Tefera Deguefe, who was a Governor of Ethiopia's Central Bank and jailed by the Dirgue in 1976, and who was Tito's "mattress neighbor" in jail, describes Tito in his autobiographical book, as intelligent and handsome and from whom he says he learned a lot about the movement. Tefera himself was no stranger to youthful politics: In 1950, he was the president of the first Ethiopian students association in North America (ESANA), where after a year, he was replaced by the more radical Girmame Neway (*Minutes of An Ethiopian Century, p.543-544)*[12].

Relation with TPLF

The ideology of nationalist forces like TPLF and that of a multi-national organization, such as EPRP, were/are diametrically opposed. For TPLF, its vision and focus was on empowering the people of Tigray and Tigray alone, whereas the EPRP's focus was on enshrining democracy and prosperity to the Ethiopian people, particularly the oppressed Ethiopian people. For EPRP, this contradiction between the two poles was deemed to be solvable through the mechanism of a united front. National oppression was explicitly recognized by EPRP, but was not conferred as the main expression and driving force of the struggle for freedom. Thus there was a place at the table for ethnonationalist forces such as TPLF in the fight against feudalism, and imperialism, and in forming a democratic transitional government. To that effect, most EPRA members naively and genuinely believed that the two forces operating in Tigrai (TPLF and EPRP) would complement each other and coordinate their fights against the Dirgue.

However, the reality on the ground was different. These two visions, rather than complementing each other, openly clashed. Each party worked hard through its *kifle-hizbi* to rally the peasants and urbanites (students, teachers, civil servants, etc.) of Tigray behind them. The EPRP was a fast growing and popular party throughout Ethiopia whose politics naturally resonated with the Tigrean masses

---

12. Teferra Deguefe. Minutes of An Ethiopian Century, Shama Books, Addis Abeba, pp.543-544

who have historically been at the center of the fight for Ethiopia and Ethiopiawinet. On the contrary, TPLF was a radical, ethnonationalist force that appealed to hate and difference and articulated the historical injustice of Tigreans at the hands of what it described Amhara oppressors. Tigrean members of EPRP were called "puppets" in derision, and the party itself described as an Amhara outfit and "*Abay Ethiopia*". Perhaps sensing it was losing ground to EPRP, TPLF demanded that EPRA leave Tigray. EPRP was adamant in its refusal. In order to diffuse the tensions between the two organizations, and to deal with the consequences of daily skirmishes, the two protagonists agreed to form a bi-lateral group to resolve problems.

From the start in 1975 until war started in 1978, at least 9 meetings were held between the two organizations to try to resolve their disagreements Looking back, and as the evidence of what transpired shows, the two organizations pursued different strategies in these bi-lateral meetings. For EPRP, which as we said earlier, envisioned making a pact with TPLF in a united front, the discussions were regarded as bumps on the road that have to be overcome to get to the united front, and hence all issues with the exception of the demand to leave Tigray, were on the table to be properly disposed of. For the TPLF, having put its maximalist demand, i.e. the demand to get EPRP out of Tigray, no issues were to be worked through unless they were part of this maximalist goal which must be achieved by any means necessary. Hence, one sees a complete waste of 2 1/2 years of negotiations by the EPRP while the sly TPLF was building its arms capacity and getting battle experience through its engagements with EDU. In the latter parts of the discussion, while an agreement was reached for each party to explain to the members of the other party their agreements and a call for peace, this never took place. Worse, during the eighth meeting held in December 1977, it was agreed to draft a joint statement and it was drafted. TPLF insisted that it would only be distributed among members and not among peasants or the militia. The EPRA distributed the draft to its members. The TPLF however did not even distribute it to its members[13].

From the above, one can clearly see how the TPLF was preparing for war, while trapping EPRA in a hopeless long-drawn negotiations.

---

13. The Generation, part ii, p.398

CHAPTER ONE: THE END GAME

The naive attitude of EPRA members towards TPLF started souring in the latter parts of 1977 after repeatedly seeing the peasant and militia victims of TPLF. There were even discussions on preparing for an eventual war; but the overwhelming rhetorical question of members was that if we fight with an ethnonationalist organization like TPLF, as a proletarian vanguard party, how could we relate with other ethnonationalist forces in other parts of Ethiopia. This attitude coupled with the rift created between the army's and the party's leadership on the question of negotiations with TPLF may have prevented the EPRA leadership from making preparations for a defensive war much less for an offensive one.

The EPRA had not arranged for its sick and wounded to be taken out of Tigray in the event of war; it had not moved around the fighting forces in a war-ready manner; it had not put in proper places party documents and other valuables. The leadership's hands were simply tied and were staring at danger vacantly. War was started and quickly finished in favor of the TPLF after 5 days. The party must be grateful to the Eritrean Liberation Front (ELF) that agreed to take into its operational areas the retreating EPRA units, although its subsequent mistreatment of EPRA in Shemshemia was despicable and tragic. This was a time when relations between EPRP and EPLF were strained. A year earlier, EPLF was rebuffed by EPRP delegates in its insistent demand to categorize the Eritrean issue as a colonial one. EPRP did not budge, whereas TPLF readily and earlier accepted this colonial thesis and endeared itself with EPLF. During the war with TPLF, some EPRA members had argued that EPLF has fought alongside TPLF, but no one has so far brought forth any concrete evidence. During EPLF's First National Congress in January 1977, in the presence of an EPRP delegation, the EPLF representative condemned EPRP and expressed total support to TPLF[14]. Just a few months before the war with TPLF, a leader of Company/hayl 500, Getnet, and hailing from the Ethiopian Air Borne, was wounded in the spinal cord during an engagement with the Dirgue forces at Wuqro. When EPLF was requested to accept him in their field hospital for medical treatment, or let him leave for abroad for treatment, they refused and Getnet died a few days later unable to receive adequate medical care.

---

14. ibid., p.253

Part of the leadership's failure to prepare for a defensive war against TPLF could be perhaps explained by the coincidental internal problems of EPRA. The factional problems that started in the urban areas and that had mostly to deal with questions of party strategy surfaced here at an inopportune moment. The army leadership was holding mass meetings to measure the scope of the problems. Many EPRA members, reminiscing the transpirations of the urban areas of not too long ago, lost their objectivity and showed a semblance of mob justice. However, to its credit, during the rectification movement that took place several months ago, EPRA had established a Members' Rights' Protection Committee. The members of this Committee ably served as defense attorneys for the accused. One of the members of this Committee was NM, and another Geleb Dafla, who fell in the hands of TPLF in the early 90's in the latest fight with TPLF in Quarra.. Thanks to its efforts representing the accused and the EPRA leadership's respect of its work, it succeeded in getting a few of the accused to be freed, and some of them to leave EPRA altogether of their own volition (Dr. Berhanu Nega of Ginbot 7 is such a case, and another is Ayele Borejo [Gebreegzei], a Sidama and a famous high school activist in Yirga Alem).

Unfortunately, while the Committee was doing its investigating work, the advancing TPLF army was at the gate. A decision had to be made. The EPRA leadership voted overwhelmingly (with the exception of Col. Alemayehu Asfaw) to punish by death 14 of the accused, and they were killed as the army started its retreat[15].

The retreating EPRA forces reached Eritrea in the second week of April 1978, almost a month after the war had begun. A group of fifteen EPRA members crossed Tembein in Tigrai and joined the army in Gondar. Although the party should be grateful to the ELF for taking in the retreating EPRA army, the treatment the army received at their hands was less than honorable. The army was not allowed to go on its planned destination (Gondar) and was forcibly delayed; the weekly supply of sorghum was meager and did not last a few days thus EPRA forces had to resort to eating all kinds of wild edibles (occasionally, a dead camel or two would wash up the camps, and their meat was eaten only to later suffer from dysentery); most were sick from malaria and malnourishment. When ELF finally agreed to let EPRA continue onto Gondar, they had cheated it of its

---

15. Asmamaw Hailu . EPRA (in Amharic), 1972-1978, vol. 1, 2003, , p.405

CHAPTER ONE: THE END GAME

arms by keeping its best arms and substituting them with their old ones. The guns were taken away by the ELF based on its policy that armed groups other than ELF fighters could not stay in ELF-liberated areas with their guns.

While in Tokombia/Shemshemia, the EPRA forces were routinely bombarded by the Dirgue's air power even in retreat. The obsession of the Dirgue to continue to attack EPRA even though other forces such as TPLF and the Eritrean forces were more menacing to its power was one of the follies of the Dirgue, and as we would see later, this was to continue until the Dirgue's downfall in 1991.

After enduring hardships for more than five months in Eritrea, ELF finally consented to the EPRA's departure to Gondar. At Tokombia, as usually happens when EPRA camps at a certain area for a lengthy time, arts and culture flourished: members engaged in poetry reading, drama staging, literary nights were common, various cultural shows and songs were aplenty (This was to repeat at Bertya on a similar scale two years later).

There was one challenge between Gondar and Tokombia, however: the Tekezie River that was overflowing its banks due to the rainy season. The EPRA much less to be equipped with boats or modern means to cross a big river was a malnourished ragtag army. It had to creatively devise the means to cross the river using local and discarded tires, sorghum mats, and rubber water cans to make rafts. 5-6 members were assigned to a raft with 2 skilled swimmers accompanying the raft by pushing it across the full river. The crossing song chorus was called "AIY,OPP" to synchronize the push of the raft by the two swimmers. The crossing of the Tekezie began on September 18, 1978 and took 6 days. During the crossing two lives were lost due to an unsteady raft overturning. The Gondar army leadership had made the EDU forces in Wolkait aware of the journey and persuaded them not to provoke any hostilities. The EPRA forces, along with their arms and packed animals and their few other possessions arrived in Gondar on October 5, 1978.

TPLF has consistently blamed the EPRP for starting the war and shooting the first shot. This is the typical TPLF clever ploy anyone remotely familiar with the organization can easily discern. TPLF had made movement and operation in Tigrai nearly impossible for EPRA and bogged it down in useless negotiations while it prepared itself for war. Besides, its subsequent actions speak volumes and answer unequivocally the question of who the aggressor was.

One of TPLF's foreign supporters, John Young, in his book[16] *Peasant and Revolution in Tigray*, puts down EPRP, and manufactures revisionist history. Says he, "the EPRP held that the road to power lay in an alliance between the working class and the radical intelligentsia, who formed a vanguard Marxist-Leninist party, which the EPRP assumed to be. While a marginal role for the peasants in this alliance was also acknowledged, it *did not* (sic!) recognize the peasantry as a revolutionary force in its own right, unlike the TPLF. Going to the countryside for EPRP was a means of increasing pressure on the Dirgue, and of providing it with rural bases of operation that could be used to support the urban insurrection that remained at the core of its strategy".

Even the fact that EPRA did not use force to get food for its army in malnourished Adi Irob is misconstrued as a non-virtue. Instead, its payment for its food from its meager resources was deliberately misrepresented by Young. He continues "if EPRP had come as liberators, they should not have to pay for their food, but should be provided by those in whose name the struggle was being fought. Moreover, the willingness of EPRP to pay even *higher than* market prices for food items to gain support may have deprived the poor of grains in a food deficit area, and thus undermined its support among the peasantry"![17].

Largely relying on TPLF militia interviews and data, John Young accused the EPRP of every crime imaginable - as the Dirgue just before him did: violence against peasants, driving up grain market prices and being wealthy, jailing and killing peasants, calling itself Black Bolshevik, not understanding the national question and calling ELF one of its mass organizations! Young then blatantly falls for TPLF drama when he says "EPRP was voted out of Tigray!"[18] Thankfully, Young admits that, Ghidey Zeratsion, a TPLF founder and an ex-leader of the organization, in an email exchange with Young, advised the author by saying that at least TPLF has to share the blame on the war.

---

16. John Young. Peasant Revolution in Ethiopia: The Tigray People's Liberation Front, 1975-91, Cambridge University Press, 1997, , p.106
17. ibid., p. 108
18. ibid., p.110-111

CHAPTER ONE: THE END GAME

In the meantime, TPLF taking sole control of Tigray after driving out EPRA, was planning to continue the attack as later events revealed. The Gondar army was divided in 4 regions and operating. The fourth region was Region 4, and its area of operation included the northwestern part of Gondar, the Wegera awraja, but mainly Wolkait area. A few months after EPRA units began operating in the Wolkait area, the TPLF launched an attack against the EPRA units around the end of 1979. They attacked a small base where non-combatants from various army departments and sick fighters had congregated. One of the victims of this attack was a young woman and early EPRA recruit by the name of Jamilla from the Tigrai region.

A few weeks after this attack, TPLF deployed three battalions for an uninterrupted military attack. In the first major attack at Sherrilla, both the TPLF and EPRA sustained heavy casualties. Unable to withstand the TPLF's advance, EPRA forces retreated. Sadly, the entire force was taking a break and some were taking a bath at a nearby river when the TPLF attacked again. The EPRA forces were caught unprepared. Losses were heavy, and the survivors retreated to the Tselemt area of Region 1. After driving EPRA away from the area, the TPLF brought the entire Wolkait area under its control. The TPLF has always justified its attack as a preemptive measure against the rapprochement of the ELF and EPRP. However, the relationship between ELF and EPRP was still strained and two central committee members were sent to mend the strain. TPLF and ELF were at war for quite some time. One of the areas of conflict was a land issue both parties claimed.

Another major confrontation with the TPLF took place a few months later. EPRA units coming back from Eritrea to Tselemt with arms given by ELF and accompanied by a small ELF contingent were met by a TPLF force. A major battle erupted and continued for days. All parties sustained heavy casualties. The EPRA units after a few weeks rest continued on to Tselemt, only to witness a fast boiling internal situation that engulfed Regions 1 and 3 (more on this later).

TPLF's undermining of the EPRP/A was not limited to its military attacks. There have always been suspicions and circumstantial evidence pointing to a TPLF/Dirgue secret joint agreement against EPRP. During the war with EPRA, the leadership asserted that the TPLF was transporting fighters on one of the main highways of Tigray, at times getting as close as five to seven miles from the Dirgue's military base in Adigrat. According to Kiflu Tadesse, a similar report was made in *Northeast African Studies*. The paper stated that the talk between the Dirgue and the TPLF was held in late 1977 and early 1978, in Axum. The TPLF never admitted such a charge[19].

Similarly, TPLF members who had infiltrated POMOA had embarked upon exposing EPRP members they knew and suspected. The EPRP believed that TPLF had collaborated with POMOA representatives of Adigrat and Mekelle and passed on the names of suspected EPRP members. In mid-1977, the EPRP detained a member of the Adigrat POMOA who was accused of endangering the lives of EPRP members. Before action was to be taken, the TPLF disclosed that he was among its members and the individual was turned over to TPLF. Towards the end of 1977, the EPRA accused the TPLF of executing a line-man - an EPRP member assigned to escort new members from the urban areas. When he was killed, he was escorting some members who never made it to the EPRA bases. It was believed that they were kidnapped by the TPLF. On the other hand, the TPLF believed that the EPRP committed similar acts against its members using EPRP's connections in POMOA[20].

Actually, TPLF was directly responsible for the closure of the Tigrai route for EPRP militants to join EPRA in Assimba. A former member of EPRP's zone 1 party committee was jailed in Tigray, and the detainee revealed that from the beginning of May 1977 to the middle of the month, fourteen to eighteen EPRP members en route to Tigrai had been arrested at the exact spot where they were supposed to meet their contact person from the EPRP Tigray zonal committee. The security forces in Tigray had detailed information about the individuals they were to arrest. They also knew the area, the day and time to meet them. They also knew where the password was hidden. There were times when EPRP members who had arrived in one of the Tigrai towns could not find anyone to escort them to the EPRA, and consequently got arrested. The detainee informed the EPRP of the names of those detained and his opinion about the events that led to the arrest. After this information was received by the EPRP urban leadership, no more members were sent through that route. Investigation proved the main source of the information

---

19. The Generation, part ii, p.404
20. ibid., p.394

CHAPTER ONE: THE END GAME

for the Dirgue security branch to be a member of the EPRP leadership in Tigray. He was suspected of TPLF links. Furthermore, the TPLF had acknowledged it did not like the large influx of EPRP members in the Tigrai area in its Tenth Year Assessment done in 1985. The informant in the EPRP Tigray structure inflicted heavy damage upon the party. The EPRP was unable to use the Tigray route from mid-May 1977 on. Since the danger in the cities had reached such a high level, large numbers of members were anxious to leave and join the EPRA. In September 1977, the Youth League demanded passage of more than 1,000 of its members and alternate routes had to be searched. Thus, EPRP was caught between the rock of the Dirgue and the hard place of the TPLF, a scenario that would continue to replicate itself as the years went by.

Organizational cross-infiltration was practiced by almost all organizations of the time to get information and do espionage on one's rivals. For instance, Mebrat Haile, a teacher and TPLF member had infiltrated Mekelle's POMOA branch and was a confidant of the decision makers there. In that capacity, she gave TPLF crucial information on members that were in danger, and what the plans of the regime were. As POMOA was nationally involved in the hunting down of EPRP members, it is logical to impugn the contributions of Mebrat in that regard. She was finally exposed and fled to the field, where she was a battalion commissar before she died[21].

Similarly, there was a Debark awraja administrator by the name of Lieutenant Gebrehiwot Gebregziabher. He was a Dirgue member representing the commandos/police Force in Eritrea[22]. He succeeded in the position the famous and dynamic Zewalle Zegeye who was killed by the Dirgue. This lieutenant was relentless and savage in his singular pursuit of EPRP/A members. He organized campaign after campaign to annihilate EPRA forces in Woggera, Wolkait, and Semien. By acting hand and glove with his boss Melaku Tefera, Gebrehiwot even took over the Woggera awraja "anti-revolutionary" campaign although that awraja was not under his jurisdiction[23]. He

---

21. Yewubmar Asfaw. Finixiwa Motam Tinesalech (in Amharic): the Uncrowned Struggle of Tigrean Women, Far East Trading Publishing, 2009, , p.52
22. Zenebe Feleke. Neber, part ii (in Amharic), Eleni Publishing, 2009, , p. 124
23. personal communication, Abune Biru

threw several members he suspected and caught, off a cliff in a blatantly inhumane fashion. He was finally killed in a helicopter crash and his remains buried at Kidst Selassie in Addis Abeba, among Ethiopia's heroes. However, to the Dirgue's chagrin, it was found out posthumously, that Gebrehiwot was a TPLF infiltrator wreaking havoc on EPRP/A on behalf of its narrow-nationalist front. Subsequently, the Dirgue ordered his graveyard to be desecrated and was defiled.

If there is a military operation undertaken by the EPRA in Tigrai repeatedly (at least four times), and each time came out unsuccessfully, (except the first one that targeted the high school in January 1976 and netted typewriters and a duplicating machine), it was the plan to raid the town of Wuqro. Each time, the EPRA's General Command provided to the hayl leadership undertaking the raid, information it reportedly obtained from the "party's committee" in the town. However, each and every time, the information about the Dirgue army's camp, the soldiers' preparedness, location and the like was full of misinformation and the exact opposite of what was given. Finally, in the next to last plan, the hayl military leadership prepared an ambush plan to intercept the army unit coming from Adigrat to Wuqro. Unfortunately, the late Taye Tola, one of the distinguished Oromo EPRA army commanders and trainers hailing from Arsi, and coming to the EPRA from the Air Borne, was easing himself under a bridge when the Dirgue's units suddenly came, and they had to be engaged prematurely. They scattered in fear to the nearby hills, and one of them aimed from very far at hayl commander Getnet's radio antenna and hit Getnet who later died (details above). In the final raid on Wuqro, depending again on faulty "insider" information, the EPRA unit was faced with an army unit that seemed to know the EPRP was coming and was ready for it. We lost irreplaceable comrades in this unsuccessful raid, like commander Hibstu, another Air Borne and a militant, and Ya'ebiyo, a Tigrean youth who matured in the EPRA to a level of providing capable military leadership at a *hayl* level, and who died during this raid in the town of his birthplace.

To this day no one knows whether the misleading information coming from the so-called "party committee" was the work of a TPLF infiltration, or a Dirgue mole (as this book went to press, Kahsay Abrha states in his book that Reda'e [a hayl 66 commissar and intelligence chief during this raid] summoned him and Fisuh

Gebrai on the eve of the raid to a hill away from Wuqro and they met urban party workers, who Kahsay says told them that *the Dirgue units were already aware of the planned raid and were prepared*. This crucial information was <u>not</u> shared with the commanders of the planned raid at that time by any of the three, and worse, even after the huge loss, when the raid was being evaluated later, perplexingly, none of the 3 revealed this information. Reda'e reportedly told the two not to say a word to anyone about this information because "it was unimportant to share the news since the General Party/Army Command had decided to surge forward with the raid no matter what". Obviously, this fact raises more questions than it answers: how did the Dirgue find out about the plan? Why did Reda'e and the two decide not to share this information both before and after the failed raid?)

The Final Nail in the Coffin: The Fourth EPRP CC Plenum

The fourth plenum of the EPRP CC was held in June 1979, at Walenta in Chilga, Gondar. According to the EPRP's constitution, a plenum had to be called every six months (a plenum is a CC meeting where 2/3 or above of the CC are in attendance). The third plenum was held in November 1976 and the last ordinary CC meeting in February 1977, followed by the politburo's (PB) meeting later that month, during the heat of the Red Terror. Thus, there were 2 1/2 years between the last EPRP meeting and the 4th plenum.

Also, this plenum was the longest meeting in the history of EPRP CC; it lasted about two months, interrupted a couple of times by the Dirgue's offensives, and by internal procedures as we will see below. No plenum has lasted the duration of the 4th plenum prior or since.

This was a plenum held following and in the face of severe organizational crises: the party has been completely chased off its urban structures; the TPLF had forced the evacuation of Tigrai by EPRA (and it was going to launch an armed attack in Wolkait soon after the conclusion of the fourth plenum); the Dirgue's attacks were incessant, and there was internal turmoil in the various sectors of the army and rural party structure. Members were questioning many aspects of the party's strategy and to many, the direction of the future looked bleak. The release of the plenum's decisions, rather than answering most questions, resulted in the opposite and exacerbated the simmering dissatisfaction.

Compounding these problems, as if the party could not thrive without creating more problems on itself, serious lapses in judgment by the leadership came to light during the plenum's proceedings. The first of these was the revelation regarding the decision to exclude Kiflu Tadesse, a CC/PB member, without his knowledge from all CC proceedings and meetings from March 1978 to June 1979, a period of fifteen months. He was now told he was reinstated and that new CC members had also been co-opted. According to him, during the time of Kiflu's exclusion, there were at least two occasions when fake meetings were held involving him. These highly unethical decisions were so unbecoming of an EPRP leadership, the plenum was hobbled right at the start when Kiflu strenuously objected to participate in the plenum unless his exclusion and the legality of the newly co-opted CC members (hence the legality of the very plenum session) were discussed. Kiflu was convinced to delay the first (his case of exclusion) and discuss it as part of the other agendas.

A few weeks before the fourth plenum, a meeting of six CC members had taken in Khartoum, perhaps to get input from a CC/PB member, the late Zer'u Khishen who was unwilling to come to the field for the meeting. It was decided at this meeting not to divulge any decisions and documents to Kiflu that occurred during the time of his exclusion.

One may surmise on the reasons Kiflu was excluded from CC meetings for fifteen months: he was one of the two CC members who stayed behind in the cities during the last active years of the party, and as such may have been held responsible for his decisions regarding the urban defeat at the hands of the Dirgue. Even after he arrived in Gondar, Kiflu has incessantly ordered the regional army leadership to provide arms that he could send back to the urban areas (personal communications with TA, who was a regional leader, and MY who was a CC member, and other sources, such as *ABS*.). Be that as it may, nothing would justify the undemocratic way in which it was decided to exclude him, and to put him through harsh times so much so he could not even have a shelter, or a department to stay with until the start of the plenum. Some 15 years later, however, Kiflu had tempered his radical impulses and at gatherings of ex-EPRP and EPRP members unsuccessfully convened to rebuild the party in 1995, he advocated for alternative and peaceful methods of

CHAPTER ONE: THE END GAME

engaging the TPLF and for being involved in Ethiopia, well before these ideas became mainstream. But very few of us at the time were willing to hear him out much less weigh the worth of his ideas.

In fact, there is some anecdotal evidence that Kiflu was held, or suspected to be solely responsible for the urban debacle. GT, who was a member of Zone 1 leadership of the ELAMA structure in Addis, and who was one of the few who left Addis in the final round, and who was a region 2 army leadership committee member since, recalls being summoned by Iyassu Alemayehu and Debteraw, to be questioned about his and the zone's experience with the EPRP CC. He told the CC that Tesfaye Debesai and Tselote Hizkias had a session with his zonal committee where they advocated why the urban armed struggle was the correct path for the party. GT recalls that the two used the examples of China and Russia to justify how in certain situations the urban struggle might be a better strategy than the rural.

Also, Hiwot Teffera, independently corroborates what GT said above. In her book, *Tower in the Sky*[24], she says three *Yebelay Akalat* came to her youth Zonal Committee meeting, explaining the new policy of staging an armed urban struggle. One of the three she recognizes from her USUAA days as Girmatchew Lemma, and she identifies the other two later in the book as Tselote and Kiflu Teffera What this meant was, and to Kiflu's partial vindication, he was not the only one pushing this fateful line, and that the CC was behind the decision[25]. However, at the 4th Plenum, according to Tsehaye, those CC members who were in Addis at the time (Samuel, Kiflu, Abebech and maybe Tadelle), told the Plenum that the issue was raised, but was not discussed due to an ongoing search and destroy by the Dirgue in the vicinity. What this means is that the teams that fanned out to various youth, labor and party Zonal committees to push for the intensification of the urban armed struggle were *not* probably carrying out a party decision.

Following this debacle, it was also curious how no one paid attention to the constitution of the party in co-opting seven new CC members. According to the constitution, the CC was entitled to co-opt only three more members until the convocation of the next

---

24. Hiwot Teffera. Tower in the Sky. Addis Abeba: Addis Abeba University Press, 2013, p. 205
25. personal communication with GT

congress (the second). However, according to Tsehaye, attention was indeed paid to the issue. Zer'u brought up the issue in Assimba saying that, especially after Tselote's death, the remaining CC could not in earnest say "we are the central committee". He suggested a congress should be called shortly, and until then fellows would be co-opted, and that the existing CC would take whatever "penalties" was thrown at it.

The fourth plenum was attended by fourteen CC members. Two, including Zer'u who was in Khartoum and refused to travel, were abroad and did not attend (the second may be AW). Half of the attendees were controversially co-opted new CC members. Those veteran CC members who did the co-opting justified their action by saying that it was a necessary step taken in order to save the EPRP, and the overwhelming majority in attendance seemed to be in support of the decision. However, in an irony, when the legality of the session was voted on after a month and half of meeting, the majority said the meeting was illegal and asked the 7 newly co-opted CC members to resign. After electing three more members (per the party's constitution), the session continued with 10 CC members for the duration of the plenum.

The agendas of the plenum were four: the assessment of the years of struggle of the EPRP; analysis of the then current Ethiopian condition; political positions of the party on various issues; and criticism and self-criticism along with task assignments.

To its credit, despite the disruptions of its session by internal and external factors, the CC completed its plenum and issued a 40-page massive document. It touched upon everything, from the party's failure in linking the issue of urban military defense to that of a popular uprising to endorsing the decision regarding the recognition of Eritrean independence. Concerning the latter, the party has always regarded the Eritrean issue as a national issue and not a colonial issue for which the party was occasionally assailed and punished by the Eritrean fronts. The communique signed by a delegation led by Tesfaye Debesay in mid-1976 was renounced by a subsequent meeting in 1977 to the anger of EPLF. However, in the February 1977 CC meeting, where 9 members attended, it was not clear why the Eritrean Question featured to be the main agenda in the face of massive repression and Mengistu's victory over Dirgue rivals that same month. Worse, the party moved away from its traditional cautionary position on Eritrea and conferred on it the right to

CHAPTER ONE: THE END GAME

independence which was subsequently made public in *Democracia*. The party's benevolent position on the Eritrean issue had led one Ethiopian historian and a one-time party member to question whether or not the EPRP leadership was nationalistic enough compared with other Marxist parties, an issue that needs more study and elaboration. Soon after the conclusion of the plenum, 4 senior members of the General Army Command, who were also among those illegally co-opted into the CC, resigned en masse (Dawit Siyum, Gazu, Roba and Yemane). This was a sad day again for EPRP. Leaders -no matter what their grievances - have a moral and ethical duty to see to it that their followers are in a safe place before they decide to detach themselves from their places of responsibility. Further, they should also weigh the consequences of their actions when they resign, and how it might affect their followers. To compound it all, to do the resignation as a group, was beyond comprehension. Kiflu, curiously says that "three of them could easily mobilize a large following against the CC had they chosen the path"[26]. Regardless of the questionable veracity of the statement, what does this mean? the issue is not the power struggle between a veteran CC and newly co-opted CC members; rather, the issue was and remains on how to make sure a leader carries out their responsibility to their followers and to their Party. The lesson from their resignation cannot be lost: No matter the weight of one's disagreements with their superiors their responsibility is to their followers and party until better times. All 4 of the leaders played crucial roles in the formation and growth of EPRA.

And naturally, the actions of the four leading senior members was imitated by the rank and file and resignation from the army and party became rampant. Fortunately, other senior members, equally disgruntled by and at the veteran CC, stayed true to their responsibilities and stayed with the rank and file to the bitter last - the most dedicated in the field (as we will see in the following chapters), and others in refugee camps and centers in Sudan, and this is the lesson worth honoring. Following the resignation of the four and the mass resignation, at least three institutions tried to maintain order and ease the peaceful transition of the party/army structure into Sudan: the Delegation assigned to call a congress and that daily dealt with the procedural/logistical issues of those resigning; the

---

26. The Generation, part ii, p.439

Provisional Army Leadership Committee named to replace the resigning four, and a Crisis Committee elected by members in Sudan to act as an intermediary between the party leadership and the members. Once again, just like the Ethiopian exiles of the Italian occupation like Yoftahe Nigussie before them a few decades ago, the EPRP patriots settled in the main towns of Sudan, such as Khartoum and Ghedariff.

Internal Turmoil and the Aftermath of the 4th Plenum's Document

The root cause for the internal turmoil inside EPRP/EPRA goes back to the decision by the party, or indecision by its structures, to be able to stop the urban offense-defense and failure to plan for a strategic retreat to rural areas when conditions allowed (for instance in 1975-76). At the same time the party decided to engage in defending itself in August 1976, it should have delinked that from a popular uprising (as the fourth plenum faulted it), and had it done so, it could probably have minimized the defense's role and duration, and instead focused on a strategic retreat to the rural areas (notwithstanding the repeated attempts for rural bases in Sidamo (September 1976 and belatedly, October 1977, and other areas). The party leadership however was a victim like the rank and file members of the temporary and fleeting "moral lifting inspiration and occasion to rejoice" when and where defense activities took place[27].

The second plenum held in August 1976, and where the CC members met for more than 40 hours[28] (Kiflu, p.119) was the most likely avenue where the impending crisis should have been foreseen, and serious plans made. Instead, the nearly 5 days meeting was spent on day-to-day affairs, CC member co-optation, and investigating the recent communique signed by T. Debesay's delegation and EPLF. Although the plenum in August and the CC meeting in June before it declared that the era of peaceful struggle was over due to Dirgue intransigence, other than proposing logistical provisions for EPRA as a solution, nothing strategic was laid out. Perhaps during its decision the following month in September to take out Mengistu in response

---

27. ibid., part ii, p. 286
28. ibid., part ii, p.119

CHAPTER ONE: THE END GAME

to the Meison/POMOA repression, alternative plans should have been considered if things went in an unplanned way. Some six months later, when the party CC met for the last time in Addis in February 1977, it spent an excessive amount of time discussing the Eritrean issue in an overnight meeting. Towards the end, Kiflu tells us three CC members whose names we don't know "raised questions about the wisdom of conducting the urban and rural armed struggle on an equal footing". Based on my personal conversation with AB, the first woman CC member of the EPRP, those who had serious reservations about the urban defense project appear to be those CC members emigrating from the US: AB herself, Samuel Alemayehu and Kiflu Tefera. (Hiwot might be wrong in thinking the third CC member that addressed her Zonal committee on the need to push the urban armed struggle was Kiflu Tefera). The CC began deliberating on the issue, but did not go far enough due to lack of time. By then, it was already dawn, and the meeting had to disperse. The meeting decided to discuss the issue at its next meeting, which never took place"[29]. Thus, the most important issue/agenda facing the party was postponed to be never picked up again.....

When the Urban Armed Wing (UAW) was formed in 1974, and activated in mid-1976 (was dormant due to EPRP's desire to pursue the peaceful struggle which the Dirgue would not allow), substantial reorganization and focus had gone into it from the summer of 1976 to December 1976 (resources allocation, organizational chart, and objective and goal clarification -procurement of arms, money and defense of vulnerable members). Again, there was little or no emphasis on emphasizing the protracted war, and planning a rural retreat. As a result, the UAW that was activated in mid-1976 was active for a while before it crashed and burned in mid-1977, and where there was no CC member to even witness the final crash.

It might be cruel and easy perhaps to use hindsight now to pass harsh judgment against EPRP's failure to strategically plan to strengthen the rural theatre of operation. CC members who were part of the decision making are probably the best resources to evaluate their experience. Most have passed away, and unfortunately, the second plenum was the last plenum where CC members who directly participated in the day-to-day affairs of the party sat and evaluated. The subsequent meetings were evaluated by CC members most of

---

29. ibid., part ii, p.188

whom had no direct experience in the affairs. The matter is so important and at the root of the derailing of EPRP's objectives, it would need a dispassionate investigation and understanding.

Even before the 40-page fourth plenum document was released, problems and questions had pervaded the party and army. As we saw above, the first was the factional issue in the urban areas emanating from the two dissenting CC members, Berhanemeskel Redda and Getachew Maru. While the faction's opposition to UAW operations may have merit, the alliance of some of them with the Dirgue brutal elements against their erstwhile comrades was beyond forgiveness. The problem then surfaced in the EPRA in Tigray. While the rectification movement done in the EPRA in mid-1977 gave space for all points of view to be aired, and for the army to rectify unhelpful methods of work, the movement left lingering questions and issues unresolved. Unfortunately, the TPLF problem followed suit and there was no time to deal with the dissident issues that were raised.

Soon after the EPRA forces in Tigray joined their Gondar comrades in 1978, questions and issues started emerging affecting the fighting spirit. During the rectification movement, such issues as the inability of the army to recruit and grow, the lack of foreign assistance, and the challenges posed by ethnonationalist forces among others were discussed. But the questions did not go away, especially after TPLF defeated the army, and as the Dirgue seemed to put more pressure on the army. Further, the EPRA and some party structures in parts of Gondar (Kinfaz, Begela, Semien) became frustrated when they realized the lack of support by some of the peasantry. There were times when peasants allied with the regime attacked the EPRA.

As in any dissatisfaction, the genuine concerns and the frivolous, personal failures and organizational weaknesses mesh, throw their lot together and become hard to categorize and solve. Both overt and clandestine coordinating committees of the opposition formed in Regions 1 and 3 (in Region 3, well before the plenum document became public). Those agitating for "change' did not have clear goals and were not a homogeneous group.

In Region 2 (Armachiho), following the release of the plenum document and the resignation of 4 senior members of the army leadership, mass resignation from the army and party structure became the order of the day.

CHAPTER ONE: THE END GAME

There was also a pre-existing tension between the region 2 leadership committee and the central command leadership that had moved to this region after coming from Tigrai via Tselemt (some members resented the fact that the central command chose for its seat a region close to the Sudan border). The tension between the two leadership committees mostly revolved around turf and jurisdiction. One flashpoint, according to GT, was the directive from the central command to the region 2 leadership to deploy 2 hayls (the region had 5 hayls at the time) to Wolkait (region 4) to help that regional army to repulse TPLF's aggression. The region 2 leadership committee initially defied the order because it argued that there was an impending attack by the Dirgue and they needed the two hayls there. This was true as later events showed. They finally relented and the two hayls were on their way to Wolkait when the Dirgue's army did a blitzkrieg and attacked a wide area of region 2 in a few days, burning houses and crops. This was a demoralizing loss both to the peasants and the region 2 army. To add insult to injury, those 2 hayls did not even make it to Wolkait when they learned that the region 4 army was defeated by TPLF, and it itself was retreating to Tselemt.

A committee composed of senior members from the Cadre school and political department tried to slow down the avalanche in region 2. They talked at length to each and every member with a resignation intent, and made a modest success of stemming the tide of resignations by promising a congress to be held and discuss all outstanding issues. Those who decided to orderly and as a group discuss the challenges moved to the Sudanese border, buried their weapons amid weeping and tribulations, and eventually went into the Sudan without holding the congress. Days before the weapons were buried, a team of EPRA fighters that were sent to China by the party for advanced guerrilla tactics training, and led by TA returned. It was hard to see the disbelief in their eyes and what was facing them. TA argued that all attempts had to be made to at least preserve the name of the party and army by leaving behind a small team. This task was not to be done by Region 2, but by remnants of Region 1.

For most members to learn otherwise of the party they looked up as infallible -admitting its many serious errors - was beyond their capacity to accept. They have sacrificed so much in living in harsh conditions hoping their party leadership would find ways to lead the struggle to better days and times. At one of the meetings where about twenty five cadres in the party's structure were discussing the plenum document, a female cadre collapsed when she heard the part that read, "the urban structures had abruptly collapsed". The discussion session had to be interrupted to take care of her[30].

Obviously, loyalty can elevate itself - and whether to a friend, lover, nation or political party- loyalty can convert to idolatry. When the party one thought was super-human was found out to be human after all, the consequences of crises were immense.

The situation in the other regions was more chaotic and damaging, especially to the peasants that were allied with the imploding EPRA forces. In the Tselemt area, a contingent of the army was in Eritrea returning with arms after engaging with TPLF in combat. When it got to its base, the remaining forces were in open rebellion and demanding that the General Command of the army to resign. The Leadership acquiesced to their demands and 3 members were replaced among from the opposition. When the contingent from Eritrea heard this, they were unhappy because they were not part of the decision and demanded a full meeting of all Region 1 members. A showdown seemed inevitable between on one hand those returning from Eritrea who argued that whatever problems they might have, they could solve them by following party and army rules and with the convening of a congress. Because of this position, they were called loyalists. On the other hand were those who recently won concessions from the Leadership by forcing the resignation of 3 members of the leadership. They were called liquidationists for their refusal to follow party and army rules. The "liquidationists" blinked first and started defecting to the Dirgue en masse.

Those army members who were to hold tight and would keep the EPRA name for more years rallied around such leaders as Tsegaye Debteraw, Mersha Yosef, Gayyim, Beker, Geleb Dafla, Iyassu and Samuel Alemayehu and Yishaq Debretsion, and would leave the Tselemt area for Eritrea by leaving a small force behind. They would be the subject of Chapter 2 of the book.

The peasant allies of EPRA were in a quandary. They knew the Dirgue would revenge on them mercilessly for their alliance with EPRA, so most resorted to do the bestial need for survival to prove their loyalty to the Dirgue by savagely killing erstwhile comrades who were doing army/party work solo, or in groups of twos and threes.

---

30. personal discussion with Abune Biru

CHAPTER ONE: THE END GAME

Tselemt was perhaps one of the best exemplary areas where the relationship between EPRA and the peasants was solid. The peasants were sold onto the EPRP politics and way of life (with the usual limitation of the peasant class giving weight to balance of power). To see that bond break in such a tragic way was beyond what words could describe. To see peasants like Aba Takelle, whose whole family were the vanguards and cheerleaders of the EPRP cause, turn against EPRP/A showed at long last we after all are human-all too human, with warts and all.....

Region 3 (the Belessa region) was the worst hit by the crisis. In a somewhat controversial move, the General Command had removed some regional leaders there in order to appease the opposition. It did not work. Gossip was rampant. Clandestine organization between the party and army structure was tangible. Discipline was absent among the army. Confused and disaffected members started defecting to the Dirgue. Others openly defied orders to fight and started asserting their independence.

When the plenum document was released, although the "liquidationists" did not get it through normal channels, some got it anyhow and a few blamed the party as *mut wokash*, or as bent on blaming the dead. In their mind, once a person is dead, he/she is above reproach or her record is not open for review. But this was just a fig leaf to what they were up to. They were secretly planning to form an independent organization. Around April 1980, the clandestine group arrested eleven regional commanders and those they perceived to be leading "loyalist" groups. The Dirgue that was monitoring all these developments made its move to give the final blow, and about 800 cadre and army members defected. When the "liquidationist" group realized what had befallen, they decided to retreat. Some went into the Dirgue; Tselemt was not an option; some went into Sudan passing through TPLF controlled area. About 37 negotiated with TPLF and were allowed to form an organization, the Ethiopian Peoples Democratic Movement, that eventually became an appendage of TPLF and a cover for TPLF's EPRDF. Some founding members of EPDM eventually left the organization, perhaps after sensing that they were being manipulated and used for TPLF's sinister purposes.

This was the tragedy of EPRP/EPRA that was simmering since the abrupt collapse of the party's urban structures, and overwhelmed by external and internal challenges that were not adequately resolved by the leadership at various times. This historical juncture could have sealed the fate of EPRP and EPRA if committed members had not decided to save what was left of the structures and rallied it for the re-launching of the party and army in the face of shrunken operating areas and demoralized remnants.

UDW -Structure and Operations

As pointed out above, the launching of the Urban Defense Wing (UDW) goes back to 1974 and its active operation did not start until early 1976. After the Dirgue declared the war of annihilation against EPRP, the CC discussed the tactic to be employed to counter the Mengistu/POMOA offensive[31]. The CC decided that it would take measures against leading figures who had perpetrated, drafted, and coerced the Dirgue into the implementation of the war of annihilation. Neither the Dirgue, as an institution, and its members in general, nor the political organizations and their general membership would be targets of the EPRP. According to Kiflu, the CC made it clear that it did not intend to engage in the offensive-defensive struggle against the Dirgue, and the MEISON, or the Sennay Likke group in general, but would retaliate against those who perpetrated and were behind the war of annihilation.

Essentially, the decision targeted those individuals who gave names of party members for execution, and those who actively pursued members and suspected members. *Democracia*, V.iii, #11 published in October 1976 has laid out the policy (some of the Dirgue officials accused of Red Terror crimes used this copy of *Democracia* and #9 in their defense to argue that the party had pledged to "return fire with fire"). The party's program made public in 1975 at Section A.II.4 has stated that it would pass judgment on those who perpetrated violence on the people, but this was a vague formulation with respect to the September CC decision which identified the types of targets.

As things unfolded later, however, the UDW was not just limited to the typical urban armed defense activities of any guerrilla movement, such as the procurement of arms and money, but faced a challenge in sticking to the party decision in "targeting targets" in the face of mounting losses by the party at the hands of the Dirgue.

---

31. The Generation, part ii, p.139

CHAPTER ONE: THE END GAME

Those guerrilla forces that engaged in scattered and infrequent UDW activities had their main forces operating in geographic areas away from the center of the regime they were fighting. Examples include, the ELF of Eritrea, China, and most Latin American guerrillas with the exception of those like the Tupac Amaru of Bolivia who had sworn to be just urban militant forces.

At its initial formation in 1974, the UDW was under the party CC through a single contact. Its operations mainly included safeguarding meetings, guarding committees and production units, and studying and training of members. As the Dirgue's repression and war of annihilation intensified in 1976, the UDW started having a definitive structure: a Military Commission (consisting of the late Yosef Adane, Zer'u Khishen and Tesfaye Debessay, among others) at the top, below which was the Rural and Urban Armed Wing leadership committee (members included Girmachew Lemma, Berhane Iyassu, Leftenant Merid, and Captain Amha Abebe). Then came in the hierarchy the Operations Committee which comprised the commanders of each unit. The lowest echelon was the unit which normally had a commander, a commissar, and two or 3 members. We can imagine, however, that this neatly laid out structure never lasted even one full year.

As the repression intensified, the UDW was expanded to a point that in a few weeks time almost all EPRP zonal committees including those in the various parts of Ethiopia formed their own military structures[32]. The urban military structure became a permanent feature of the EPRP and the mass organizations. Along with the restructuring, the interzones and the zonal committees were deciding the targets of operations with all the implications this carried.

This meant that the earlier policy where, after reaching a decision about a certain target, the Addis Abeba IZ was supposed to forward to the Military Commission, which checked to see if the target fell within party policy, was abandoned.

EPRP, whose superior organizational skills resulted in the formation of zones and interzones covering the entire nation, whose militant forces were organized in party-affiliated mass organizations, such as women's, youth, labor, etc. had most of its members and supporters in urban structures when it started implementing the UDW. Although attempts had been made to start rural armies in

---

32. The Generation, part ii, p.151

such places as Shewa (Kessem), Harereghe, Keffa, and Sidamo, the two provinces EPRP operated rurally were just Tigray and Gondar. So, the impending danger against the exposed overwhelming members of EPRP in the cities was clear to see. As a result of that danger, when in the final hours of 1978 the party was under duress to save the lives of its militants, a group of about 40 militants made it from Addis to Korem (Wollo), and yet, due to the repression, no contacts were available to accompany them to EPRA areas in Gondar. They had to stay in caves in the outlying areas for weeks.

Of the notable operations of the UDW, one of the most memorable was the Sendafa Operation of September 1976 where the successful operation netted 15 pistols, 100 automatic weapons and a round of ammunition that was quickly distributed to the UDW units. Also, the unsuccessful attempt on Mengistu Hailemariam's life on September 23, 1976, and a bank robbery that same month that resulted in the party getting 1.2 million Birr are the famous ones. The EPRP CC passed a death sentence on only 3 Dirgue members - Mengistu Hailemariam, Major Getachew Shibeshi for the Jimma massacre, and Colonel Teka Tulu. Regarding POMOA, the decision included as targets only those who had designed and drafted the policy of the war of annihilation[33].

UDW Activities versus EPRP Ethical Standards

The escalation of the UDW activities had double jeopardy for EPRP: on the one hand, it exposed the tens of thousands of Party members and sympathizers to the Dirgue's repression and torture; and similarly, in carrying out attacks against targets, it also tested the lofty aims of the party and challenged its rules and laws. EPRP is a party that was willed onto the Ethiopian political stage by unique historical circumstances that prevailed in the country some 40 years ago. It was a party that proclaimed to liberate the Ethiopian peasant from years of feudal bondage; it was a political party that set to work to do away with cultural and nationality oppression, and make Ethiopia a country where all it citizens irrespective of geography, language and station in life were going to be equal before the law;

---

33. ibid., part ii, p.154

CHAPTER ONE: THE END GAME

EPRP had noble goals about gender equality and brought women in great numbers to its cause for their liberation and equality. EPRP is simply a progressive political party guided in its heydays by a progressive ideology. Because of its emancipatory message, and a vision of a new and compassionate Ethiopia, EPRP was able to rally tens of thousands of members and numerous supporters.

The party had rules and bylaws that demanded the highest ethical standards from its members and affiliates. In order to be a member, a prospective candidate has had to go through a probationary period, and fulfill the criteria set for membership. These include exemplary behavior, conferred high esteem by the community in which one lives, being hard working, and one has always to be seeking to improve oneself, and one that holds the interests of the oppressed far above his own, and one endowed with a sense of justice, fairness and a sense of sacrifice for the cause.

These are high standards for an ordinary mortal to meet and always keep. And EPRP has had in its ranks thousands of such upright Ethiopians who gave themselves up as exemplars for the cause.

Unfortunately, and sadly, the urban defense operations severely tested EPRP's high ethical standards. As it is, operating as an outlawed opposition party anywhere has its confining limits to live up to rules and laws. When that is compounded by the hounding acts of a repressive regime, such a party is bound to violate international norms of engagement, and its own constitution and bylaws. A good example of this is the African National Congress which had to explain some of its less honorable deeds in front of a Truth and Reconciliation Committee.

For EPRP, especially, once the hierarchy and policy put in place by the party broke down, and the activities of the UDW were decentralized and outsourced, the party clearly veered away from its studied and based-on-approval targets. There were a few instances Kiflu cites that merit commenting:

1. One of these operations was on Colonel Teka Tulu, the Dirgue security chief and Mengistu's right hand man. He was selected as a target in September 1976, but the UDW units had hard time tracking him. Therefore, the units had to wait in ambush for a long time in the bushes surrounding his Gulele home. This aroused the suspicion and anger of his

neighbors, just showing how unpopular and unsupported such UDW acts were by the people. One evening the unit encountered a large and growing crowd. The residents asked the EPRP unit members about their identity and when their suspicions were confirmed, they tried to capture them. When the unit members ran, rather than shoot innocent people, the residents gave chase and threw rocks at them. Then a member of the unit blew a grenade and scared the residents and thus the unit managed to escape. Following this incident, the operation against Teka Tulu was cancelled[34]. It is very hard to imagine how members of a party that relied on the people for sustenance and fought on their behalf could feel at such sign of alienation and public outcry.

2. The unit that killed Dr. Fikre Merid did so at a chance meeting. It is stated that he was believed to be one of those who drafted the policy of the war of annihilation[35]. We do not know if his case was submitted to the CC, and that if he was an approved target. The fact that he was killed during a chance meeting might make it look appear as an arbitrary act.

3. Despite the precautions taken, Kiflu says some mistakes were committed by the UDW units[36]. The case discussed is someone killed in January 1977 because he was mistaken for Tesfaye Tadesse. Tesfaye was among the first people to put out a paper disclosing the identity of some EPRP members, and therefore he was a wanted man. An EPRP member testified that it was him, and he was killed only to discover later that it was not him...

4. During the trial proceedings of Dirgue officials in early 2000 for Red Terror crimes they committed, some of the defendants argued that EPRP was the main instigator of the confrontation and presented a long list of what they said were victims of the EPRP. Of these Fikreselassie Wogderess, Mengistu's deputy, gave an elaborate and detailed account of what he unsuccessfully thought would be a good defense against the allegations against him. It was an all-out deja vu attack against EPRP, this time in a court room. Of the

---

34. ibid., part ii, p.157
35. ibid.
36. ibid., part ii, p.158

CHAPTER ONE: THE END GAME

gruesome murders he alleged to have been committed by EPRP, one was the case of a Berhanu Mulugeta, an EPRP resident of Keftegna 12, Kebelle 11, and who is alleged to have killed 24 people. Berhanu was of course killed by the Dirgue, and the information that he killed 24 people seems to have been extracted from him under torture[37], or as the Dirgue frequently did, EPRP may have been blamed for murders the Dirgue or its civilian allied committed. Assuming some portion of this bit of information is correct,(and of course, this is a big assumption), again, it is fair to ask how many of Berhanu's victims were approved targets.

Of course, in a revolutionary situation where events and people are moving at a fast pace, where there is little time for reflection, and especially for an underground opposition party where the overarching concern is survival, the question of legality and prudence might sound luxurious. Besides, in a war situation, for a fighter to see his comrades die right in front of him as a matter of daily routine, and in what he perceives to be in a grossly unjust way, rationality takes leave and emotion and passion take over. However, even with all these factored in, the excesses of the UDW appear to be a permanent stain on an otherwise glorious history of the EPRP.

Almost any revolutionary movement of the 60's and 70's including those whose primary base of operation was in the countryside used urban guerrilla tactics to advance their causes. Latin America seems to be the continent where urban guerrilla warriors proliferated, in such nations as Brazil, Argentina and Uruguay (the Tupamaros). After democracy was returned to Uruguay in 1985, the Tupamaros returned to public life as part of a political party, and they are today the largest single group within the ruling left wing. A couple of the Latin American urban warriors of the 1970's are now presidents of their countries through power legitimately won at the ballot box - Jose Mujica of Uruguay (2009) and Dilma Rousseff of Brazil (2010).

On the other hand, under no circumstances should these evaluations of EPRP be misconstrued to let the Dirgue off the hook.

---

37. Special Prosecutor's Charges Against Col Mengistu H/M et al...and the Decisions of a Federal Higher Court (in Amharic), September 2008, p.124

EPRP

EPRP's self-defense acts, however repugnant, pale in comparison with the Dirgue's Red Terror, and later Netsa Ermija (license to kill). The Mengistu regime officially sanctioned the Red Terror campaign of total liquidation of the EPRP as a political group in state Proclamation 121 of 1977. Between February 1977 and March 1978, the Dirgue issued hundreds of orders and directives to state agents and cadres to kill. It also received reports of summary executions, torture, and extra-judicial killings of EPRP members[38].

Ethiopian centers of interrogation functioned under the Ministry of State and Public Security (MSPS). The Dirgue trained and armed local death squads and pro-Dirgue kebelles. It also created a paramilitary group, the Dirgue Special Forces and put their activities under the Dirgue Campaign Department (DCD). The DCD which coordinated the affairs of the MSPS, nebelbals, kebelles, and the DSF was itself under the command of the Dirgue's standing committee, chaired by none other than Mengistu. This elaborate bureaucracy of murder often worked efficiently.

On April 30, 1976, the DCD ordered the DSF to eliminate anyone who participated in the planned EPRP nationwide protest against Dirgue on May Day. The DSF carried out this directive that led to the deaths of thousands on that fateful day[39] (p.121).

According to Gebru Tareke, "although the Terror was launched under the overall supervision of Mengistu, its first phase was inspired and coordinated by Meison with such slogans as "White Terror with Red Terror", "Intensify the Red Terror", and "Democracy with the gun". Though it knew too well that the ghastly contest was between progressives, Meison nevertheless inappropriately reinvented terms in order to cast the EPRP in the mold of the Russian reactionary generals who prosecuted "White Terror" against the revolutionary Bolsheviks who responded with "Red Terror". It was a self-flattering, but false analogy. It also mischievously attacked the leaders of the EPRP as the disgruntled children of the dispossessed classes, calling them anarchists and nihilists in order to stir up class animosity. It worked direfully against the EPRP which had already alienated a cross-section of the urban poor by its ill-considered attempt to kill Mengistu; the dispossessed and underprivileged saw him as one of

---

38. Edward Kissi. Revolution and Genocide in Ethiopia and Cambodia, Lexington Books, 2006, p. 119
39. ibid., p. 121

CHAPTER ONE: THE END GAME

their own, a plebeian, because of his humble social origins and the progressive image he portrayed. The rhetoric or psychological warfare was as wicked as the physical violence was appalling.

Gebru continues, "the contest quickly became a mismatch, and the sheer scale of the brutality committed begs the imagination. Code-named Operation Mentir, the offensive to wipe out the EPRP in the capital comprised the Union of Marxist Organizations (Emaledh), "the revolution defense squads", the 291 urban dwellers' associations, and the security and paramilitary forces that were the praetorian guards of the Dirgue. The operation was waged relentlessly for 5 months during which time two major house-to-house searches lasting three to five days, were conducted to flush out EPRP's cadres"[40].

Generally, on top of the debacle brought about by the expanded urban squad activities, and compounded by it, EPRP members in the cities were faced with crucial problems: because of the continuing martyrdom of members, surviving members were overworked as they took over additional responsibilities; keeping appointments became increasingly difficult; committees were forced to break discipline and meet horizontally to keep things moving; the feeling by surviving comrades that situations were dictating their activities rather than a planned guidance from the leadership; the continuing culture of underestimating the Dirgue, and the overestimation of the party's and army's status; running out of safe meeting places, and holding meetings as comrades walked by; and the eventual demise of committees and the start of single contact work. As GT put it, the final days were like riding at a high speed in a driverless car to our eventual demise.

Hannah Arendt, a famous American Jewish philosopher of the 1960's, was unfairly condemned by Israel and many Jews for coining the phrase "banality of evil" to describe the atrocities of the Nazis' Adolf Eichmann, who after being hunted down, was being tried in Jerusalem in 1961 and whom she was covering as a reporter. By banality of evil, Professor Arendt meant that even the most ordinary people could commit the most vile crimes because they believed like Eichmann, that they were doing their job. Thus, In Ethiopia under

---

40. Gebru Tareke. The Red Terror in Ethiopia: An Historical Aberration? http://www.ethiopiafirst.com, May 2004, p.8

the Dirgue, many *kebelle* officials and *abyot tebakis* took part in gruesome torture and murder.

As the losses mounted, the party was forced to consolidate the various structural squads under one unified command[41]. The leadership, or what was left of it, issued bizarre assignments to the unified command that went against EPRP's high ethical standards, and luckily in most cases, either the human resources or the equipment needed to carry out the assignments were unavailable and most of the assignments were not carried out.

Finally, and sadly, the urban debacle came to an end on its own due to heavy repression, without any one in the leadership deciding to stop it.

The Cause:
The Import of Unresolved Issues?

The political parties such as EPRP and Meison that emerged during the 1970s were products of the student movement. The Ethiopian Student Movement that traces back its beginning to the 1950s was the only progressive and organized movement at the time and for many decades to come. Starting at Addis Abeba university and the various colleges, it eventually fanned out to the various high schools. The university mandatory National Service program helped plant the seeds of progressive ideas outside Addis Abeba in the provinces.

Student activism was not a domestic affair. Student unions and organizations were equally active in Europe and North America. The more durable student organizations were the Main Campus Student Union (MCSU), The National Union of Ethiopian University Students (NUEUS), and the University Students Union of Addis Abeba (USUAA) inside Ethiopia (and once USUAA was established, the other student unions ceased to exist); and abroad, the Ethiopian Students Union in Europe (ESUE) and the Ethiopian Students Union in North America.

During the course of the struggle, students articulated the demands of the day through such slogans as "Land to the Tiller", "Poverty is

---

41. Kiflu Tadesse. The Generation, part ii, p. 152

CHAPTER ONE: THE END GAME

not a Crime", "Academic Freedom", etc. The students put out massive amount of protest and organizational literature to rally their members and supporters. The famous ones included USUAA's "Struggle", ESUE's "Tiglachin" and "Tatek", and ESUNA's "Combat" and "Challenge". The forms of struggle included demonstrations, mass rallies, organizing guest lectures and class boycotts. Many activist students were not able to finish a 4-year college course on time. Some repeatedly went to jail and served time. There were at least two airplane hijackings as a form of protest, the first successful and carried out in 1969, and the second a not successful attempt, at the end of 1971 (an Ethiopian war hero, Brigadier General Tesfaye Habtemariam discusses in his book the formation of an anti-hijacking unit in Ethiopia where he himself served in that unit during the critical years of 1969-1972)[42].

When Berhanu Dinke, Ethiopia's ambassador to the US, 1961-1965, resigned his ambassadorship in June 1965 in protest against human rights abuses in Ethiopia, three student leaders of ESANA (the predecessor of ESUNA), Hagos Gebreyesus, Meles Ayalew and Berhanu Abebe, publicized their support of the move, and were summoned home by the Ethiopian Government. Berhanu's resignation letter was read subsequently at a student rally in Addis. Berhanu since has written a book about his experience on one side of the book, and a novella on the other, titled "*Kesar and Abyot/Albo Zemed*"[43].

Even graduating and employed students were part of the struggle by helping cover some expenses for the struggle. In general, until the watershed year of 1969, the civil and peaceful unrest progressed in a linear fashion with a few bumps. In fact, in the early 1960s, the Emperor even attended the annual student poem competition where it was not uncommon to read radical poems in front of the Emperor.

In 1969, Wallelign's paper on the National Question was published, and it was soon followed in 1971 by the Algerian Group's paper on the same issue authored by the pen name of Tilahun Takelle. At the same time, the 11th Congress of ESUE held in Berlin and the 19th Congress of ESUNA held in Los Angeles, brought to the fore the nature of the question and the seeds of split within the

---

42. Tesfaye Habtemariam (B/General). Yetor Meda Wullo (in Amharic). Addis Abeba, 2005, p.53-62.
43. Berhanu Dinke. Kesar and Abyot/Albo Zemed

unions (another irony is the fact that students who were opposed at the time to the notion of the rights of nations and nationalities, students like the late Senay Likke (for the Dirgue) and Andreas Eshete, have now ended up being architects and apologists of TPLF's ethnic federalism).

More significantly, the tense relation between regime and students changed for the worse, and Tilahun Gizaw, the then president of USUAA, was murdered in 1969. Many University student activists believed that peaceful struggle with the regime was coming to an end, and agitated for leaving Ethiopia for abroad to contemplate the kind of organization and enhanced methods the struggle would employ in the coming decades.

Given the shocking and total absence of student activism in EPRDF's Ethiopia today, one can only fondly recall the memories of a past era with undying hopes that one might see before one dies the same political and organizational activism from this generation. As stated above, the unions in Europe and North America have been afflicted since the 1970's with potential differences related to organization, the National Question, and political line. Many believe at the root of this difference was a competition to control and dominate the powerful student movement abroad and inside the country.

Bahru Zewde says "As it turned out the tension and friction that have been evident in the early 1970s came to a head at a meeting in Berlin in April 1973. That meeting brought together the leaderships of the two trends that eventually surfaced as EPRP and Meison. On the surface, the divergence arose over the nature and role of the reconstituted World Wide Union of Ethiopian Students, which was restructured as the World Wide Federation of Ethiopian Students. In actual fact, the formal debate over clauses and phrases concealed a crucial struggle between the two budding leftist organizations... Nothing illustrated this fact more dramatically than the mutual recriminations that the two leaders of the organizations, Berhanemeskel Redda and Haile Fida were seen to be exchanging on the sidelines of the meeting"[44]. Bahru said this in a book he edited summarizing a retreat he organized in Adama/Nazret in September 2005 inviting a spectrum of former student movement activists (it

---

44. Bahru Zewde, ed. Documenting the Ethiopian Student Movement, p. 16

was not clear why Bahru did not invite senior EPRP members like the late Yonas Admassu, his colleague at AAU, but instead invited someone like Genenew Assefa, whose contributions at the retreat were at best scant).

According to Melaku Tegegne, one of the participants, "the differences started in the student union in Netherlands, and later encompassed Europe, and eventually spread to the World Wide Federation. In retrospect, I think the differences were more organizational than political; it was a reflection of the rift between the groups that were later to organize as Meison and EPRP. Despite Haile's repeated trip to Algiers and lengthy discussions, no consensus could be reached between the two groups. In essence, they tacitly agreed to disagree"[45].

Regarding efforts to bring all progressive forces under one umbrella, Meison states that in July 1974, it formed an organization called the "Ethiopian Democratic Movement". To that effect, it adds that through its leader, Daniel Tadesse, the organization had contacted the "Abiyot" group of Getachew Maru, and a result of their close cooperation was a joint authorship of a news journal called "People's Voice" issued in March of that year. This cooperation was, however, short-lived as the two groups could not come to an understanding on the Eritrean Question. According to Meison, the "Abiyot" group insisted on Meison accepting Eritrea's colonial status which Meison rejected. From here, Andargatchew wrongly conflates the issue and attributes to EPRP as accepting Eritrea's colonial status which is a wrong statement as we will see in detail later[46]. Outside of this, Meison's effort through its "Ethiopian Democratic Movement" and its journal "the Progressive's Voice" seems to have only enabled Meison consolidate its organization and netted it new members, but failing to produce the desired unity of all leftist progressives.

Then, in 1975, there were hopeful signs that the two large leftist organizations were to undertake negotiations for this lofty goal.

According to Kiflu, the negotiations between the two parties continued after the groups' leaders came back to Ethiopia, and

---

45. ibid., Melaku Tegegn: p.73
46. Andargachew Assegid. Bachir Yetekeche Rejim Guzo (in Amharic): Meison inside the Ethiopian People's Struggle, Central Printing Press, 2000, p. 401

Tesfaye was the EPRP leader assigned for the task[47]. But as is known, the talks did not bear any fruit.

According to Meison's version (through the work of Andargatchew Assegid), the following were the facts surrounding this issue: both organizations named delegates to the talks, initially Dr. Tesfaye Debessay and Kiflu Tadesse for EPRP, and Haile Fida and Andargatchew Assegid for Meison. Andargatchew was replaced months later by Dr. Negede after the Land Distribution Proclamation. The discussions were held from February to April 1975. Allegedly, EPRP insisted that unless there is unanimity on the need for a PPG (people's provisional government - a slogan and a notion both organizations shared for over a year until Meison changed course and opposed it around the first quarter of 1975), that it was impossible for the two organizations to work together. As a result, the two agreed on minor issues such as on popularizing revolutionary ideas, on the distribution of their organs among each other's members, and to hold further talks. Once again, Meison changed its delegate and the latest discussion was between Dr. Tesfaye Debessay and Dr. Kebede Mengesha. In weeks, Dr. Tesfaye went underground and the talks were permanently discontinued[48].

According to Kiflu, Meison had experienced an internal power struggle, and former positions were reversed and the leadership was changed. Andargachew too seems to share this view. But neither Kiflu nor Andargachew provide names of the losers and winners in Meison's new realignment. Contact between the two groups was maintained until the land proclamation in February/March 1975. "Haile[Fida] had not shown up for two of his appointments, and when he did, he informed Tesfaye[Debessay] about the new "theory" of "Critique-support". Haile stated that Meison had decided to support the Dirg while continuing to be critical. Tesfaye then asked how it was possible to criticize a government which legally forbid{sic} criticism?..whatever Haile replied, the answer satisfied neither Tesfaye nor the EPLO central committee".

Thus the talks that could have potentially saved the course of the Ethiopian Revolution and perhaps the history of the country broke down and all hope was dashed. And the leading party leaders on

---

47. Kiflu Tadesse. The Generation, part ii, p. 198. See also details on p. 71-72, and in part i, on p. 227
48. Andargachew Assegid, p. 222

CHAPTER ONE: THE END GAME

both sides fell victim to Mengistu's terror: On the side of Meison, Haile Fida, Nigist Adane, her husband Desta Tadesse, Terefe Wolde Tsdaik, Kedir Mohammed, Hailu Gerbaba, and Eshetu Ararso died, while Daniel Tadesse and Kebede Mengesha committed suicide. On EPRP's side, Birhane Eyasu, Yohannes Berhane, Kiflu Tefera, Girmachew Lemma, Markos Hagos, and Berhanemeskel Redda died, while Tesfaye Debessay committed suicide. It is only fair to note here that for those EPRP members and other unaffiliated Ethiopians who lost their lives when Meison was collaborating with the Dirgue for 15 months, in its self-criticism, it takes responsibility for a 5-month period from March 1976 through August of the same year, although Meison adds hastily that it was doing this in self-defense, and that the real Red Terror had started in 1977 after it stopped collaborating with the Dirgue, and at that time it too was a victim[49].

Haile Fida, Meison's leader, while at Addis Ababa University in 1960, wrote an essay titled "*Man and His Destiny*"[50]. In it, he reflected whether or not there was such a thing called "Fate". He said, "limited though man may be, he still has the freedom to create things that will serve either as his salvation or his doom". His and his party's association with the brutal Dirgue sadly ended up in their doom, and wasn't Haile prophetic about his fate and future?

For a period of time in 1974, the two organizations advocated the same political positions (they both even supported Gizeyawi Hizbawi Mengist -Peoples' Provisional Government). Until February 1975, *Meison's* paper, T*he Voice of the Masses,* was just like *Democracia* was, critical of the Dirgue, supported CELU's ill-fated strike, condemned the killing of General Aman and 60 officials of the ancient regime, opposed the *Zemecha,* and denounced the Dirgue's war in Eritrea[51]. Then things started changing.

Subsequently, Meison stated in its organ, Yesefiw Hizb Dimtse that no agreement could be reached with EPRP on the assessment of the Ethiopian situation, alliance of forces, and the nature of the Dirgue. And from here on, the relation between the two organizations soured and went south.

---

49. Meison's self-criticism: July 1989, p. 49-50
50. Haile Fida. Man and His Destiny. UC Journal, pp. 14-16, in Voices From the Past, AAUP, 2010, PP.218-221
51. Kiflu Tadesse. part i, *Independent Publishers, 1993,* p. 157

EPRP

Some leading Meison members seemed to think that EPRP relying on a presumed alliance with the Eritrean fronts was in haste to initiate an armed struggle (this is on top of their outrageous allegation that the EPRP murdered its own leaders, such as Tselote Hizkias and Binyam Adane (see Andargatchew's book, and also Meison's self-criticism of July 1989 most of which is incorporated in Andargatchew's book). Andargatchew Assegid alleges that EPRP/EPLO was being pressured by the Eritrean fronts to "show its force" by dictating terms and destabilizing student unions[52]. Even those who initially supported EPLO shared this view. Efrem Dagne, now a businessman, and leader of the student union in the USSR in the 1970s says " then my organization[EPLO] began to forge closer links with ELF. Before long, the organization informed us through Kiflu Tadesse of the needs to discuss the importance of armed struggle. We argued that if we initiated armed struggle without first educating and organizing the people, the peasant would wipe us out. Kiflu & Co. countered that ELF would provide the necessary military training equipment. I objected strongly to this, saying that both Eritrean fronts were bent on secession, as they insisted that Eritrea was an Ethiopian colony"[53]. Further, he adds, "...the rift between EPRP and Meison goes back to before 1974. Nor could it be reduced to semantics of 'yashenfal' and 'yachenfal'. We returned to Ethiopia with our differences. We failed to narrow our differences partly because of the close links that EPRO(EPRP) had developed with the Eritrean fronts"[54].

It must be remembered that while supporters and leaders of the two organizations were fighting over some issues such as, the naming and structure of world-wide students Federation/union, over the national question, and over armed struggle, it was clear that they had formed clandestine political parties -Meison in 1968, and EPLO/EPRP in 1972. Thus, the fight in 1973 at the Berlin Congress was really a dress rehearsal for the fight that was to take place inside Ethiopia after the Yekatit revolution, and especially after the land proclamation.

---

52. Andargatchew Assegid. p. 303
53. In Bahru Zewde, ed. Documenting the Ethiopian Student Movement, Efrem Dagne, p. 143
54. ibid., p. 145

CHAPTER ONE: THE END GAME

Melaku says during the founding of EPLO, "we were led to understand that the ESUE leadership as well as two members of ESUNA were to be excluded from membership of the party". (perhaps with the knowledge or suspicion that the bulk of ESUE leadership formed their own clandestine party). He adds, "as the chairman of the organizing committee, it was Berhanemeskel who addressed the [founding] meeting. He stipulated that it be placed on record that 4/5th of the Marxists in Ethiopia were in attendance. He further made it clear that even though the European group was not present at the conference, the time may come when unity with that group may be achieved. To that end, it was desirable that 1/5th of Marxists were absent should be documented".

He then goes on to say that the politburo was tasked to find ways and means of starting talks with Meison (although Melaku says no one at the time knew the existence of Meison)[55]. But Kiflu says that when Haile traveled to Algiers, he broached the issue and invited the Algeria group to join them[56] (Andargachew too confirms this version)[57].

The 2 groups (EPRP and *Meison*) seemed to have the following differences, and neither side appeared to be big enough to compromise and overcome the gap: (1) that the Ethiopian people were not ready to seize a revolutionary movement, and that a revolutionary situation will take a long time to take place (EPRP appeared vindicated when the Yekatit revolution came about in February 1974); (2) *Meison* partisans appeared to be against armed struggle, while EPRP was enthusiastic about it; Senay Likke's formulation of "via Bole or Bale" seemed to succinctly summarize it;(3) initially there seemed a discernible difference on the National Question, but after the 1971 ESUE Congress, both sides seemed enamored with the Tilahun Takelle position on the issue and their positions converged; (4) then in April 1973 at the congress of the World Wide Union of Ethiopian Students Congress, things came to a head, and the split was sealed. Of immediate issue was the organizational structure of the student union. The groups that favored EPRP wanted a federal structure, while the ESUE group of

---

55. ibid., p.147
56. Kiflu Tadesse, part i, p. 78
57. Andargatchew Assegid, p. 76

Meison wanted to keep the union. The federalists won the day, but *Meison* partisans later met and decided not to join the federation.

When a year later the Ethiopian Revolution surged, partisans of the two camps started returning to Ethiopia with unresolved issues on their minds.

Professor Salem Mekuria's 1997 film, "*Deluge*", is a very well done cinematographic depiction of the differences between the two groups and the ramifications. Revolving around the main characters in opposite camps- her own brother Solomon as an EPRP partisan, and her best friend, Nigist Adane, as the *Meison*'s alter ego, Salem brought home the tragedy faced by that generation as a result of the split. Epitomizing the tragedy is the real character in the film of Nigist's mother who sorrowfully narrates her dilemma as her own children were waging a pitted fight in the family's home and outside (Nigist on this side, and Binyam and Yosef on the other).

In the early 1990's the heavy burden of picking up the wreckage of the two organization's relational debris, fell on the shoulders of Mersha Yosef of EPRP and Abera Yemane-ab of Meison, neither of whom were at the helm of power during the critical years of the mid- to- late 1970s. The cooperative working model the two set in motion in the establishment and operation of the Coalition of Ethiopian democratic forces (COEDF) was a modus operandi history did not allow two decades back. The EPRP leadership in COEDF, Mersha and Fassika, had to contend with significant opposition inside EPRP by some members who refused to forget the sins of Meison and the damage it wrought on the party. Abera, in particular, paid the heaviest price starting in 1994 when he was one of COEDF's delegation to a Peace Conference at the Ghion Hotel to which EPRDF had initially agreed and later reneged. Abera was thrown in jail by EPRDF on trumped up Red Terror charges. Although the courts threw the charges out for lack of evidence, Abera was unable to leave the jail and the country and rejoin his family until 2012.

Relation with the Eritrean Fronts

Some members of ESUE and ESUNA had either written Othman Saleh Sabeh (one of the founders of ELF, later split to lead his own faction) or inquired about assistance or cooperatively working together. One ESUNA activist says they talked to him when he came to the USA, and told him Ethiopian progressives supported

CHAPTER ONE: THE END GAME

Eritrean self-determination, and since the objective of both struggles is achieving socialism, there was a lot to cooperate about. His answer was that since there are suspicions by the Eritrean fronts about those coming from the center of the country, they can trust only if the Ethiopian progressives accept unequivocally Eritrean independence[58].

This position of Othman Sabeh was to epitomize the demand of the Eritrean fronts in subsequent years. Any equivocation, as the EPRP did plentiful, was to earn their wrath.

To wit, Sabeh was instrumental in introducing the party's delegates tasked with preparing for the armed struggle (Kiflu and Berhane) to Arab diplomats. He also helped secure passports for EPLO organizers[59]. To that effect, he facilitated their training by the Palestinian fronts and others, and saw them through until they left for Eritrea. He gave them a letter to give to Isayas who by then had split from ELF, and was the leader of the nascent front, ELF/PLF, later EPLF. Isayyas read the letter, put it in his pocket and muttered that Sabeh is only a foreign affairs representative and had nothing to do with military issues. Sabeh is reputed to have recommended to Isayas to give the newly-trained EPRA units all the field arms they needed[60]. Isayas delayed EPRA's transit to Tigrai for over 1 1/2 years blaming the on-going war between his forces and that of ELF. In the meantime, he was breathing down the neck of Berhanemeskel, the group's only official contact with Isayas, to accept Eritrea's colonial relations with Ethiopia, and its independence. Without getting a straight answer such as the one he got from TPLF forces who were there at the same time, Isayas seemed to have decided to punish EPRA units.

While they were being delayed, the EPRA units held heated discussions among themselves about the Eritrean question, and some differences were discernible. There are unconfirmed reports that Berhanemeskel might have promised Isayas that he would use his influence as secretary-general to sway EPRP's CC to accept Eritrea's colonial status and its independence. This may have resulted in Isayas relenting and letting the EPRA units leave for Adi Irob. Even if the unconfirmed reports are true, Berhanemeskel might have said that just to get the forces to Assimba. As a matter of principle on the

---

58. In Bahru Zewde, ed., Abdul Mohammed, p. 79
59. Kiflu Tadesse. part i, p. 97
60. Asmamaw Hailu. EPRA, P. 227

Eritrean Question, Berhanemeskel was adamant in his opposition to the position the delegation led by Tesfaye Debessay took in 1976 deferring the question and appearing to concede to accept independence which the Party CC subsequently abjured (*On The Mass Line*)[61].

Isayas's suspicion was reinforced by among other things, the resolution of ESUNA's 22nd Congress held in August 1974, that ridiculed Eritrea's claim of colonial status, and its petit bourgeois leadership[62]. Of course, For Isayas, ESUNA was not an independent mass organization, that finally deprived its support for the party, but seemed to be an appendage. At the end of 1976, Tsehaye, Debteraw, Gayyim, Gurmu and Tesfaye went to EPLF to ask for some assistance. Again, the same demand was put. Subsequently, Tesfaye/the delegation signed a joint communique that underscored Eritrea's right to self-determination, including up to independence. Tesfaye/the delegation had no such mandate, and as a result, he was criticized by the party, and the agreement was pronounced null and void, and was not distributed to the public despite the agreement's call[63]. When Tesfaye heroically killed himself, The EPLF to their credit, eulogized him in their monthly magazine, *Vanguard*, October 1977 edition[64].

One could imagine how furious the EPLF was, and biding its time for a revenge. It got it in mid-1977 when EPLF held its first congress and invited EPRP, along other numerous invitees. Representing EPRP/A, Debteraw, Tsehaye and Roba were the delegates. The late Tariq Aziz was Iraq's delegate. There were European socialist and communist party delegates, and Middle Eastern diplomats. The EPRP/A delegation was told right from the outset not to talk to any other delegation without authorization from EPLF officials. The Yemeni delegate wanted to talk to them and was looking for an opportune moment. When they secretly met, he told the delegates not to cooperate with the dictatorial EPLF, and instead to work with the Dirgue which reportedly was soon to call for a united front of all democratic forces in Ethiopia.

---

61. Berhanemeskel Redda. On the Mass Line, 1977, p. 12-13
62. ibid., p. 274
63. Kiflu Tadesse. part ii, p. 121
64. Ghelawdewos Araya. Ethiopia: The Political Economy of Transition, University of America, Inc., 1995, ch.4, p. 124

CHAPTER ONE: THE END GAME

At the end of the congress, Isayas' deputy, Ramadan Mohammed Nur, gave the closing speech. He singled out EPRP for condemnation, and glorified TPLF. He asked fraternal parties and fronts to condemn EPRP and its machinations to thwart Eritrean independence![65]. Following this, many EPRP members in Eritrea started disappearing, and the relations never recovered.

On the other hand, ELF had never been as insistent as EPLF to demand of the party a colonial category for Eritrea. ELF allowed entry and delivery of the batch of weapons the party received from Palestinian friends around 1977. Of course, it was ELF that gave the retreating EPRA units safe haven and passage to Gondar when the army was forced to evacuate Tigrai 2 years later.

EPRP's position on the Eritrean Question, that could not be called cut-and-dried, admitted the complexity of the issue. Unlike TPLF, that unhesitatingly accepted the colonial thesis, and as a result reaped the fruits of its unprincipled position, EPRP had to navigate through the maze of the intricate historical relations between Eritreans and the rest of Ethiopians. To imply that because EPRP relied heavily and optimistically on the help it was going to get from the Eritrean fronts, it neglected to consolidate its alliance with the remaining leftist forces, requires substantial evidence to stand on its legs.

As we saw above, the student union members and leaders have heard an earful from Othman Salah Sabeh before even EPRP approached him for facilitating training assistance. The fact that EPRP never accepted the colonial thesis advanced by the fronts partisans should also say volumes about EPRP's expectations on the limits of the help to be rendered by the fronts. The initial EPLO forces that came to Eritrea were surprised to see some students who were activists back at Addis Ababa University now under the banner of EPLF. Such activists included Tesfu Kidane and Yohannes Sibhatu[66] and Afeworki Teklu[67]. Yohannes Sibhatu was an editor at *The Ethiopian Herald*[68]. Another progressive who went over to the EPLF was Taemeselasse Beyene. He was the chairperson of the progressive multi-national, and multi-organizational group that was

---

65. Asmamaw Hailu. p. 226-7
66. Asmamaw Hailu. p.42
67. Kiflu Tadesse. part i, p.151
68. Bahru Zewde. p. 47

instrumental in the drafting, and implementation of the 1975 Land Distribution Proclamation. As soon as he was invited to join the Dirgue's People's Provisional Organizational Office, he escaped to Eritrea[69].

Both Tesfu and Yohannes and many other democratic Eritreans who made the mistake of joining an ethno-nationalist force in EPLF, than staying true to the tradition of their youthful commitment of struggling for a better Ethiopia, were murdered by Isayas's intelligence units as "*manka'e*" (bats). Perhaps because at the initial stage of EPLF's formation as a breakaway group from the traditionalist ELF and as a progressive movement, this might have been an attraction to Eritrean progressives. With their democratic ideals, and autonomous free will, they could not toe the EPLF party line for long (Neither was ELF a saint; it had liquidated its own free thinkers dubbing them "*falool*") (anarchists).

Back to EPRP's equivocation on the Eritrean Question: At that time, the question was not studied very well and debated either within the student unions that preceded EPRP, or within EPRP itself. The question that was discussed and debated was the broad category of the National Question, and the context was mostly a Marxist-Leninist rendition. So, if EPRP refused to categorize the Eritrean Question as colonial, it did not feel comfortable to put the Eritrean case on a par with other nations and nationalities in the rest of Ethiopia and call it a "National Question". Therefore, what the party decided to describe it was as a "Question that resided in the broader notion of the National Question", and for good measure, added that as long as the party accepted the right of nations to self-determination, including and up to secession, including the Eritrean case, the party has discharged its revolutionary duty. And occasionally, and at its last plenum in particular, the party called for Eritrean independence. EPRP repeatedly called for the Eritrean Question to be resolved peacefully, and democratically, and condemned the Dirgue's harsh wars on Eritrean civilian population. This never placated the Eritrean fronts, particularly the EPLF, as we saw above. Nothing illustrates this better than what Amare Tekle, a former EPLF mole in Ethiopia's Foreign Ministry, and even in old age, a polemicist, says on the issue in response to Professor Bahru Zewde's take on the issue. Says Amare to Bahru "*you claim that the*

---

69. Andargatchew Assegid. p. 296

CHAPTER ONE: THE END GAME

entire Ethiopian left had consistently supported Eritrean independence (via "secession", if not decolonization) is historically incorrect. All available records of meetings between the EPRP, MEISON and the EPLF indicate that, in spite of their theoretical support for secession, these two groups and others had in fact shied away from recognizing the right of Eritrea to a political existence outside Ethiopia. True, agreements were signed; but agreements were broken not much after their signing. It was only towards the end, for example that the TPLF and later the EPDM recognized the Eritrean struggle as an anti-colonial struggle and supported Eritrean independence. It is not without a certain amusement, therefore, that I noted your exhortation of the remnants of the Ethiopian left to reconsider- indeed to change-their position..." (A Response to Professor Bahru Zewde)[70].

Tsehaye correctly describes the categorization problem. He says it cannot be dealt as a national question because there is no nationality called Eritrea. There are 9 nations/nationalities within Eritrea. The Ertitrean question was the creation of European colonialists and to a certain extent the Eritrean petti-bourgeois that came into being as a result of the colonial heritage (personal communication).

Looking back today some 3 decades later, it seems the party's equivocation at the time reflects the dilemma and ambiguity displayed by Ethiopians to this day. One evidence that can be presented is the 1998-2000 wars Ethiopia under the TPLF/EPRDF fought with the Eritrean government under EPLF. This was after the TPLF/EPRDF had proclaimed that it has within its hands the solution to the biggest political problem that bedeviled Ethiopia for decades. TPLF, after accepting Eritrean colonial status, and benefiting from the partnership it forged with EPLF, even by deploying a brigade-equivalent armed assistance for EPLF in fighting against Ethiopia under the Dirgue, and after dislodging the Dirgue, arranging Eritrea's so-called referendum, and petitioning the UN to grant Eritrea its independence, could not solve the Ethio-Eritrea problem.

Although, one could say with certainty that there is unanimity among Ethiopians in disagreeing with TPLF's disposal of Eritrea in a sham referendum, the agreement ends there. Today, some, notably, citizens like Professor Yacob Hailemariamhave methodically argued that one of the ports currently under Eritrean possession, Assab, legally belongs to Ethiopia. To that effect, Yacob and others have

---

70. Amare Tekle. A Response to Prof. Bahru Zewde, *www. dehai.org*, January 22, 1999

marshaled and submitted unassailable evidence[71]. On the other side of the spectrum, intellectuals *like Professor Tesfatsion Medhinie,* an Eritrean that has for many years vehemently spoken against the Eritrean fronts, and advocated a peaceful solution, takes issue with the "Assab Camp". He thinks it is counter-productive and equates the movement with the Dirgue's division of Eritrea into two administrative regions in its final days, that according Tesfatsion had angered many Eritreans. Instead, Tesfatsion argues for what he calls "an open confederation", in which Eritrea will retain its nationhood along with its two ports, but envisions, eventually, the two nations may come back together and form a single country one day. While envisioning this, Professor Tesfatsion appears to expand it by also suggesting that the Ethio-Eritrean Confederation might also serve as a model for other East African countries to join it gradually. A third position is one supported by the likes of Professor Daniel Kinde that states that a federal arrangement might be the best choice for the two peoples[72]. Then there is the position of a good number of Ethiopians not articulated by any intellectual as far as I know. And that position says "they have opted to go. Good riddance. Good luck with their new home, and we should focus on ours".

And within EPRP, the Eritrean Question was never laid to rest in the February 1977 CC meeting. After ebbing and flowing in the next decades, it was once again to flare up at the Third Party Congress in Bonn in 2000 and almost divide the party leadership into two camps between those who advocated recognizing Eritrea's de facto independence, and those adamantly opposed to it.

EPRP in the Eyes of Foreign Writers

Most foreign writers have tried to take a dispassionate and detached position on the Ethiopian revolution. However, their conclusions and interpretations of events are obviously informed by their ideologies, convictions and preferences. To illustrate that, we should perhaps start with the Cuban writer Raul Valdes Vivo. In his

---

71. Yacob Hailemariam. Who owns Assab? (in Amharic); Question of Ethiopia's Gateway to the Sea, 2012
72. Daniel Kinde. The 5 Dimensions of the Eritrean Conflict, 1941-2004: deciphering the geopolitical puzzle, Signature Book Printing, Inc. 2005, p.368-374

CHAPTER ONE: THE END GAME

book, *Ethiopia's Revolution*[73], he shows in an unabashed form his political partnership with the Mengistu regime. For Vivo, those who opposed Mengistu and his regime are nothing but reactionaries. Says he, "it should also be noted that a great many students have adopted an entrenched anti-militaristic stance, that could only be justified if the armed forces had taken the side of the oppressors; in effect, because of this, many students have themselves ended up on the side of the oppressors (sic!), whether or not they want to admit it. The so-called EPRP, that engages in counter-revolutionary terrorism in the cities, originally drew its ranks from the students. As was only to be expected, they had their inspiration in Maoism. Of course, also present in the petty bourgeoisie's loathing of discipline, organization, and giving way to the masses".

John Young, a TPLF partisan, in his book, *Peasant and Revolution in Tigrai*[74], says "the leading element [of the opposition] was the Marxist-Leninist EPRP which demanded a quick end to military rule and the formation of a people's government. This question increasingly came to the fore and tensions between the government and its radical urban critics became violent as *the EPRP started a White Terror* campaign in 1976 against the government, which in turn responded with its far more lethal Red Terror campaign. Initiated in Addis through the kebelles, the government spread the urban terror throughout the country.

Another long time TPLF partisan, the late Paul Henze, weighs in in his "*Layers of Time*"[75]. For Henze, "the party was an outgrowth of the shadowy Ethiopian Peoples Revolutionary Movement, a radical grouping that appeared in the late 1960s among Ethiopian students in Europe and N.A". Perhaps drawing on his espionage resources, he adds that Haileselassie security services had evidence that the Soviets regarded it as an embryonic communist party and *used it as a channel for supporting student agitation in Ethiopia after several Soviet and East European operatives were expelled in 1968/69.* He then goes onto say "EPRP was Marxist but anti-military and rapidly attracted a large

---

73. Raul Valdez Vivo. Ethiopia's Revolution. New York. International Publishers. 1978, P. 65-66
74. John Young. Peasant Revolution in Ethiopia: The TPLF, 1975-91, CUP, 1997, P.59-60
75. Paul Henze. Layers of Time: A History of Ethiopia. NY. St. Martin's Press, 2000, p. 293

following of *ill-disciplined* intellectuals, students and junior government officials. The eagerness of EPRP to claim the right to lead the revolution soon put them at odds with dominant Dirg elements and their relation with EPLF, TPLF and Meison also came to entail a great deal of rivalry".

Among those who do not fall for the false dichotomy of white v's Red Terror, Christopher Clapham and Edmund Keller are the leading voices.

According to Keller, "the left opposition was predominantly urban-based, while the right operated almost exclusively in rural areas. We may include in this group all dissident activities ranging from those of students, teachers, trade unions, individual publishers in the underground press (which thrived until the latter part of 1977) to those of the extremist organization known as the EPRP. The EPRP, Meison and POMOA practically disappeared during the Red Terror. The Dirgue triumphed over the civilian opponents not surprisingly since it controlled the military". Then, in a footnote, Keller adds, "Meison and POMOA disappeared completely, although some of the leaders remained active politically, resurfacing either within the new ML parties formed in 1978, or in the ethnic opposition movements, particularly the OLF. The EPRP survived as an organization, but it became much smaller and weaker, a marginal movement no longer active in the cities"[76]. Further, Keller adds "the feeble but irksome terror of the EPRP was now (1977) answered by the massive terror of the State".

Keller also talks about the ideological differences. Says he, "Meison was willing to accept the idea of military rule, at least for a moment. EPRP was diametrically opposed to the idea. The debate between the two groups first took place in the pages of pamphlets, newspapers and did a lot to shape the thinking of the general population on what should be the nature of the new Ethiopia. In addition to their contradictory positions on the issue of military rule, EPRP and Meison differed on the kind of democracy they envisioned. Meison favored "controlled democracy" guided by a vanguard party. The EPRP pressed uncompromisingly for an unlimited "people's democracy". Speaking of the press, Marina &

---

76. Edmund Keller: Revolutionary Ethiopia: From Empire to People's Republic. Bloomington. IUP, 1988, p.41(N.13); P. 161; P. 197

CHAPTER ONE: THE END GAME

David Ottaway in their book, "Ethiopia: Empire in Revolution"[77], state that "underground groups joined in what amounted to a de facto civilian campaign to force the military from power. The most notable of these was the EPRP, which eventually became so vocal that by the spring of 1976, the Dirgue allowed the state-controlled press to express its viewpoints and courted its support.

Clapham is more philosophical and more holistic about the positions of the Western left on Ethiopia. "Western left comment has generally been hostile sometimes violently so. This is partly the result of the fact that quite a number of Ethiopian Marxist intellectuals took up the cause of EPRP which was from the start violently opposed to the Dirgue. Another strand was that development of links between the Western left and separatist Marxist guerrilla movements, notably EPLF[78]. On EPRP's ethnic composition, which, of late has been ignorantly thrashed and makes out EPRP to be a northern Ethiopia party only, Clapham states "by comparison with Meison, its leadership tended to be younger, to have been educated locally or the USA rather than Europe, and to be drawn from the north. To some extent, ethnicity influenced membership in other ways; in south-western Shoa, for example when Oromos were likely to support Meison, Gurages tended to opt for EPRP, while in Harrar, it similarly gained some support from Aderes."

Other writers commenting on that period include Kjetil Tronvoll who says both the EPRP and Meison were victims of the Dirgue's Red Terror: in 1977/78 the state launched a military campaign called the Red Terror against political fronts. Tens of thousands of Ethiopia's intellectuals and politically-conscious men and women were killed during this period, while an even larger number fled from the cities to the countryside and abroad.

John Markakis highlights the problem inherently associated with calling oneself a "proletarian vanguard". Others also make similar claims. EPRP claimed that is a vanguard in its political position and the purity of its line. The soldiers called themselves Workers in Uniform. In another book, he co-authored with Nega Ayele,

---

77. Marina & David Ottaway. Ethiopia: Empire in Revolution. New York. Africana Publishing co., 1978, p.9
78. Christopher Clapham. Transformation and Continuity in Revolutionary Ethiopia. New York. CUP, 1988, P. 17

EPRP

Markakis says the Dirgue regime's inept propaganda effort gave the EPRP massive publicity[79]. He explains EPRP's defensive response by saying "the EPRP struck selectively, and even gave its enemies advance warning". Finally, "the EPRP suffered heavy causalities, but fought on undaunted"[80].

Nega Ayele, an economist and a lecturer at A.A. University, was a member of the EPRP's political department. He died with his comrades including the most known foreigner member of the EPRP, a British geologist teaching at the university, Dr. William Hastings Morton, Yohannes Berhane, a CC member, Melaku Markos, a de facto CC member and secretary of the zonal committee overseeing Sidamo, Gamu Goffa, Bale and Arsi. Markakis, in a memoriam to Nega, says of his activism, "typical of an uncommon generation".

John W. Harbeson says EPRP was one of those that threatened the Dirgue. "the government's postponement of civilian and more democratic rule contributed to its apparent retreat into counter-revolutionary posture. The EDU opposed the Dirgue from the right but never threatened its rule as seriously as did movements seeking the liberation of Eritrea from Ethiopia or as did the EPRP which disputed the government's claim to rule.

Perhaps more than anyone else, Harbeson analyzed in much greater detail the political differences between Meison and EPRP on such issues as (1) the nature of the post-imperial state; (2) the role of elections; (3) nationalities self-determination; (4) socio-economic development[81]. The late Harold G. Marcus, in his "History of Ethiopia"[82], says Meison had willingly cooperated with the Dirgue in suppressing the EPRP, its political rival, in order to build its own power base among peasant associations and kebelles. Once the EPRP was gone, however, Mengistu then turned on Meison".

---

79. John Markakis & Nega Ayele. Class and Revolution in Ethiopia. Trenton. NJ. The Red Sea Press, 1986, p. 164.
80. ibid., p. 162; p. 167
81. John Harbeson. The Ethiopian Transformation: the Quest for the Post-Imperial State. Boulder, Westview Press, 1988, p. 150-157
82. Harold Marcus. A History of Ethiopia. Berkeley, UC Press, 2002, p. 200

CHAPTER ONE: THE END GAME

Why a Radical Movement, and Not a Reformist One?

The Ethiopian Student Movement out of which EPRP and other leftist parties emerged was a radical movement by any account. Of the parties that grew out of it, EPRP was undoubtedly the most radical. For Messay Kebede, Ethiopian students rejected the liberal position, not because it was inappropriate but because it contradicted their prior ideological commitment to radicalism[83]. Ali Mazrui, the famous Kenyan professor who was invited to give a lecture to Addis Abeba university students in December of 1973, just 2 months before the breakout of the Ethiopian Revolution, said of the students "the most radical African students he had ever addressed[84] ". The prior commitment to ideology" of which Messay spoke had its roots according to him in the miseducation of Ethiopian students. He rightly argues that due to a lack of national ideology, the Ethiopian education system was deficient.

Nothing shows this deficiency clearly as the lack of robust history courses explaining the reasons for Ethiopia's independence. Messay says instead, an 8th grade history book was "the *Old World-Past and Present*"[85]. He continues by saying that unlike other revolutions, anti-imperialism opposition to internal reactionary forces did not follow the path of a nationalist stand advocating the defense of the traditional culture.

Although this is a theme Messay repeatedly analyzes and dissects in his books, his analysis does not account for the dilemma of Ethiopian radicals in melding traditional culture with a radical ideology. They did not totally neglect the culture as Messay alleges. But they were not able to invoke it forcefully and synthesize it with Marxism-Leninism, and their youthful defiance and the international fad of the ideology might have been the greater culprits. A good counter example is the actions and policies of another democratic movement in feudal Ethiopia of the 1960s - the Confederation of Ethiopian Labor Union (CELU). From its inception in 1963, CELU

---

83. Messay Kebede. Radicalism and Cultural Dislocation in Ethiopia, 1960-1974, University of Rochester Press, 1999, p.2
84. Mazrui, Ali. 1978, p. 262
85. Messay Kebede., p.58

did not entertain a radical ideology, and was led by relatively older folks with family and community responsibilities unlike the students. CELU leaders in the 60's and early 70's included at least 4 university graduates, and the rest were elementary to high school levels.

It can be said that the two democratic organizations in feudal Ethiopia were the student unions (both inside the country and abroad) and the CELU. (The Ethiopian Teachers' Association -ETA- formed in the 1960s, could also belong to this select group. However, ETA was similar to the student unions in many aspects, and tremendously contributed to improve teachers' working conditions and gave a boost to the overall social justice struggle).

Some of their similarities included both elected their leaders, both had constitutions, and both had their organs (CELU's *Voice of Labour* and USUAA's *Struggle* and the papers of the student unions abroad, such as *Challenge* and *Combat*).

CELU's first constitution was a translation of the constitution of Workers' Union of Kenya. The Amharic translation was done by Dr. Bereket Habteselassie and Professor Mesfin Woldemariam. The latter also helped find an artist to design CELU's logo. These two men advised CELU in its early stages, including a $500 gift by Professor Mesfin, money obtained from the sale of his famous book, *the Geography of Ethiopia*[86].

Their leader for the time of interest (1963-1975) was Beyene Solomon, an Ethio-Eritrean with humble beginnings and no or little formal education. In his autobiography, he says "an appropriate relationship has to be established with the government. Not too close, and not too distant. But better to be closer than distant"[87]. These are the wise words of a pragmatic labor leader who practiced what he believed as we see below in advancing the interests of Ethiopian workers.

In line with this, when the Emperor made the office of the Prime Minister more powerful by adding to it more duties, CELU promptly sent a letter to the Emperor thanking him for pioneering changes in government[88]. In 1962, the Emperor was urged by his more conservative advisors to delay the issuance of the Labor Decree that

---

86. Beyene Solomon. Fighter for Democracy: The Saga of an Ethiopian Labor Leader, Publish America, 2010, p. 61
87. ibid., p.234
88. ibid., p.112

CHAPTER ONE: THE END GAME

recognized the rights of Ethiopian workers for the first time to form unions and codified their bargaining rights. Labor Minister Getahun Tessema was a progressive voice that added his weight behind the Decree, and the Emperor declared that if the country was going to do it later, it might as well do it now, and issued a proclamation in September 1962.

In 1968, when CELU built its modern office, high government officials were invited and attended the inauguration. When students went on strike in the late 1960's and were jailed, Beyene went to the PM's office and protested their jailing saying they were workers' children and their protest could ignite strikes in CELU. The PM who was not seeing anyone that day was open to see and talk to the labor leader.

On May 25, 1973, the Emperor joined celebrations with African labor leaders in Addis in recognition of the formation of the Organization of African Trade Unions Unity. On July 23, 1973, for his 80th birthday, CELU gave a gold cup to the Emperor as a birthday gift.

The smooth relation between the government and CELU was so much so CELU was able to field candidates for parliament to advocate labor legislation favorable to workers. To that effect, in 1973, three labor leaders, Sintayehu Geda (Diredawa Textiles), Sileshi Belatchew (Wonji Shoa), and Mewail Mebrhatu (Kagnew, Asmara) were elected to parliament. Imagine USUAA going this route!

CELU also had allies in the international labor movement. These included the International Labor Organization (ILO), the pro-west International Confederation of Trade Unions (ICFTU), American affiliated AFL/CIO and AALC (African-American Labor Center), and the pro-east World Federation of Trade Unions and the African-based, OATUU. These organizations helped CELU in training its members, in financing and equipping its offices, and in hosting its leaders for visits. Although student leaders were invited in the early days to international student meetings, CELU had wider exposure. For instance, in 1964, its leaders were invited to the May Day celebrations in Moscow, and in 1968 they witnessed firsthand US presidential elections.

Finally, when Somalia's first invasion of Ethiopia took place in 1964, CELU's leadership and union leaders in Addis went to the Emperor and Beyene said if the Somali army did not leave Ethiopian land, 50,000 workers would stand behind their army and government to repel the invaders[89]. The public offered money to the war effort and the government formed a committee for the purpose of fundraising led by the Minister of Interior. The members were: Dejach Kifle Ergetu (minister, Interior), Dejach Kebede Tessema (vice-minister, Interior), General Iyassu Mengesha (Chief of Staff, Army), Secretary of the Ethiopian Chamber of Commerce, and the leader of CELU, Beyene Solomon. The money raised was used to build an airport at Gode, and to improve army base facilities there. One would hasten to compare CELU's stand on the first Somali invasion with the stand of EPRP 13 years later on the second Somali invasion. Influenced by Marxist internationalism, EPRP erroneously condemned both the aggressor and the invaded regimes, instead of putting the blame squarely on Somalia, and supporting the national effort to repel the invasion. Of course, the Dirgue and its supporters later exploited this void and manufactured all sorts of stories of sabotage to completely discredit EPRP.

However, it is important to mention here that Berhanemeskel Redda, expelled from the party CC (effectively from the party) in November 1976, took a better position on the Ethio-Somali war than the position taken by the EPRP. In his major monograph, *On The Mass Line,* he explained his position in detail. His position still suffers from the same Marxist dictum as the EPRP in calling out for the so-called "rights of nations to self-determination up to and including secession",(at least he was consistent in his error espousing the same line he popularized under the pen name *Tilahun Takelle* from Algiers about a decade ago). He, however, pointedly blamed Somalia for its irredentist invasion of Ethiopian territory, and demanded for the invading Somali army to unconditionally leave Ethiopian territory[90].

An Ethiopian worker without the protection of labor laws meant salaries were very low, employees were fined and disciplined for petty offenses, there were no medical payments for work-related injuries and illnesses, no paid maternity leave, and often women who went on maternity leave were not allowed to return to their jobs. Whenever there was a decision to protest, CELU rounded up its affected members, carried the Ethiopian flag, and marched onto the Emperor's palace to request redress. Thus, CELU, by creating a smooth relationship with Haileselassie's government, and aided by a

---

89. ibid., p.81
90. Berhanemeskel Redda. On the Mass Line, p. 6-9

CHAPTER ONE: THE END GAME

progressive minister in Getahun Tessema, was able to fight successfully (often) on behalf of its members.

On the other and, the other democratic movement in the country, the student movement, related to the regime entirely differently. The regime responded to the students' class boycotts and demonstrations with repression followed by forgiveness. Balsvik says "student political activism was able to continue precisely because the regime's response to it was inconsistent, fluctuating between repression, ambivalence and paternalism[91]. Neither the regime nor the students broke this cycle to change the relationship into a working relationship in the model of CELU. As a result, CELU was much more anchored in tradition and Ethiopianism than USUAA or the unions abroad were. For instance, when it called for a general strike in 1963, and that action made the Emperor unhappy, CELU sought the mediation of Ras Imiru, an act unthinkable to be undertaken by the student radicals[92].

After the murder of Tilahun Gizaw in 1969, instead of deciding that peaceful struggle had come to an end, and that a higher form of struggle was now the order of the day, the students never contemplated to reach out to the government. Instead, they left the country to Europe and the US.

USUAA and CELU, although the only two democratic organizations in the nation, did not coordinate their struggles. In USUAA's eyes, CELU was perhaps an appendage of the CIA, and not worthy of any partnership in a progressive cause. They went their separate ways, until after the revolution when EPRP members such as Girmatchew Lemma, Samuel Alemayehu, Lemma Siyum, Ali Hussein, and Kiflu Tadesse joined it, a few of them as members of the editorial board, publishing CELU's journal, *the Voice of Labor*.

As the Dirgue attacked CELU starting in May 1975, the party decided to organize an underground labor organization and organized it by zones just like its youth and party structures. One of its unsuccessful actions was the 1976 September strike which was a failure and resulted in the unnecessary exposure of labor partisans.

---

91. Randi Balsivik. Haileselaasie's Students: The Intellectual and Social Background to Revolution, 1952-77, Michigan State University, East Lansing, 1985, p.184
92. Beyene Solomon, p.77

The Marxist-Leninist Ideology Influence

EPRP's choice of a radical socialist ideology largely explains the practice and policy of the party. According to this ideology, the concentration of capital in capitalist societies and the contradictions inherent therein make the transition to socialism inevitable. Socialism involves public ownership of the means of production and thereby the abolition of exploitation, of privilege and inequality deriving from the unequal distribution of wealth. There must be no discrimination based on race, nationality, gender or religion. There must be equal opportunities for education, healthcare and social amenities. Socialism is in the interest of all mankind and will make the universal development of culture and welfare, but the main force in the fight for socialism is the working class as the producer of all values and the class most resolute in abolishing wage labor.

Capitalism cannot be radically altered by cumulative reforms. It can only be swept away by revolution when the class consciousness of the proletariat and the economic conditions under capitalism are ripe for this. Socialism is not only a political program but a world view based on the premise that reality is susceptible of scientific analysis. Dialectical and historical materialism offer the scientific tools for such analysis.

The working class cannot capture state power by its struggles and fights alone. It requires a proletarian party made up of its advanced elements and other petit bourgeois and bourgeois elements who have committed class suicide and have taken up its cause. In oppressive societies, the party is not elected by open ballot, but rather is formed secretly by like-minded people who then organize the party from top to bottom. The operating principle is democratic centralism where lower echelons report to upper echelons, and where units and individuals know what is relevant to their function only. In its Leninist version, polemicized arguments are the standard styles against one's opponents, and these may include insults and epithets. Violence is justified and glorified as revolutionary in order to defend the class interest, and drive the class enemies into submission.

The self-designation of a leftist party as the vanguard of the working class, and hence the vanguard of the revolution was also an associated problem. There was no peaceful adjudication of the self-entitlement when others also so designated themselves. The claims and counter-claims by the EPRP, Meison, ECP, and Mengistu's

CHAPTER ONE: THE END GAME

working class party were areas of dispute. The notion of "vanguard" had elements of messianism, defined by Wilson Moses as (*Black Messiahs and Uncle Toms*), the belief that a person or a group had a "manifest destiny or a God-given role to assert the providential goals of history and to bring about the kingdom of God on earth. "It's a form of utopianism that implies faith in man's perfectibility, a willingness to serve as conscience for the rest of humanity, sometimes as a suffering servant, or a sacrificial lamb, sometimes as an avenging angel", Moses adds[93].

To its credit, however, in various conferences and *Democracia* editions, particularly in response to the Dirgue's call for a United Front (UF), EPRP had outlined its vision of a Front that would be constitutive of all significant political entities and mass organizations of the time. According to *Democracia, vol. ii, Special Edition*, OLF, TPLF, ALF, ENLF and mass organizations were mentioned to be invited and form a UF (Meison had aligned with the Dirgue at the time and was a co-sponsor of the proclamation with the Dirgue). This was obviously contrary to the dictates of political vanguardism. EPRP did not insist that it alone would or should replace the Provisional Military Government of the Dirgue. Critics might say that this was slated on the fact that EPRP knew it was the dominant party then, and it would naturally dominate the UF. But this has been a political truism of a democracy predicated on one-man-one-vote - that the majority or dominant party or ethnic group relies on the might of numerical strength.

The experience of socialism in the 20th century had been framed in such a way that it was divorced from democracy. Democracy and socialism had become diametrical opposites. This perversity is curious in that socialism is after all an emancipatory program. It is an ideal predicated on extending and expanding the formal definition of democracy. The roots of this divorce between democracy and socialism are many. The primary one is the notion of the dictatorship of the proletariat. A party that confers on itself the title of a proletarian party not only holds in low esteem other classes and parties in its partisan project, it has also no room for other parties that make the same or similar claims. In fact they will be hounded as

---

93. Wilson Jeremiah Moses. Black Messiahs and Uncle Toms: Social and Literary Manipulations of a Religious Myth. Penn State University Press, 1993

pretenders and fakes. Thus, the democratic rights of others to operate in a multi-party political environment is a priori foreclosed.

Following this, after Marx's death, socialism has taken root in conditions of under-development: what Fred Halliday describes as "if socialist revolution is an attempt to expand and consolidate the "realm of freedom"...such revolutions have taken place overwhelmingly in the "realm of necessity"[94]. In these backward societies, where the proletariat is insignificant, the issue of even implementing socialism is a big question. Where societies have not even experienced and matured in the practice of democratic rule, tolerance, and technological advance, the attempt to implement socialism by a self-professed proletarian party has been disastrous from Yemen to Ethiopia, from Cambodia to Angola.

With these ambiguities and contradictions, Marx died in 1883 and Engels followed in 1895. From 1899-1914, many competing interpretations and appropriations of the socialist project took place. During this period, Marxist thought had been clearly defined as a stand-alone school of social thought. However, various European countries infused accepted Marxism with their own traditions. In Britain, socialism owed its character to the ideas of utilitarian philosophers like Bentham, and Mill. During this period, in order to match Marx's socialist theory with a working class movement, a loose federation of working class parties and individuals formed what is called the Second International. No sooner had it formed when differences started creeping. The first major difference was whether or not Marxism could be developed and enriched for changing conditions. One group answered this in the affirmative, while a second, dogmatic group denied that possibility. Then the second major blow to the International was the impending World War 1. Marx's notion of the solidarity of the working class was severely tested as workers primarily rallied behind their bourgeois regimes against other workers and nations. The third and final division was on the question of ethnic self-determination, an issue with practical significance for nations in Eastern Europe and the Balkans.

All the while, there were active dissensions within the Marxist cult around issues such as the peaceful transition to socialism without violence (articulated by Edward Bernstein), around the argument of

---

94. Fred Halliday. The Ethiopian Transformation. London. Verso Editions and NLB, 1983

CHAPTER ONE: THE END GAME

ethical socialists objecting to the Marxist notion of privileging the proletariat, and demanding that all human beings regardless of class be treated the same. The victory of the Russian Bolshevik Revolution threw most of these dissident arguments on the wayside.

The Russian Communist Party displayed most of these tensions. Believing that all differences of view in the last analysis reflected class antagonisms (a false Marxist dictum), Lenin naturally plotted and fought those with differences with a singularity of mind. The differences of the Mensheviks and Lenin's Bolsheviks traumatized the party until their final split in 1912. After the capture of state power by the Bolsheviks in 1917, the non-Bolshevik press closed down. The opposition socialist parties -the Mensheviks, the Socialist Revolutionaries were terrorized and liquidated. The autonomy of the university was suppressed in 1921. Lenin constantly repeated that the so-called freedom of the press was a bourgeois deceit. Thus, the abuse of the socialist ideal did not start with Stalin, as it is sometime alleged. It hails from Marx and goes to Lenin and the early days of Bolshevik power.

Socialists like Rosa Luxemburg understood Marx's notion of the dictatorship of the proletariat to mean socialist pluralism, and were stunned when the Bolsheviks banned in 1921 all parties except the Bolsheviks. Lenin died in 1924. His state allowed no appeals, no checks, no balances, and no distribution of power. Stalin followed and perpetrated one of the greatest crimes in human history in the name of socialism by purging friends, comrades, intellectuals, and causing the deaths of millions of peasants. His show trials in his kangaroo courts stained socialism forever. China's ten year cultural revolution, 1966-76, a madness justified in the name of strengthening socialism, was also a part of this socialist stain, only made worse when Pol Pot took over Cambodia and killed at least 2 million people, and in another madness forced the evacuation of all cities.

Although USSR and China made tremendous advances in technology and modernity under socialist parties, the permanent damage done to socialism was irreversible. One of these damaged goods was the Communist Party of the USA which was allied with the Communist Party of the USSR. Despite massive evidence presented to it about Stalin's genocide, the CPUSA members were initially hesitant to consider the proof. As is often the case, many renowned writers, film makers, entertainers, and artists were members of the party. Communist party members were the bedrock of American culture from theatrical productions to famous songs.

During the Spanish Civil War of 1936/37, the Abraham Lincoln Brigade of the US contingent sent at least 1,000 party members to the international force supporting the republicans fighting against the fascist Franco rebellion.

Finally, when Stalin's crimes were too huge to hide, and when he signed a pact with Hitler in 1939, many members were disillusioned and abandoned the party. However, the US Congress started investigating communist party members for unAmerican acts, and many were blacklisted in Hollywood and beyond. Stalin's perversions contributed directly to the emasculation of socialism worldwide before existing socialism had hiccups twice, in 1956 in Hungary, and later in 1968 in the Prague Spring, before it mightily and finally crashed in 1989.

Notable books were written by former communists about the tragedy of communism and their own experience: Examples include *"Darkness at Noon"*[95] by Arthur Koesler, *"Witness"*[96] by Whittaker Chambers, and *"The God That Failed"*[97], a collection of essays by disenchanted communists. The Polish philosopher Leszek Kolawokski was an intellectual leader of the 60s Left until his defection to the west in 1968. A year after EPLO/EPRP was formed, Kolakowski organized a conference at Oxford which asked, and which in his conference paper he answered in the affirmative, "Is There Anything Wrong With The Socialist Idea?". 16 years later, however, when existing socialism was fracturing, the late Joe Slovo, a South African communist and a leading member of the ANC, wrote a treatise and answered in the negative to rally the dispirited troops, asking : "Has Socialism Failed?".

Marxism-Leninism can also be held indirectly responsible for masking and delegitimizing the power and contribution of the American Constitution, a pioneer and most democratic constitution

---

95. Arthur Koesler. Darkness at Noon, Scribner, 2006
96. Whittaker Chambers. Witness, Regnery, 1987
97. Arthur Koesler, ed. The God That Failed, Columbia University Press, 2001. *Some leftists, when they became apostates, went all the way to the other side. American leftist of the 1960s, David Horowitz, is one such example. When in the 1980s he co-authored an essay riling against socialism, titled, "Goodbye to All That", the Washington Post editors changed the title to "Lefties For Reagan", and published it revealing his new rightist activism.*

CHAPTER ONE: THE END GAME

the legacy of which was disparaged as "imperialistic". Before the American Constitution was ratified in 1787, no regime in history, not ancient Athens, not republican Rome nor the Swiss nor the British had ever adopted a written constitution by popular vote. True, the American Constitution barred for a long time slaves and women from participatory democracy. But prior to 1787, no slaves or women had voted anywhere in the world. With its Bill of Rights and additional amendments, the American Constitution has set an example for the rest of the world in helping fashion it a democratic governance. What makes the American Constitution so powerful and appealing is its ideals of the separation of power between the Executive, Judiciary and Legislative branches - an arrangement devoid in Marxist Leninist nations, that eventually directly contributed to their descent into dictatorship and eventual demise.

One wonders whether it is fair to demand and expect from the leadership of EPRP and Meison in 1974-6 to take this communist perversion into account and balance it with the positive aspects, such as third world and colonial liberation, and work more diligently at unification. There are records showing the Party leadership was cognizant of the problems and made modest suggestions to avoid them, even then it might still be a wish to demand for more, abetted by hindsight and the subsequent down spiral of the nation.

Even West European Marxist parties who were geographically closer to the futility of Marxism, and who had the resources to see pseudo-communism at work more than their Ethiopian counterparts had to wait until the late 80's to shake loose the obsession.

Some say the differences between *Meison* and EPRP were so basic, talk about the two coming together was a wishful thinking. Upon closer scrutiny, however, the argument does not hold water. Political wisdom has been in display often in the world when seemingly rival groups forge unity based on a common platform, giving precedence to their similarities than their differences. It seems theoretical differences are not new to Ethiopians, and that oftentimes they had been handled in the most civil manner. *Blata* Mersaehazen Woldekirkos, in his autobiography, narrates such incidents. In 1680, during the reign of King Aelaf Seged Yohannes, a theological divide emerged among the followers of Orthodox Christianity regarding the nature and relation of God, Jesus and the Holy Spirit. At that time, it was between the Kibaats and the Tewahdos; 100 years later during the reign of Atse Yohannes, however, it was between the Two Births and the Three Births. After a heated debate where each side was represented by their best church scholars, the Tewahdos won, and the King said, "I am with the losing side; I am a Kibaat believer, but kudos to the Tewahdos for their excellent debates and their victory". Then in 1788, at Borumeda, the theological debates continued and the Two Births/Tewahdos were declared the victors ("*Tizitaye - Mersaehazen Woldekirkos, 2002, Aster Nega Publishing, p.111-113).*

Who knew all this at the time? Such intellectual inheritance was not largely bequeathed to the radical generation by its forefathers. It started coming out only in the last decade or so in a major way. Thus, it is small surprise that the radical generation sought in Marxism the solutions to all the problems of the nation.

The Third International organized under Stalin's leadership, while mobilizing international communist forces to aid Spain that was threatened by fascists, did nothing to help Ethiopia earlier when it was invaded by fascist Italy in 1935. In fact there is anecdotal evidence that Stalin ordered ship dock workers in Russia who refused transit of Italian cargo in solidarity with Ethiopian freedom fighters to reverse their decision and go back to work(while this might have been so on national interest grounds, it is however undeniable that the USSR was one of the nations that consistently helped Ethiopia's case at the League of Nations during the Italian invasion). The only help Ethiopia got from the socialist camp in its hour of need, if it is any consolation, was when Howard Kock, screenwriter for the movie *Casablanca,* described a character *Rick,* the hero played by Humphrey Bogart, as someone who "run guns to Ethiopia". Imaginary guns that never materialized! The Argentinian Che Guevara seems to be the lone and true consistent internationalist, who after helping liberate Cuba, gave up a ministerial position, continued his international fight for justice by going to Congo in the early 1960s, and despairing over tribal politics there, went to Bolivia, and met his fate there.

In fairness to socialism, however, there have been some significant accomplishments by a few socialist states. For instance, Cuba, socialist since 1959, not only has it been able to provide its citizens with free medical care, schooling, and other social services, but also has been on the frontline in assisting less developed Third World countries with its doctors and technicians. Likewise, revolutionary socio-economic transformation under Mao's China is believed to be partially a contributing factor for today's super power status of that nation by laying the socio-economic foundation.

CHAPTER ONE: THE END GAME

In his 1987 paper presented to the 2nd Annual Conference on the Horn of Africa, Melaku Tegegne had some critical remarks about EPRP. Melaku argued in the paper that EPRP failed to implement the works of Marx and Lenin, and that it practiced "Marxism transformed", whatever that notion meant. Based on this premise, in 4.2 of his paper, he said "the EPRP had as a whole a lot of ideological problems of deviation and disarticulation. This can be attributed mainly to the lack of integration with the working class proper (sic!) and lack of ideological training"[98]. One wonders if Melaku still maintains these views, or if they were the views of a former Marxist caught up in the radicalism of the times...

On the other hand, there were others criticizing not EPRP per se, but the radical left in general and from the opposite direction. Speaking of the obsession of Ethiopian students with Marxism with doctrinal purity, Tesfaye Demmelash writes "the stress on doctrinal purity and unity within ESUNA in fact entailed the application of methods of scriptural exegesis to Marxist texts, based on the belief that there is only one correct interpretation of the writings of Marx, Lenin, Mao and their followers, and that the interpretation is spontaneously given by the texts themselves. And the defense of the true Marxism so understood, that is, is Holy Writ, from "reformist" and "revisionist" heretics became a central ideological concern of the ESUNA faithful[99].

Some of the critics exaggerated the danger posed by the leftist movements regarding the integrity of the nation. A long time student activist and one of the earliest, Hagos Gebre Yesus used the term national nihilism to denounce the radicals' endorsement of the right of self-determination in a famous article that used a biological metaphor: "*the Bankruptcy of the Ethiopian 'Left' Meison-EPRP, a Two-Headed Hydra: a commentary on the ideology and politics of national nihilism*".

Another Ethiopianist, Balsvik said that the feeling was rife that ideology had become more important to the students than the survival of Ethiopia as a state. Generally, the Ethiopian left, particularly EPRP, was on the run chased and maimed by the Dirgue on one hand, and by the TPLF on the other and having no "red

---

98. Melaku Tegegne. EPRP: A Historical Background and a Critical Assessment of its Experience, 1987, p. 42.
99. Messay Kebede, p. 113

diaper babies" of its own, children who grow listening to left-wing chatter and reflection at the dinner table.

Despite the overwhelming historical odds against it, the radical generation has enduring legacies which even its ardent critics need to grudgingly accept. One of these is the struggle for Land to the Tiller and the Proclamation that made it a reality in 1975. The radical students started demanding for Land to the Tiller going back to 1965. The land holding issue was a bedrock on which nationality and economic oppression were anchored, especially in south and southwest/east Ethiopia. The March 1975 Proclamation distributing land to peasants effectively ended serfdom in Ethiopia, and did away the virulent form of nationality oppression.

Another was the radicals' fight against distasteful foreign cultural influences, and struggle against what they termed "cultural imperialism". The commodification of current Ethiopian life, and worshipping of anything western from naming commercial establishments to copying uncritically western lifestyles would make the martyred radicals turn in their graves.

In the post-socialism world, the heir of the USSR, Russia, has descended into a crony capitalism and dictatorship, although Gorbachev initiated political changes first in attempting to reform the system. The Chinese went the other way by prioritizing economic reform, and at least saved their vast country from disintegrating. However, they too ended up in a one - party dictatorship where, despite the huge economic gains, corruption is rampant and they are infamously propping up similar one- party dictatorships elsewhere. Until a blue print is designed for a more perfect governance in the contemporary world, social democracy seems to offer the best hope for improving the lot of humanity.

CHAPTER ONE: THE END GAME

Attendees of the Ethiopian Teachers' Association (ETA) meeting in Jimma, August 1975. The meeting *passed* resolutions critical of the regime. Shown in the back include Kassahun Bisrat, Assefa Dereso, Mequanint Ejigu, Yohannes Berhane, Mesfin Gelaneh and two female teachers. Among those sitting in the front include Kibebe, Shumet Sishagne and Berhanu Ejigu.

A few activists from the school of engineering at HS1. Nolawi Abebe, 2nd from left, and Mekonnen Belay, a one-time A.A. IZ member, shown on far right, were victims killed by the Dirgue. These engineers were la crème de la crème -most were awardees of the coveted German financial stipend given for distinguished academic work.

CHAPTER ONE: THE END GAME

ቄይ ሽብር ይፋፋም ተበሉ ተሰጥዋቸው ሊረሽኑ የተዘጋጁ (መጋቢት 3 1969ዓ.ም)

Youth Victims of the Dirgue with disparaging slogans affixed on their backs and just before they were mass murdered, March 10, 1977.

Chapter Two: Licking the Wounds

EPRA's Retreat into Eritrea to Relaunch and Re-Create Itself

As the internal problems started consuming EPRA in the different regions, two of the senior army leaders, Tsehaye and Abebe Debteraw went from Armachiho into the hinterlands of Tselemt and Belessa. In Armachiho/Felfel area, the remaining party leaders in charge were Tadelle, Yonas, Lemlem, Mersha Yosef and Kiflu.

In the hinterlands, the army that was abuzz with mutiny and anarchy, demanded the resignation of the senior leaders, much less allow them to help start solve the problems. As a result, Tsehaye dutifully complied, while Gayim refused to resign on the grounds that the members of a single region (Tselemt) had no authority to force his resignation. The late Hiruy, a former Interzone member, made the trip to the Felfel area and broke the grim news to the party leadership there.

Tadelle, and Yonas as a duo, and Mersha separately started going to Tselemt, and the former's trip was aborted in an area called Janora and they had to return to Felfel. Based on my conversations with Mersha, with Hiruy as his guide, he continued onto Tselemt, but Hiruy refused to continue the journey after guiding Mersha to an area called Sifra Gebeta in Tsegedie.

Peasant comrades holding in their hands pieces of cloth sewn in red, met Mersha and lamented that "some members have torn off our insignia (EPRA's), and surrendered to the Dirgue". 14 days after he left Felfel, Mersha arrived in Tselemt. Alebachew, a CC member of EPRP now, guided Mersha on an 8-hour on- foot journey to Gilbena, where Debteraw and Gayyim were camped. Alebachew had to use a cane in the journey to keep steady and going. Gilbena was through and through EPRP, and the local song memorializing this went like this:

አትደምቅም እያሉ ፈዘኞች ሲያሙሽ፤
የኢህአፓ ከተማ ግልቤና አንዴት ነሽ

Initial consultations amongst the senior army leadership resolved that the struggle had to continue in the face of what seemed insurmountable problems, and because the leaders who were in Tselemt have already been resented, Mersha had the opportunity to launch a meet-and -consult sessions with teams, gantas and hayls. At this time, senior army leaders who were under the control of the Region 3 rebels who went over to TPLF, released their victims, and Fassika joined them at a place called Ternasha.

The attempt to discuss and find solutions did not pick up steam; on one hand, most army members were not convinced that with the current structure and capacity of the army, the problems would be solved. Making matters worse, and sensing the internal turmoil, the Dirgue's army was daily harassing and pushing EPRP units to further destabilize them. At this time, it was clear that no meaningful conference could be held in Tselemt to resolve the army's problems; instead, it was decided to make a trip to Eritrea and hold the meeting there. Debteraw was sent to Sudan to notify of the plan to hold a conference in Eritrea to the party leadership that left for Khartoum following the 4th plenum, leaders such as Iyassu and Samuel Alemayehu. Iyassu, Samuel, Debteraw and Tsehaye (who had earlier left for Sudan, and according to Tsehaye: "I left for Sudan because there was no Region 2 and not because I left the party. The reason for my decision was the following: while Debteraw and I were doing our best to resolve the problem, some information will come through the cadre structure destabilizing the situation even worse. After the resignation of Roba and co., I concluded that the problem lies in the CC. I told Debteraw and Gayyim that I do not see any purpose in doing what we were doing in the regions. I said that we need to go and call a CC meeting and solve it once and for all. When they objected to my idea, I told them that I will be leaving and arrangements were made for me through the cadre structure to

CHAPTER TWO: LICKING THE WOUNDS

Region 2. When I got to Armachiho, I met Yonas and Tadele about to leave for the Sudan. They told me about the fate of Region 2).

Bertya

Before the army made the trek to Bertya, it was decided to leave a squad behind in Tselemt to give the semblance of EPRA presence and in the interest of continuity. Gayyim and Jabbir (the latter was a senior comrade and a central committee member from the Eritrean ethnic group of Bilen, and a third year Addis Abeba university business major when he joined EPRA. Jabbir was one of the last comrades whose trace was lost in Quarra while on a mission with another squad) volunteered to lead a squad that would stay behind. Beyene Gura'a was also a volunteer with them.

During their rapid movements, the squad members had to cover large areas and avoid undue attention. However, a member of a banditry team who saw the squad opened fire and critically wounded Gayyim. Subsequently, he was captured by the TPLF from whom he escaped during an operation near Mai Tsebri, and walked all the way to the Waldiba monastery eluding his captors. (actually Gayyim was not "captured". See the details later).

Bertya is a river bank in Barka Awuraja that was under the control of ELF at the time, and EPRP's leadership made a prior arrangement with ELF's leadership to convene at a safe area there. In Bertya, the army that now numbered 600-700 men and women continually met and discussed for nearly five months. On some days, there were two or three sessions. Those who wanted to continue the struggle wanted assurance that there was an objective situation in Ethiopia that made it possible to continue the struggle against the Dirgue. The issues were generally divided into two: on one hand, contradictions and differences between the rank-and-file members and the leaders; and on the other, the issues needing fleshing out, fundamental issues such as the question of democracy, the nationality question, principles, strategy and tactics of the struggle.

Finally, almost everyone was convinced that most questions had been settled. Jigsa was elected commander, and Mersha was elected as the commissar of the army, and Beker was the deputy commander. Gayyim and Fassika were co-opted into the party leadership. It was time to head back to continue the struggle. To that effect, local guides who knew the way back were arranged, and provisions prepared. Suddenly, on the morning of the departure date, a group of about 12 army members had escaped to the Sudan taking with them the best weapons, watches, and communication radios. The defectors at Bertya were Mekurya, Semere, Hiwot, Kesete, Aklog, Demmelash, Kelbessa, Fitsum, Fasil, Simret and 3 others (*ABS*). A few of the local guides who knew the area and who were supposed to guide the army joined the escapees. The incident created havoc among the remaining members. Those close friends of the escapees who chose to stay behind were looked suspiciously by the rest. The rank-and-file demanded that the close friends had to be disarmed. For a traumatized army, guilt by association was a trivial to worry about.

The army leadership was tasked with compiling a list of the "close friends". A mass meeting of the army was convened, and sentries assigned. One of the first members to be called from the list, and to be disarmed was a cadre of the mass organizing committee (kifle-hizb) called Mulat. Jigsa was the assigned senior leader to take the arms from those slated to be disarmed. Along with him, Beker and Mersha were standing in line. As his name was called, Mulat stepped forward, pretended he was going to tender his weapon, but instead started firing three shots before he was shot down by the sentry. The first shot killed a hayl commander called Siber, a comrade from Gamu Goffa. The second bullet killed Berhe, a comrade from Tigrai, and the hayl commissar. The remaining close friends on the list were rounded up and quickly disarmed. An inquiry commission was set up to investigate whether or not they were guilty and part of a conspiracy. The maximum penalty was dismissal from the army. The army leadership apologized to two members who were wrongly listed and suspected, and those members continued with the army to the bitter end. As a result of this incident, the army was delayed by 15 days from moving back to Tselemt.

One of the decisions by the army leadership was to immediately undertake a military operation as soon as the army moved to Tselemt. This was undoubtedly planned to plant a dagger in the Dirgue's back on one hand, and to inspire supporters and members on the other. It has been awfully a long winter for members and supporters, and no encouraging news had come their way in a very long time. On the way back to Tselemt, the EPRA units saw about two battalion of TPLF's units at a river. It was a sudden encounter. Neither side wanted to spoil the surprise and the chance meeting.

CHAPTER TWO: LICKING THE WOUNDS

Nothing happened, and the EPRA units moved on and spent the night at the Waldiba monastery.

Realizing that the EPRA was not yet done and finished, TPLF started distributing leaflets in the area demanding that EPRA units leave the area, reminiscent of what they demanded of EPRA in Tigrai in 1978. The army instead expanded its areas of operations. While the threat of the TPLF increased daily, the Dirgue had not stopped its harassment of the army and its supporters by sending squads. After a few months, the EPRA units fought a big war against the TPLF, and had captives and gained materiel. However, the army was divided into two, and one segment carrying its wounded, and captured weapons retreated into a lowland area called Gichew. Gichew is near the farm areas of Humera and Abderafi, and Sifra Talian. The other segment of EPRA units retreated to Telello/Godguada in Wolkait. The two EPRA segments for a time failed to communicate.

A squad was operating in Wolkait to guard the wounded and the sick. At a place called Midquas Barud (Barud maqlecha), a Dirgue squad attacked the EPRA squad, and an army member called Gugsa, from Tigrai, and the army's deputy commissar, was killed. Mersha, the commissar, was severely wounded on his right hand, and his wrist bone crushed. The wounded stayed in a cave, and local supporters brought food and water to the wounded in the cave under the cover of darkness, cautiously eluding TPLF. Leaving two of the severely wounded in the cave, about 5 army members left the cave and luckily on the third day encountered an EPRA squad. Abebech (Mumina), a female comrade who lives in Denmark now, and a field nurse who joined the army as others were leaving it en masse, attended to the wounded and cared for them.

Iyassu, Oumer, and Asgedom left for the Sudan for possible diplomatic work, while Jigsa and Beker were the commanders. It was at this time, a promising military commander beloved by members by the name of Gigar was killed in these confrontations.

In the lowland area called Gichew to which the bulk of the army retreated in 1982, the army stayed there for a little over a year and used it as a base. Self-reliance, although a key component of the party's principles, has not been widely practiced. However, here in Gichew, there was some hope. As necessity is the mother of invention, one of the big causes that pushed hard the EPRA units to look into self-sufficiency in Gichew was the situation of comrades in the Sudan. The party had underground and semi-underground members in organizational cells in the major cities of Sudan, such as Gedariff, Medenie, Port Sudan and Khartoum, and border towns like Tiha (there was a brief period during these years when the party had started functioning officially with the full knowledge and cooperation of the Sudanese authorities so much so EPRP members and supplies were transported by trucks back and forth. This was drastically to change 4 or 5 years later). The party had rented houses called shelters for comrades coming into Sudan on organizational business and where sick and wounded comrades rest and recuperate. The party had always been under financial constraint, and this was particularly so during the years from 1980-1984. The party therefore embarked on a few projects to alleviate its financial burdens and get money to pay the rents of the shelters in Sudan and to feed and care for its sick and wounded there. Those projects included farming and harvesting sorghum, honey collection, buying cattle in Ethiopia and selling them at a profit in Sudan. Comrades in Sudan who had gainful employment also helped by contributions to the party, most contributing the lion's share of their incomes.

The first United Front between the EDU and the EPRP was formed here. Major Kidane and Wagshum Newete were the notables on the side of EDU. They brought about 30 EDU fighters, and EPRA units trained them and armed them. There was a proposal on the part of the EPRA leadership to merge the EDU and EPRA units. About 75% of the army supported the idea, while 25% strongly objected to it on the grounds that "a proletarian army cannot merge under any circumstances with feudal forces".

At this time, Jigsa left the army and went to Sudan. The EPRA units expanded from Gichew into Armachiho, Qola Wegera, Ajirei, Janora and Tsegedei. A seminar was held at Jansuma.

The Tragedy in Armachiho

At the seminar in 1982, a hayl commander by the name of Desalegne was criticized for his failure to comply with the army's code of conduct. He and 10 others deserted the army the following day, and met at a river with a band of travelers and traders coming from the Sudan into Ethiopia. Some of these travelers were members and supporters of the EPRA and the party. The defectors opened fire with automatic weapons and killed instantly Bitweded Adane, a

CHAPTER TWO: LICKING THE WOUNDS

famous anti-Italian patriot, and Abebe Jember, a local family scion and a party member.

As they say, misery loves company. This crazy incident created a huge stir among the local populace. In order to contain the damage, EPRP members distributed communiques throughout the area churches. The leadership of the army/party at this time included Iyassu, Mersha, Samuel, Debteraw and Fassika. The community of Armacho was divided over the issue, some saying that EPRP is behind the murders, and others strongly refuting that. There were ambushes and skirmishes with casualties on both sides. Futile attempts were made at reconciliation.

There was a growing demand in the army to fight back. In order to cool off tempers and divert attention, the army attacked a town in Chilga, the town of Aykel. However, when the army came from the operation, it was ambushed by the local peasants at a place called Sanku. An able EPRA commander by the nickname of "Danger" was killed along with 5 others. The battle expanded to Lower Armacho and claimed the lives of Zelleke Jember (a leader of Tach Armachiho, a supporter and brother of the martyred Abebe Jember) on the other side, and Hadish Beyene, a veteran of EPRA. The leader of Upper Armachiho, Berihun escaped. It is thought the 11 notorious killers/traitors who were the root causes of this mess went over to TPLF.

Thus, EPRA/P lost the goodwill, support and love of the people of Armachiho after carefully cultivating and winning their trust over a long period through a network of cadre and army work.

As if it were the work of a permanent curse, the party could not shake the crises that piled on it one after another. As soon as it gets over one crisis after much sacrifice, the next one lurks in the winding road and jumps on it. As a result of the tragedy in Armachiho, the party and the army were once again forced to vacate their areas of operation - a trend that has been the trademark of the army since 1978 after it evacuated Assimba forced by the TPLF. Luckily, at least for once, and albeit for a brief period fortune smiles on EPRA/P at its next destination as we will see in Chapter 4.

However, despite the trials and tribulations, EPRP had been regarded largely as a beacon of hope among the peasants it operated in, and it had tried and succeeded in improving the hard and dark life of peasants, although not to an extent it would have liked to. That accomplishment is the subject of the next chapter.

EPRA's Regions in Gonder:
1-Tselemt; 2. Chilga/Armachiho; 3. Libo/Belessa; and 4. Wolkait Tsegedie

Chapter Three: Eihapa Aleme Dur Aderech Lamei

ኢህአፓ አለሜ፤ ዱር አደረች ላሜ

The Background

The title of Chapter 3 was an Amharic song by young and adult shepherds alike, reflecting the mood and feelings of peasants. It meant "due to the presence and justice of EPRP, my cow can now spend the night out with no fear on my part of it being stolen, or hurt". In other words, the saying reflected the widespread feeling and optimism among peasants that a new day was in order, and that justice and fairness are now at long last the operating modules.

In order to understand the full meaning of this, one has to survey the hard life of a north Ethiopian peasant. During times of absent or little rainfall, the peasants suffered from famine. The landscape was parched and dry, with no green pasture for domestic animals, and no crops for peasant families. The choice mostly was to leave the weak, the sick and the elderly behind and migrate to faraway places in search of food. The Wollo and Tigrai famines of the early 70's and mid-80's are extreme examples of such. Because the land was stripped of forests, it was very hard to find firewood to even cook wild vegetables, or to keep a family warm in cold climates. For those peasants whose homestead and farmlands were located on slopes and hills, the farms' topsoil is washed off during the rare events of torrential rainfall, thus severely limiting the productivity of the farms. Besides, each peasant farmer owned a tiny plot of land. In cold climate areas, such as the Semien Mountain areas, they could only harvest one crop (mainly barley) a year. In temperate regions like Eastern Tigrai, beles (qulqual) was the only available food mostly during times of drought. Making matters worse, crops were from time to time attacked by locusts that performed a carpet bombing style and cleaned out everything green. In fact, Berhanemeskel Redda, in 1964, when a student at Addis Ababa University, had written a short story on the plight of a peasant facing a locus menace, titled "*Gebre-Aregawi's Hopes'"*[1]

Misery attacked the north Ethiopian peasant from every direction. For those residing in the hot (kola) lowlands, malaria reigned supreme. The highlanders (degegnoch) fared no better. The extreme cold, and the rocky escarpment made life meaningless. Women have to travel long distances to fetch water. At some places in northern Ethiopia, wooden ladders and ropes were the only means of transportation to reach a mountain top, or to cross a mountain. The ladders consisted of several poles, and tree branches, and were placed against a steep cliff. The pieces were tied together with wobbly tree barks and ropes. To fight the extreme cold, the peasants wore two or three layers of sheep skin, and burned a fire at night using dung and dry leaves. Their weathered faces made them look older than they really were. Because they did not wear shoes, their feet were cracked by the cold and the thorny bushes they daily tread on. And after all, life expectancy was very low among these peasants, and reaching old age was a reverence.

On top of the small plot of land, land and domestic animal theft was rampant in most areas, particularly targeting poor peasants. The practice of stealing sheep, cattle, goats, donkeys and horses was mostly committed by well-armed professional thieves and well-armed rich peasants. Government agents had never been the allies of poor peasants. Agents of the state, such as judges, soldiers, police, tax collectors and chiqa shums treated peasants extremely badly. Thus, these agents could not protect them from local bandits and criminals. On the contrary, the government officials expected bribes from these poor peasants. If a victim went to a faraway court, the judge almost always ruled in favor of whoever bribed him with the most money, or items -honey, butter, cattle. Judges often were unencumbered to tell a losing party that he was not as competitive as his rival to please the

---

1. Berhanemeskel Redda. Something#3, p.32-39 in Voices From the Past, Addis Abeba: AAUP, 2010, PP.77-86

CHAPTER THREE: EIHAPA ALEME DUR ADERECH LAMEI

judge. A peasant normally would spend weeks and months looking for his stolen cattle. In a society where blood feud was common (and parts of northern Ethiopia had a checkered history with this backward culture), owning a gun was the ultimate marker of a man's standing in the society. It signified that the man could defend his and his family's honor. Whenever a dispute erupted, people had to fend for themselves and those who could took the law into their hands. Surrounded by hostile and untamed nature, with corrupt officials around them, and with well-armed criminals in every corner, the life of a peasant was extremely challenging.

Women's Specific Oppression

A peasant woman worked non-stop, from early dawn until she went to bed at night, and from her pre-teen days to her old age. One would never see a woman sitting by idle and relaxing. Women helped on the farms doing farm chores such as weeding. At home, very early in the morning, a woman starts grinding grains. Then she prepares the meals for the family, packing her husband's lunch which he takes when he goes out for the day, or she delivers at lunchtime. If she has a small baby, all these chores are done while the baby is on her back.

There is so much to be done at home: baking *injerra*, making home-brewn drinks- sewa in Tigray, and korefe, in the Semien Mountains. She spinned and weaved threads and cotton to help make the family's clothes- *netella, kemis, and gabi*. She collected animal manure and firewood for fuel.

It is not uncommon to see a group of women, each carrying a big clay pot placed on their backs with a rope. On the average, it might take women two to three hours to fetch water. This is largely due to the fact that they live on hills and ridges, away from the malaria-infested lowland areas. There are no wells or streams nearby their homes especially during the dry season. The water obtained from the daily trek is used to make beverages, as drinking water, for sanitary purposes, and for domestic animals and chickens consumption.

Except for meeting the demands of their daily chores, women are not allowed contact with the outside world. Even when EPRP men and women visited their houses, most women hid away, or insisted that visitors should come back when the man of the house comes back in the evening. This is likely due to the fear of perceived or real adultery and rape.

There are incidents of rape among northern Ethiopian peasant women. Usually, just like most places, wives who have been raped there would not divulge the crime. A wronged husband would scheme to take revenge on the wife of the suspected perpetrator. A woman who had been raped would be punished by her husband by being sent away to her relatives, or by being beaten. Since the dowry the woman brought to the marriage could be divided in a divorce proceeding, the amount plays a role in the course of action a husband contemplates.

In northern Ethiopia, marriage for girls took place at a very early age (to their credit, both TPLF and EPRA campaigned, with some success, to stop this practice). Often, the parents of children entered into a marriage agreement including even children who have yet to be born. The parents of the boy give a sheep or an ox to the girl's parents. While boys were a bit older, girls married even as young as 9 year old. A little girl often slept with her mother-in-law until she was considered sexually ready[2].

If the contracted marriage took place between a young girl, and somehow older boy, the parents of the boy employed a divorced young woman, often poor, to serve both as a maid and concubine to satisfy the sexual appetite of the boy until his young wife is old enough to meet his sexual needs. In the meantime, the boy's parents cared for the girl in their house.

According to Makonnen, "the only benefit the concubine received for her service was food, lodging, and annual purchase of a new dress. Since there were more women in Beyeda (Siemen Mountains) than men, young concubines usually fell into such agreement out of despair of finding a suitable husband. This unfortunate arrangement was common among the very poor women whose parents could not provide their daughters with animals and other material goods as dowries, representing their contribution to the common property of the marriage. The men usually saw to it their future wives came up with enough wealth to help start their new lives[3].

---

2. Mekonnen Araya. Negotiating A Lion's Share of Freedom, lulu.com, 2011, p.168
3. ibid., p. 169

CHAPTER THREE: EIHAPA ALEME DUR ADERECH LAMEI

The Religious Divide

Blood feuds sometimes took religious lines. The relatives of a murder victim felt they had a duty to avenge the murder by killing the murderer or a close relative related by blood. This created a vicious circle of blood-letting. Often, after being exhausted by the killings and counter-killings, people submitted to arbitration to stop the cycle, an attempt which almost always failed.

In northern Ethiopia, there were pockets of blood feuds involving Christians and Moslems. Moslems resented the fact that their ancestors and themselves have been relegated by Christians to remote and inaccessible areas with little cultivable land. For many years, there was peaceful coexistence, at times blemished by breakdown of law and order. The minority Moslems made pottery and weave traditional Ethiopian clothing which they sold to the Christians. Often, Moslems carried their weaving rudimentary equipment to Christian areas and made clothing for their customers at their places. They received cash or grain as payment. Moslems also were petty traders, buying goods from semi-urban centers, and taking them deep into rural areas, and selling them for a small profit. Because of the steep topography of their areas, Moslems had to carry their stuff themselves instead of employing domestic animals.

This interrelationship contributed to the largely peaceful coexistence. However, when Christian thieves tried to steal cattle from the Moslems, the Moslems engaged them in gun battle, and the lives of one Christian or two are lost. This rolls the wheel of blood feud cycle, north Ethiopian style.

Because of Christian arrogance and contempt for Moslems, it is almost always certain the instigators and guilty party in such incidents are Christians. The situation breaks the peaceful coexistence, and inter-communal trade is hampered, thus hurting both communities. When at last EPRP mediators imposed as settlement on the communities, a fragile peace was able to hold with each community warily watching over the other.

Similarly, EPRA fighters operated among another religious minority in northern Ethiopia, the Bete Israel or the Felashas. This minority, like their Moslem brethren, was also denied land ownership by the majority Christians. As a result, Moslems became mostly traders and handicraft men, while the Felashas specialized in smelting and turning scrap metals into farming and household tools, and making pottery.

EPRP fighters and community organizers worked among many ethnic and religious groups in northern Ethiopia and gained their trust and love: the Felashas, Moslems, Christians, Kimants, Woytos, Tigreans, Agews, and others.

Fighting Against Peasant False Beliefs and Bad Practices

Literacy among northern Ethiopian peasants is minimal. There were almost no schools. The only institutions remotely close to learning and numeracy are churches, but even here, most of the clergy are illiterate, or semi-illiterate. A segment of these, the debteras, dabbled in sorcery as well. Such a society is vulnerable to false belief systems, spirits, and the like, and are gullible to charlatans and so-called healers faking as knowers of the present and fortune telling. Before the arrival of EPRP, the practice of witchcraft, and beliefs in spirits/kole was rampant in northern Ethiopia. Almost every one wore one or more amulets to ward off evil spirits.

Although inroads were made by EPRP to change such bad beliefs, since they had held sway over the society for such a long time, it was not easy for them to part from the practices. The limited medical help EPRP fighters gave the peasants (acupuncture, basic hygiene and sanitation teaching, and some tablets) established some belief system change in science than in spirits.

Another bad practice was what Makonnen witnessed in Beyeda about female mourners mutilating themselves at funerals to express their grieving[4]. They peeled off their facial skin with their fingernails, exposing the underlying flesh and bleeding their faces, while at the same time pulling out hair from their heads, and further causing blood to trickle down. While the women disfigured themselves in such gory fashion, the men made circles and gently wept chanting praises to the deceased.

Makonnen says that the EPRP organizers asked the elders at the funeral why they did not interfere and stop the women from harming themselves. The answer was that it was a customary ritual for women

---

4. ibid.

CHAPTER THREE: EIHAPA ALEME DUR ADERECH LAMEI

to express their deeply felt sorrow. If a woman abstained from being overly demonstrative in her grief, she would be considered not showing enough sadness and not caring for the condition of the deceased.

After getting approval and agreement from the elders, the EPRP organizers, including Makonnen, made a speech and a decree outlawing the practice right there and then. Some elders and priests stood up and spoke supporting the decree (which included penalty for transgressors). From that time on, the practice had ceased, and one hopes, the censure has continued to this day.

Why the People Have Good Memories About Eihapa Aleme?

The people in northern Ethiopia were initially hesitant and suspicious to embrace EPRA/P. This was largely due to the false propaganda repeatedly fed by the Dirgue authorities. These authorities went even as far as telling the people those EPRP men and women were aliens with oversized ears and noses. Once the people saw that they are looking at ordinary Ethiopians in EPRP, and when their abandonment of their comfort for the peasants' sake dawned in, the gradual strengthening of the bond took hold.

As EPRP fighters took over city after city, the local officials took flight, and EPRP organizers were the de facto administrators, and judges. Almost every peasant had a case to be adjudicated. Most of the cases involved land issues. While the organizers settled some of the cases, others were deferred to the local's elders to be fairly dealt with.

In both Tigrai and Gondar, EPRA units had modest success in implementing land distribution among peasants. In Tigrai, when the army started land distribution in one community, others quickly demanded that land in their areas also be distributed. The fact that TPLF also engaged in land distribution made the progressive action popular. Land distribution gave rise to self-administration and changed the power relation of peasants at a community level.

The local chiefs who took flight were almost always joined by notorious armed robbers and thieves to fight EPRP. The thieves were severely dealt with in all the areas EPRP operated, and knew their interest would be adversely affected as EPRP implemented the rules of fairness and justice. To the peasants, the justice EPRP rendered liberated them from endless suffering and showed a new ray of hope.

The peasants many times expressed their gratitude by sharing what little they have with EPRP fighters and organizers. They would slaughter a sheep in honor of EPRP for a festive dinner (a rare deed otherwise, only done on special holidays). When EPRP organizers refused, the peasants regaled them with the stories of the previous authorities who demanded the fattest of their sheep for their dinner.

During harvest time (winnowing and thrashing), it is not uncommon for travelling EPRP organizers to be invited by peasants to be offered home-brewed beer (sewa, tella or korofe), and some hearty meal. The most common festivals are, of course, the annual celebration of patron saints. Abune Aregawi in Aduwa, and St. Mary in Mekane Yesus are examples. Weddings are another merrymaking gatherings. These occasions offer not only an opportunity for the party organizers to do political and organizational work among the people, they are also festive moments where people and party lay back, eat and drink, and relax.

Thus, Eihapa Aleme Dur Aderech Lamei, was etched in a memorable rule of law fire that binds together the people and the party and that may be stoked one day in the future.

And let history record that this is the collective history of every one, underground or above, that at one time traversed the path that was/is called EPRP, although now many may be disengaged, of different political persuasions, or still carrying the burden of history on their weak shoulders.

Chapter Four: Returning to the Golden Years

Quarra

EPRA, throughout its history, was characterized by unmet needs and destitute life. The army had never had a uniform; food was always scarce and the army had to largely depend on the peasants for support although occasionally it bought its supplies and provisions from the peasants at fair market price. Bojboj was a familiar dish that was a mishmash combination of leftovers and various dishes combined together and eaten with delight because of larger servings.

The most serious problem of all was in fact the inability to grow the army. The fact that the urban structures were decimated meant that there was no longer a supply of potential recruits to the army from urban centers. And the peasantry was not that willing to join a destitute army, except for a few enlightened folks. As a result, in all the areas the army operated except in Quarra, growth was a big issue.

When the army moved to Quarra after the Armachiho debacle, this all changed for the better. The theory of self-reliance was a key principle for EPRA. However, it was in no area implemented on a larger scale as in Quarra under the leadership and creativity of Gayyim. Farming by army members in fact started back in Gichew as stated earlier where the party was self-sufficient by farming and harvesting sorghum and engaging in honey collection for use and sale. Here in Quarra, the major farm areas were Mertrad, Dirhassen, and along the Gelegu river.

In Quarra, almost everything went well. Hence returning to the Golden Years. Indeed, EPRP announced its existence in August 1975 with a flourish and with a promise of golden times. Things started well with its superior organization, and attractive political line that mobilized women, young people, ethnic groups, workers and peasants in their thousands, in an unprecedented scale. . However, in 4 short years, its urban presence came tumbling down, and affected its long-term strategy. For a second time, it got a chance at Quarra to implement its program. The late Fitawrari Ayele Abaguade, a Kimant by nationality and a pro-EPRP government functionary and local chieftain in Chilga and Quarra, said at the time, "EPRP had finally arrived home"[1]. Indeed. When the Fitawrari died, his will stated that his second son join EPRA carrying his automatic weapon that could fire 40 bullets at a time.

The successful attack the army undertook at Aykel earlier amplified the army's fame and facilitated its settlement in Quarra. Subsequently, it successfully attacked Salia, the main city in Quarra, enhancing its fame and obtaining a huge cache of weapons. The land was fertile and was bordering Sudan. The army was expanding with new recruits, especially from the minority ethnic groups of the Beni Shangul, Agew, Oromo from Wollega and the Kimant. It was able for the first time in its history to train its new recruits adequately and target practice was common and undertaken for an extended period using live ammunition. By 1981, the army was operational with a battalion army members. The army, using the tractors it captured from the Dirgue, started extensive farming, honey production, and commerce with Sudan. It even started renting trucks and equipment to the Sudanese along the border. There were mills that ground cereals into flour, and vegetable oil processing facilities. The army even had an Internal Revenue Service (gumruk) that levied taxes on traders and pastoralists. The property of stubborn and incorrigible thieves and bandits was confiscated (the army had traditionally penalized these outlaws by leaving some of their property for the upkeep of their innocent families). The army stopped the lawless cattle raids and attack among and on pastoralists. The army distributed fishing nets to help the locals supplement their diet, and the planting of new protein-rich plants, such as soybeans was popularized. The army provided free tractor farming to poor communities, such as the Gumuz (Beni Shangul).

---

1. personal communication with Mersha Yosef

The army also opened no less than 20 elementary schools throughout Quarra, and hired teachers and administrators to staff them. Many health clinics were also operational. The geographic expanse of the army's administration extended into Chilga Awraja, Bahirdar area and Metekel, Agew Midr Awraja, Wembera and the Wollega border. The army had influence in the administration of border towns under the control of the Sudanese, such as Tiha. The comrade responsible for the army's property management was Eshete (Geleb), a central committee member and an Eritrean by birth that died at the hands of TPLF while resisting arrest (his brother, Kibrom Dafla, joined the EPLF and he was in Asmara until his defection in 2012 -personal communication with Dr. GA).

The party and army made sure that Ethiopia's borders were sacrosanct, and that its forestry was not violated. Penalties were handed down on those guilty of arson, and deforestation.

The Second Party Congress

EPRP's First Party Congress was held in Berlin on April 9, 1972. In Quarra, the army had some communication with what was left of the urban structures. This was largely possible due to the fact that several dedicated comrades whose organizational chains had been crushed had not ceased searching for the party, and used such means as communicating with comrades they knew in earlier years to re-establish contact. These were members mostly from Gondar, Addis and Bahir Dar that sought the party through their own efforts by various means.

The Second Party Congress was held from March 21 to April 4, 1984, twelve (12) years after the First Congress. The time was ideal for convening a Second Congress. A Congress preparatory committee was named by the leadership that included Samuel, Mersha and Iyassu. Maaza (Aberash Berta) was assigned to come out to Sudan to type Congress documents. Aberash Berta, who lost an eye during a battle in Tselemt, is now one of the disappeared victims of EPRP. Genet Girma and Khasay from Europe, and Bisrat and Tiruneh, from the US came to Quarra as delegates to attend the Congress. There were also delegates from Sudan that came into Quarra. It is important to remember that in the EPRA, the party has managed to the last days to maintain a separate structure (albeit loose) of party members within the army as distinct from youth league members and other members who were simply soldiers.

For the first time in its history, the party used secret ballots to elect its leaders at the second congress. Among those who were elected as the party leadership were: Mohammed, Fassika, Mersha, Melaku (the highest vote getter), Gayyim, Debteraw, Jabbir, Eshete (Geleb) and Samuel (Later a few more like Matewos were coopted). Following the long-standing tradition of EPRP candidates, most of the nominated strenuously objected their nominations to the leadership. Some who were shepherding the army through the immense crises had legitimate reasons to decline. However, the army insisted that they take up the positions, and most did. A couple of them still refused the nominations. Iyassu declined the nomination. Another one, Oumer, an Aderei/Hareri, whose responsibility, along with Mohammed, a Guragei, was as the party's representative in Kahartoum, Sudan, doing diplomatic work and facilitating party supply routes, declined to accept his election in absentia (Oumer was among the first EPRA units that trained in Palestine, and came to Tigrai through Aden/Eritrea. His name at the time was Roble (real name AA), and now lives in Toronto, Canada).

In 1986, Fassika and Mersha were assigned to help organize ex-EPRP members in the Diaspora, especially in Europe and the US. Two years earlier Melaku was sent for the same purpose but was unsuccessful. Soon after, he asked to write the history of the party and was excused to emigrate to Europe. As we will see in the next chapter, the two (Mersha and Fassika) did tremendous work in bringing back hundreds of ex-members into the party's fold, and equally important, in helping form the first broad-based, anti-TPLF coalition of political forces, civic groups and individuals, the coalition of Ethiopian democratic forces (COEDF).

The Signature Accomplishments of the 2nd Congress

The 1960s and 70s, the formative years and urban heydays of the EPRP, were revolutionary and radical times. Marxism-Leninism (sometimes along with Mao Zedong Thought) was the dominant ideology. The party's program was largely a reflection of the implementation of Marxism in Ethiopia's semi-feudal and semi-

CHAPTER FOUR: RETURNING TO THE GOLDEN YEARS

capitalist socio-economic structure. In short, the program was centered on proclaiming EPRP as the sole proletarian party destined to enshrine the dictatorship of the proletariat, through the nationalization of the commanding heights of Ethiopia's economy, and subscribing to the solution of Ethiopia's nationality problems through the Marxian formula of "the right of nations to self determination, including and up to secession".

Nothing seemed to be wrong in this platform. Students were rebelling from Mexico to Paris and winning concessions from their governments; colonized peoples like in Vietnam and Algeria were fighting their colonial masters and scoring astounding victories; the Soviet-Chinese camp that was the moral center of the radical revolution was not only catching up with the West in terms of technology, but surpassing them, for instance by putting the first man in space. So, for EPRP and the Ethiopian left to be mesmerized by Marxism, was only a natural outgrowth of the seductive luster of the revolutionary times existing then.

By the mid-1980s, things had started to radically change. Marxism has overstayed its welcome. It has lost much steam. What was promised to be a paradise on earth had turned out to be "darkness at noon", as the title of one ex-communist succinctly put it. The dictatorship of the proletariat transformed into the dictatorship of a few elites, and eventually one dictator. The gulags of Stalin's Soviet Union, and the hard labor dissenters were sentenced to, and the psychiatric wards they were falsely committed to, were laid bare for the whole world to see. Things were not much different in the rest of the Soviet Union's satellites in Eastern Europe. After over half a century of dictatorship against their own societies and the workers in whose names power was usurped, these countries started cracking under the heavy weight of their suppression.

Marxism was in short discredited. Through the medium of Mikael Gorbachev in the Soviet Union, existing socialism started unraveling, and the component parts of the USSR seceded from the empire and Russia was left standing as the sole heir of the legacy. Liberalism was once again in vogue. Marxism completed by the mid-1990s its unceremonious retreat, save in a few enclaves like Cuba and North Korea. Even in these hermit states, doctrinaire Marxism has to give room to some form of private ownership, or state-private partnership.

Liberalism won on the gravesite of existing socialism, and its more vocal supporters started boasting that the end of history has dawned, and proclaimed that the age old battle between liberalism and its foes has been successfully won by liberalism and from here on the world was going to march along on this liberal path. Subsequent events taking place beginning in the late 1990s have shown that this was a premature gloating. However, since going into this part is not the project of this book, suffice it say that every decade or so, we see visions for the soul of a large portion of the world locked in battle and shaping history: the Enlightenment and the Church in the 18th and 19 centuries; The 20th century hosted a number of battles on many fronts: colonialism and wars of liberation; socialism and liberalism; Nazism and liberalism. And now, in the 21st century, we see Islamic fundamentalism that filled the void of socialism, locked in battle with the West.

So, by the mid-1980s, EPRP was confronted with a different world from what the world was in its inception and maturing years. In addition, in the last 12 years of its existence, it had faced tremendous odds and had paid huge sacrifices. A moment has finally arrived to take stock of the changes in the outside world, and map a strategy to take the struggle. The very fact of selecting its leadership at its second congress using secret ballots was a sign of the times. Then, one by one, its planks and platforms gave way to new ones. The following are the main ones:

- Marxism-Leninism was jettisoned as a guiding ideology for the party. What this meant was that the party no longer fought to bring about the dictatorship of the proletariat.
- Instead, the party accepted the theory and practice of multi-party democracy. Although the party had in the past indicated the right of other parties to peacefully contest political power and form a coalition government albeit transitionally (such as during its call for a provisional people's government; in its response to the Dirgue's call for a united front; and in working out a solution on dealing with TPLF), the second congress was the forum where with clarity and finality the party stated that all parties were equal, and none privileged by history, and competition amongst them was the engine that was supposed to mark a vibrant democracy. To that effect, the party affirmed the need for a transitional period in

CHAPTER FOUR: RETURNING TO THE GOLDEN YEARS

Ethiopia consisting representatives from all political parties, and civic groups, and made this transitional charter part of its political program.

- This is also the stage where the Marxist dogma of secession had its long overdue burial. As stated earlier, the party aped the Marxian slogan that the solution to Ethiopia's "National Question" was the right of nations to self-determination, including and up to secession. As most Marxists naively believed at the time, most in EPRP also believed that as long as socialism wins and a proletarian party is in power, no nationality would secede, and workers would rather strengthen their unity under the motherland rather than fragment. However, the experience in Ethiopia and elsewhere was frightening, and the party's own experience bitterly showed it that narrow nationalist forces were not to be placated. So, now, the party reformulated its program in such a way that self-determination of nationalities was still preserved in the program, but that right did not this time include the right of secession. The party believed that the problems of nationalities could be solved through democratic means without resorting to secession. It went further and proposed a federal solution to the Eritrean problem as a solution for the war that has been going on for some 23 years at that time.

- The party also revisited the land question in Ethiopia at this congress. It is a well-known fact that the Ethiopian left had called incessantly for "land to the tiller" in its student days (the first official demonstration urging "Land to the Tiller was in 1965). When the Dirgue nationalized land in 1975, the euphoria that followed was one for the history books. Although the land proclamation act freed the Ethiopian peasant, especially the peasants in the south and east of the country from serfdom and historical injustice, its full power was not realized. This was because the government emptied the proclamation of its vitality by bureaucratizing it through such successive proclamations as forced communalization, fixed market prices, government-allied peasant associations, etc. One of the catalysts of the 1974 Ethiopian revolution was the 1973 Wollo Famine that distressed the nation and turned it en masse against the monarchy. The 1975 land proclamation was hoped to end the shame of famine and hunger. However, nine years after the proclamation, another massive famine hit the country in 1984. It was with this background in mind that the party at its congress decided that peasants should be entitled to individual holdings codified by law, and that this right should include a peasant's ability to lease all or part of his/her land as they see fit.

To this day, land is owned by the government, just as in the Dirgue days. The country has not been ridden of famines, year after year many millions living on the charities of foreigners. To add insult to injury, the government that owns the land is now giving it away to foreign businesses in what is notoriously called a "land grab".

- Extending its economic policy into other spheres, the party tempered its earlier "nationalization" policy and gave space to private investment, and acknowledged a bigger role to what private investors could play in the country's development. This was done by still emphasizing the critical role the government would play in certain key areas, but simply widened the role of private capital in a mixed economy.
- Finally, a mobile radio communication system was launched to popularize the party's position among Ethiopians, and it was named 'Finote Democracy Radio" - The Path of Democracy, and it played a significant role until it was silenced by TPLF's attacks which will be our next topic.

Despite these milestones, some of the publications around this time still continued to reflect the old positions: the following were some of the more notable publications that failed to reflect the positions adopted at the Congress: a September 1986 booklet/study guide on Protracted War, a March 1985 study guide on the objective condition, and a March 1986 booklet titled " When We Say a Proletarian Party".

The Second Congress was a watershed event in that it instilled at long last a sense of stabilization among members, and for the first time in the party's history, most of the party central committee members were with the army. Seven members were in the army command, the second hierarchy below the central committee members. Some of the command members were at the same time

CHAPTER FOUR: RETURNING TO THE GOLDEN YEARS

central committee members: Jabbir, Geleb (Eshete), Gayyim (alternate CC member). The other command members were the commander Beker, his deputy Berhe, HaileAbay (Ambaye), and Hailemariam. The structure also included the usual departments: intelligence; medic; army training, political department, logistics and mass organization.

**

No sooner had the party concluded its Congress in March when the Dirgue army moved in April into Matebia and Seraqo towards Quarra. The Dirgue army was led by the Chilga awaraja governor, and had 800-1,000 well-armed soldiers. In early May, at Dubaba, EPRA forces along with the local people started the counter attack. The forces of EPRA that took part in the defensive war were no more than 4 gantas, and after a 4 -hour battle, they were able to rout the Dirgue forces. This victory enhanced their image among the people.

After re-stabilizing the area for a couple of months, and some preparation, at the beginning of July, the army raided Dangilla planning to extend its zone of operations. The EPRA forces were able to get weapons and also succeeded in releasing political prisoners and doing agitation work among the residents. Again, the fame of the army and the hope it created among the people soared.

For the next one year (summer of 1985 to summer of 1986), the party/army was engaged in attacks and counter-attacks with the Dirgue army in a swath of land as wide as Quarra and Achefer in Gojjam. Wars were waged in Kumer, Alefa, Gazgei, Bambuk (in Metekil), Manqush, Omedla, Yismala (Achefer's main city), and Jawi. When a semblance of relative peace reigned, internal stabilization and re-structuring of the army took place. During this time, the army was careful not to get into conflict with Ansar movement rebels of Sudan who were using the Ethiopian border to launch attacks across the border against Niemeri's Sudanese forces. When the party sent Gumuz emissaries to these rebels, they complied with the party's request, and no hostilities ensued.

By October 1986, the army grew two-fold, and at Salia (Tewodros Ketema), it was re-organized into 4 hayls (each with 2 gantas, and each ganta up to 100 fighters), and with one, stand-alone ganta.

At this time, in Jawi, the army was faced with a controversial issue regarding a commercial farm run by the Dirgue regime. Believing that the farm was part of the regime's effort to attack EPRP, EPRA units raided the farm, and hijacked a trailer truck loaded with fuel. While the army used the fuel, it burned the tuck.

However, attacking a farm meant for development invited a critical assessment by the party leadership, and at the end of December the party CC came out with a policy prohibiting such attacks against development projects. However, this policy did not stop EPRA forces in March 1986 from peacefully taking over the camp of a geological team doing mineral exploration, and taking over two Toyota pickup trucks. The fear was that roads were being built deep into rebel-held areas, as part of the exploration, and EPRA units were concerned that the Dirgue would continue to attack them if the project went ahead.

This fear, almost a year later, was to result in a major controversy as we will see below when the EPRA forces attacked a major development project at Pawi, that of Tana Beles.

EDU: A Distraction during the Golden Age

In April of 1986, the party and army were surprised by unannounced visitors: news came that an unidentified armed group had camped at the border. It was soon found out that these visitors were members of EDU's forces. Soon after, a member of EPRP's foreign committee came from Khartoum and broke the rather stale news about EDU. As there were no prior arrangements and announcements, the army had to improvise to deal with the new situation. The EDU forces had to be fed, medically taken care of, and provided areas of joint operation. When the rainy season started, communication with them was difficult; but still a hayl was assigned to operate with them in certain areas around Seraqo, and mostly in Chilga awraja. They participated in a few wars and obtained weapons based on the number of their participants. They tried to access their former members and re-recruit them into EDU.

Around January and February of 1987, however, problems started to surface. Some EDU units started demanding food by force from some peasants; started penalizing innocent citizens without cause; allied with thieves and bandits and disturbed the peace; overreached their assignment by demanding taxes from traders; involved in defaming EPRP/EPRA in some areas. The problem posed a challenge to the EPRP leadership. The party and army knew that there were some honest leaders in EDU like Aba Girmai and Aleka

CHAPTER FOUR: RETURNING TO THE GOLDEN YEARS

Tesfai that wanted harmonious relations. Organizational discipline was not one of the attributes of EDU.

The problems continued through September 1987. The worst areas of the confrontation were Seraqo and Matebia. New transgressions started to emerge: some EDU members started harassing small groups of EPRA units; in some cases, they demanded small EPRA units to disarm and hand over their weapons to EDU; some demanded that EPRP had to move over to Gojjam since it was allegedly operating in areas EDU fighters liberated.

EPRA units were frustrated and demanded action. Finally, the EPRP leadership directed all EDU units to come to Matebia and to help solve once and for all these problems. Using the lack of supply for their units if they all came to Matebia as an excuse, EDU refused. In order to facilitate the logistical problems of EDU, the party leadership gave EDU ten thousand Ethiopian birr. This still did not move EDU, and they instead continued harassing EPRA units.

In September, EPRA graduated several new recruits, and subsequently decided to wage war on EDU and quickly evict it into Sudan. In a war that took less than a week, and waged on two fronts (upper and lower Matebia), EDU was routed- Very few were wounded or died from either side, while the majority of the EDU forces surrendered. Although defeated, EDU camped near the border and the Sudanese regime was urging it to counter-attack. However, the EPRA units attacked EDU once again, and tried to make sure that it was no longer a threat as a fighting force. Leaving a small squad (with a support of a nearby battalion) to monitor the border, the rest of the army moved into the hinterlands to continue unfinished business with the Dirgue. However, the respite from EDU only lasted 8 months.

In April, freshly armed by the Sudanese regime and invigorated, EDU was itching for a fight to settle old scores. The lone battalion in the area, even with the support of the local militia, could not have stopped the EDU forces other than delaying their march for a few days.

At a village called Shukuria, the EPRA forces ambushed at the rear side of the thousand- plus strong EDU army. A senior EDU leader who was later released (Ato Zemete Beyene), along with 10 others were captured. EDU however, undeterred by the temporary setback, launched an attack two days later and pushed back EPRA forces, fully taking over the lower Matebia area.

Having its rear protected by the Sudanese, and buoyed by its recent victories, the EDU forces pushed further into Aysega and Serferedin, long EPRA-controlled areas. The party leadership and the command had directed the battalion and militia fighting EDU not to engage in frontal and conventional war with the EDU forces. Instead, they were supposed to use small and mobile forces to harass and defeat EDU. However, fearing that if unchecked, the EDU forces would overrun Quarra and EPRA's base area, the battalion engaged the EDU forces frontally and sustained major losses. Members of the battalion command and departmental senior members were martyred and wounded.

This created a deep sense of resentment in the army and the party. As a result, the army command decided to call off planned skirmishes with the Dirgue and to pull all battalions from the hinterlands (at Gazgie and Alefa) to the war zone. The militia and new recruits at the training center were ordered to be on the ready and prepare supplies for the war front. In the meantime, the Sudanese army was openly helping EDU by treating its war wounded, and replenishing the EDU supplies. Emboldened by these, EDU declared to the people that they were going to drive EPRP out into the border areas of Gojjam.

The EPRP command decided to ambush the EDU forces by encircling them at their base at Mertrand and attacking them, before they had a chance to fan out in various directions to overwhelm Quarra. The battle started on April 18 in the wee hours, and the EDU forces were totally annihilated: dead, wounded and captured, only a few managing to escape into Sudan. The Sudanese army stationed as their rear was terrified at their stooges loss and retreated into Tiha. Again, the party and army lost experienced and senior comrades. In this battle, EPRA lost 12 comrades, three of whom were battalion commanders -Dibekulu, Asmare and Zergaw, and one, Hailemariam was a Command member, while another Command member, Meskerem was wounded. On EDU's side, 200 were killed. A mop up operation was followed, and the remnants of EDU were hunted down, and they were never heard from.

The victory over EDU and their unofficial ally the Sudanese regime aroused the nationalistic feelings of the local people. Thousands of people came from Gojjam and Gondar border areas to demonstrate at Mertrand against the settlement policy of the Sudanese army inside the Ethiopian side of the border. The demonstrators elected representatives to discuss with the Sudanese army officials on how they should vacate the Ethiopian lands. The Sudanese army command stated that it would pass the Ethiopians' messages to the authorities in Khartoum, and took no further action.

Development and War: The Twin Sisters

For almost a year, again, from February 1986 to January 1987, the army continued expanding its areas of operation, engaged in skirmishes with Dirgue units, and consolidated its structures. Members of its mass organizations units covered wide areas of Gojjam and Chilga awraja. Support from the local people, especially from the Gumuz was at an all time high. In November, the army re-organized itself again.

It formed 5 battalions (each with 4 hayls) as fighting forces. This meant, at this time the army had at least 4,000 armed and properly trained members. Teams of the mass organization departments laid out democratic administrative structures in all army-held areas. These included peasant associations and justice tribunals that the people themselves set up. There were thousands of militia support groups organized into units. The army's operations included not only fighting against the Dirgue units, but also hunting down thieves and bandits.

In early December 1987, the Dirgue in a project called Tana Beles, started building roads and feeder roads that traversed the areas under EPRA's control. Starting in Pawi, the main road passed along the edges of Lake Tana, and ended in Bahir Dar. At the same time the project included building channels to take water from Lake Tana into the Beles Valley, and building micro dams at desirable locations to facilitate the development plan. By mid-December, barely 2 weeks since the start, the army convoys protecting the road building team, came to Gazgei and Zibstu in Achefer, a direct existential challenge to the party and army.

Almost a quarter of a century later, in April 2011, TPLF's Meles Zenawi delivered a speech in Guba, Benishangul, to purportedly mark the commencement of the Millennium Dam project, a Dam later re-named the "Great Ethiopian Renaissance Dam". The dam is estimated to cost 3.3 billion Euros, and all the money is expected to be raised from domestic sources, as no international agency or bi-lateral state has agreed to partially fund it. If built, it would be the largest dam at any point on the Nile. The regime's ambitious power generation plan calls for the generation of up to 8,000 mega watts (MW) by 2016, of which "the Renaissance Dam" is expected to generate about 5,250 MW. The Dam is expected to hold 67 billion cubic meters of water, thus creating a reservoir almost twice the size of the natural Lake Tana (maximum capacity 32 billion cubic meters). This man-made lake would provide opportunities for fisheries and cultivation.

The timing of the opening ceremony of the Dam was inopportune: it was at a time when the TPLF/EPRDF regime was preoccupied with fear of the North African and Middle Eastern people's power coming to Ethiopia, a revolution by that time had thrown from power Egypt's and Tunisia's long-reigning presidents. It was also threatening the leaders of Syria, Libya, and Yemen. So, many Ethiopians thought the Ethiopian mass media frenzy with this news was a diversionary tactic, and a ploy to get remittances from the Diaspora by dangling a 5% paying treasury bonds to finance the construction of the Dam.

The Dirgue's development construction in 1987 was funded and manned by an Italian construction company called Salini. This is the same Salini that is winning construction bids also under the EPRDF. Within a few days, the EPRA Command decided to attack the convoy and hamper the progress of the project. In the attack, the EPRA units captured two Italians, burned over 20 large and medium-sized cars and trucks, and annihilated the Dirgue armed units. The Dirgue sent reinforcement units that same day, but EPRA units attacked them at night. According to the author of a carelessly written book on EPRP, *Yedem Meret*, the author alleges that EPRP negotiated with the Italian government over the fate of the hostages, got a substantial amount of money, and with the money bought in Paris, France, an apartment building used as office and residence.

The Dirgue did not stop its attempts to go after the EPRA. In March, It planned a major attack coming from three directions, and its goal was to overwhelm Quarra and if possible to drive EPRA into Sudan. The forces in three directions were to merge at Quarra: one force coming from Gojjam (Pawi); the second coming from Gondar (Chilga) and the third from Metema via Matebia. The force starting from Pawi was a logistics force, and confronted EPRA at Mariam Wuha, and was annihilated. EPRA units got weapons, radio

CHAPTER FOUR: RETURNING TO THE GOLDEN YEARS

communication equipment, and a pack of animals with food supply. The Dirgue units sent in reinforcements, and EPRA units encircled the new force. Both sides sustained huge losses and the Dirgue units fled the battle area. The second force suffered a similar fate.

The third force coming from Matebia was able to penetrate into Quarra, but sensing that its other forces had not arrived, it quickly retreated.

Thus, the Dirgue's subsequent attempts at counter-attack, especially to free the 2 Italian hostages proved useless. However, this did not mean there were no costs to pay as a result of the Dirgue incursions: peasants had to flee their homes and stay in the bushes for several days; their houses were burnt down; and the cattle they left behind were slaughtered.

In early November 1988 (almost a year after the first Italian hostages were taken), EPRA units engaged in an ambush at an area between Qunzla and Yismala, and captured for the second time two Italian citizens. Again, the Dirgue made futile attacks to get the two hostages and failed.

The EPRA forces treated the Italian hostages in a humane manner, for instance, by letting them go out on hunting. After their release, they became friends of the party. The late Professor Alem Eshete of the University of Rome had asked to come to Quarra to discuss the release of the hostages. He was denied, and had to return to Rome from Khartoum. The Italian Communist Party arranged a conference in Rome surrounding the issue, and Mersha, Iyassu and Mohammed were the principal speakers.

Around this time, for the first time in the army's history, training in the use of heavy guns, anti-air plane missiles (Sam-7S), and explosives was given. The army steadily grew by leaps and bounds. What started as a 2-ganta army when the EPRA first moved to Quarra in 1984/5, two years later in 1987 resulted in the creation of a new division it called a column. A column had two battalions, and a number of heavy machine gun hayls.

As we can see, the peaceful Golden Age of EPRP/A was only marred by the never-ending, back and forth war between EPRA and the Dirgue. This was to be expected. The Dirgue was not to let its sworn enemy EPRP that it drove from the cities in 1978 now grow and expand under its nose a decade later. To sweeten the deal, EDU also rained on EPRP's parade albeit for a brief period.

EPRP

What the Dirgue and EPRP as two multi-ethnic entities failed to see was the power of the two ethno-nationalist forces that was menacingly growing exponentially and threatening both entities and the country for which each purportedly fought for. To the very last, the Dirgue pursued EPRP, and the latter returned the favor. There is nowhere any record where the EPRP leadership posed to see the big picture danger and brainstorm possible strategies to thwart the impending danger. The same could not be expected from the militaristic and violent Dirgue. However, one Brigadier General assigned to the Gojjam region as a Gibrehayl commissar by the name of Gebremeskel Azbtei demanded of the political committee secretary to make peace with EPRP and instead focus on fighting the secessionist forces. The secretary reported Brigadier General Gebremeskel Azbtie's "transgression" to Col. Mengistu who promptly called him to Addis where he languished without a task until the EPRDF forces moved in[2]. After jailing him for 2 years, the General was released by EPRDF and now lives in Addis Abeba. Perhaps as a result of mixing priorities, the party around this time prepared an outline of a policy for allowing and legalizing marriage in the EPRA, which heretofore, was not a condoned and codified act. The members however commented that the time for this was not now, and that they would revisit the issue at a later date.

After its war with EDU, EPRA units continued the attack and counter attack against the Dirgue for the next 2 years (May 1987 to April 1989). As known, during a respite from the wars, they consolidated their structures and did internal consolidation. Thus, in 1987, they fought wars in Alefa, Pawi, (for a third time, they captured one Italian, bringing the hostage number to 5), Jawi, Delgi, Janoha.

At the end of these wars, the EPRA went back to internal consolidation where for the first time it gave a select cadre of 20 army members training on explosives as a stand-alone course. This was given at the end of a 3 1/2 months cadre school training, which was the fifth course this time, and attended by a few members of the foreign committee members from Sudan. Although the army was steadily growing, the party noticed that there was still a shortage of

---

2. Zenebe Feleke: Neber, part ii, p. 306. The party secretary was Captain Begashaw Atalay, and he had the support of Major General Asrat who was the area's leader, in the marginalizing and eventually sacking of Brig. General G/M Azbtie.

CHAPTER FOUR: RETURNING TO THE GOLDEN YEARS

qualified leaders to take political and military leadership positions at the highest echelons.

In 1988, wars were fought at the following battles: Guba/Isidi (as a result of the complete annihilation of the Dirgue forces, a Dirgue unit stationed at the border was terrified and surrendered to the Sudanese authorities instead of joining the EPRA); Yismala (not a successful operation by EPRA's standards, and to make matters worse, the Dirgue's air force bombarded the retreating guerrilla army); in an irony of history, on the very day senior Dirgue generals were carrying out a coup against Mengistu, his units in Gojjam were bombarding Gojjena in Gazgie which they thought was EPRA's logistics depot.

Moving towards southwestern Gojjam towards Wollega, the EPRA fought battles in Wombera and its capital Debrezeit, Bullen and Mura the same year. The next year (1989), another unsuccessful raid was waged by EPRA at Dibati. The Dirgue units were well fortified, and the EPRA suffered considerable losses. Zigem and Kilaj were attacked by EPRA, and the youth of the towns and the surrounding areas joined the army following the victory.

One of the highlights of 1989 was the fact that the army as a result of its growth decided to divide its forces into two big regions and one sub region. The first region consisted of the Northern Sector encompassing Alefa/Gazgie, Seraqo, and the Achefer/Dangila zones. The Southern Sector consisted of Wombera/Dibati, Mandura, Guangua/Agew Midr to the Wollega Border. The sub-regions were Quarra/Matebia and Metekil.

To cover these new zones, a column (recall it had 2 battalions), Column 82 was assigned the Northern Sector, while Column 90 was assigned the Southern Sector. Stand-alone hayls were assigned to cover the sub-regions. At this stage, the army had 2 columns, 3 battalions, over 5 stand-alone hayls, 2 heavy machine gun hayls and numerous support departments. The same year (1989) after these assignments, the Northern Sector fought for 4 months a defensive war against the Dirgue that was trying repeatedly to break into their areas. The Dirgue units used heavy machine guns including Stalin Organs (MI-25), and rocket launchers.

The Southern Sector was in a similar war situation. As the area was newer, a lot of the work was organizing the people and militia forces, and fighting the Dirgue units as necessary. As in all liberated areas, the people formed their own peasant associations and justice tribunals. The people were enthusiastic with their support, and at one point raised up to 40,000 Ethiopian birr for the army. The last time the Quarra area displayed such enthusiasm for an institution was perhaps when Kassa Hailu (later Atse Tewodros) emerged from the area and his power expanded tremendously, which resulted in relative and temporary peace in the area.

During these Golden Years, up to 10 Kenyan leftists came to Quarra to train for launching a possible armed struggle in their country. The training/stay may have been facilitated by the famous Kenyan writer Ngugi.

CHAPTER FOUR: RETURNING TO THE GOLDEN YEARS

EPRP/A in Quarra and Gojjam

EPRP's new logo in the backdrop. The hammer and sickle were gone after 1985. The new logo was designed by artist Solomon Hailu, a longtime political prisoner of the Dirgue and a torture victim.

Chapter Five: The Sun Sets On EPRP's Golden Age

The TPLF War on EPRA -Round 3

As the reader might recall, TPLF had declared war on EPRP in 1978 in Tigray and forced it to retreat to Eritrea. That was Round 1. Then, in successive battles, in Round 2, it had forced the army to leave the Wolkait/Tselemt area. The final push for a TPLF that was defeating the Dirgue forces, and had only EPRA between Gojjam and Addis Abeba, was Round 3.

As the provocations of TPLF intensified, EPRP started mobilizing the populace and its army. One of EPRA's organizers during this period was Haile Abay, a Tigrean from Adwa who later lost his life at the hands of a bandit while working alone in Quarra.

As patriotic citizens sensed the dangers to EPRP and Ethiopia, thousands started flocking from Sudan in lorries and flooded the Quarra lands. A portion of the militia and regular members of the Dirgue also abandoned their units and started joining EPRA. There was little time to train all these citizen soldiers, and more importantly, to instill them with the frugal and hermit-like values of EPRP. Some tainted the army with their loose morals and maintaining discipline was a major problem in the ballooning army.

Starting in August 1990, TPLF openly embarked upon laying the ground work to attack the EPRA forces. Senior members of TPLF started arranging interviews through print and air media where they freely attacked EPRP/EPRA. The party was characterized as "bourgeois", "capitalist", "anti-people", and "chauvinist", and was sentenced to be liquidated. EPRP also obtained evidence that they were preparing their army and militias for a showdown. Indicating a joint strategy, EPLF too joined the fray. Its leaders, Isayas in particular, in interviews, attacked what he described as "chauvinists and the Dirgue that together would be thrown into the dustbin of history".

To counter these provocative acts, EPRA forces started preparations to defend themselves. As part of the preparations, in November 1991, they convened a large conference in Salia inviting peasants and representatives from Quarra, Metema, Matebia, Semien Gojjam/Zibist, Alefa Taqusa/Seraqo/Gazgie, and Western Gojjam/ Metekel/Guba and Dangur woredas. The representatives included mothers, members of the militia/hizbawi arbegna, peasant association leaders, and notable individuals. The agendas included the current Ethiopian situation, and the danger posed by narrow ethno-nationalist forces, the role the people should play to avert the dangers and to help the EPRA. The meeting lasted 6 days, and passed resolutions.

One of the decisions passed was to call for peace, and assign among the conferees people who would travel to all liberated areas to explain to the residents the decisions of the conference.

True to its violent behavior and true to the last days, the Dirgue kept the pressure on EPRA forces despite its debacle and encirclement in the Northern wars by TPLF and EPLF forces. From February 1990 to October, it engaged the EPRA uninterrupted by deploying its battalions and divisions to stop the EPRP from expanding into Gojjam and Wollega. When these wars failed to produce the desired results, it tried another tactic by using local saboteurs sneaking in the rear and fomenting trouble in the villages. One famous family among these saboteurs was Fitawrari Al Gemmer and his sons. They ambushed small EPRA units, and sabotaged the free movement of people and supply.

To pacify the situation, on the Wombera front, EPRA made peaceful overtures, and the problem was peacefully resolved. However, on the Guba front, EPRA units had to attack these saboteurs and their supporters before driving them to Sudan or to Dirgue-controlled cities. The Dirgue was in a way successful in its tactic to tie down the EPRA and to arrest its expansion, because the EPRA units had to stay over 3 months in these areas to pacify the situation and stabilize it.

CHAPTER FIVE: THE SUN SETS ON EPRP'S GOLDEN AGE

In January 1991, the last re-structuring of the army was completed with the fresh graduates of the training school. 3 columns and 3 battalions were formed; over 20 stand-alone hayls were formed, of which 4 were heavy machine gun hayls carrying 60 and 80 mm mortars and 50 caliber machine guns. Departments were also tweaked; the supply and logistics department was expanded to cover its responsibility for transport, farming, ranching, and supply purchase. This department took up close to 2 battalion manpower.

No sooner had the army re-organized itself when the Dirgue started crumbling and the incoming TPLF forces started attacking EPRA units and militia forces from February 1991 through June 1992.

In the face of the impending danger, the EPRP CC held a plenum in December 1991. It made decisions regarding the mobilization of the army and people; it expanded the Army Leadership Committee from its 10-man strength to 14; including the first two female Command members (Meaza [Aberash Berta] and Tirsit who prior to this assignment were members of the Political Department), and the other two additions were members of the CC, Yishaq Debretsion and Sitotaw Hussein - three of the four are still on the party's disappeared list, while Tirsit passed away a few months later due to the stress and strain of the existing conditions then. With the two women departing from the Political Department, the Department was folded and its tasks taken up by the Command.

The Army leadership created a 7-man provisional Command and started preparing for the inevitable confrontation with the TPLF aggressors. In mid-February, the TPLF/EPRDF forces took control of Bahir Dar, in Gojjam province. By the end of the month, both Gondar and Gojjam provinces were under the full control of TPLF forces. The EPRA units were busy taking in both Dirgue units and their weapons and assimilating them in their lines.

During this time, the EPRA units encircled a well-armed Dirgue Division stationed in Dibati, Metekel and directed it to peacefully surrender. Failing that, they sent in local emissaries and waited patiently for 2 days. However, the Dirgue units tried to break the encirclement and suffered huge losses. The few that managed to escape ran away to Chagni, knowing full well that that town was under TPLF's control. The arms and ammunition obtained in this battle was a huge boost to the Southern Sector EPRA army as its recruits were low on ammunition.

In the following several weeks, EPRA units were racing against time and against the TPLF to get their share of weapons, fuel, food, vehicles and parts from the retreating Dirgue army. While the provisional Command members were busy leading the army's attacks and property procurement, the remaining Command members were deployed to safe keep the party's property; ensure the safe retreat of sick and wounded comrades. The standing order by the Command was to avoid frontal confrontations with TPLF, and work hard and fast on assimilating thousands of new recruits joining the EPRA. In the meantime, TPLF sent out press releases alleging that EPRP is attacking its units, and preparing for war. This has been an all-too-common tactic employed by TPLF in Rounds 1 and 2.

The following were the major battles between TPLF and EPRA forces fought over a year's period (April 1991 through June 1992)

1. Having evicted the Dirgue from Gondar and Gojjam, TPLF's next strategy was to squeeze EPRA units and drive them into Sudan, or force their surrender. The first incursion by TPLF forces was around the areas near Lake Tana, closing the routes from Addis to Bahirdar, from Bahirdar to Gondar (through Kunzila), and from Metema to Gonder. Then, in April 1991, a massive force occupied EPRA's liberated city of Maksegnit, near Dangila. Two EPRA battalions, along with the local people, counter-attacked, and the TPLF units withdrew from Maksegnit.

It was clear to anyone that followed TPLF's strategy that it would massively retaliate its loss at Maksegnit, and the provisional Command was cognizant of this eventuality. Accordingly, it directed the column that was involved in the counter-attack at Maksegnit to quickly evacuate the area and be on high alert. However, contrary to the Command's directive to the column leadership, and despite the urging of several members of the column to quickly leave the area, the column leadership camped nearby for 2 full days.

2. As expected, TPLF mobilized several brigades and they all traveled day and night and converged near Maksegnit and surrounded the Charra area. The next day, early in the morning, the TPLF forces started attacking the surrounded EPRA units. It was nearly impossible for EPRA forces to break the encirclement, although they fought valiantly. The column commissar (Alemayehu) killed himself; the commander of the column (Denbelo) was wounded and captured, and the deputy commander (Chaqlei) disappeared during the battle. The rest of the junior commanders

CHAPTER FIVE: THE SUN SETS ON EPRP'S GOLDEN AGE

gathered the remnants of the battle, and were able to rejoin their forces.

EPRA's loss at Maksegnit, where it could have been fully avoided, and in which TPLF snatched victory out of the jaw of defeat, adversely affected the morale of EPRA units elsewhere. The two battalions that suffered in this battle were the most battle-tested and superior fighting forces of EPRA. Therefore, the loss negatively affected the future fighting spirit of EPRA forces. The unanswered question was how could an experienced column leadership defy the Command's directive to leave the area fast, and instead camp for 2 days, making the column vulnerable to TPLF attack?

As a result of this loss, the Command decided that all forces and departments should be neither sedentary nor scattered. They started moving together, and this situation created a crisis in rations supply. The training camp still had thousands in training, and they were now vulnerable to this encircle-and attack strategy of the TPLF.

After its victory in Charra, TPLF successively attacked EPRA areas:

3. They first invaded the Southern Sector of Dejen and Wombera out of their bases from Pawi and Chagni. Fortunately, the main fighting force of the EPRA was not in this area. Only new recruits, and local militia assigned logistical tasks and a medical facility staff were in this area. The TPLF forces rounded up EPRA's cattle, medicine, and property and headed to Almehal, a border area where they looted the army's and the people's property, and burned up, and returned to their camps in Pawi.

At this time, the army's main policy was still intact, namely, not to confront TPLF frontally. In line with this, as soon as the TPLF evacuated the areas they overran, the EPRA units quickly went back and stabilized the people, procured property, and when possible harassed TPLF units with small units. In the Southern Sector, hundreds of new recruits started streaming to the EPRA following the takeover of big cities by TPLF and the crumbling of the Dirgue. The Sector's training camp was teeming with new recruits, and training them and quickly assimilating them with the fighting forces was a challenge.

4. At the beginning of May/end of April, while EPRA units were preparing to operate in central Gojjam with 4 battalions, and had gathered in Shendi in Kolla Damot, the TPLF units coming from their Burrei and Finote-Selam bases, made a surprise attack. The

EPRA units, assisted by the local militia, defended themselves and counter-attacked. The TPLF forces were completely routed, and the local militia went after the scattered and running TPLF forces and captured them and their weapons. This victory boosted the morale of the locals and the EPRA units. In the following two days, the army started its trip to central Gojjam by traversing the main road connecting Bahirdar and Addis, towards Burrei. In the City of Sekella, the army hoisted the Ethiopian flag in front of a proud and welcoming populace, and explained to the residents the impending danger posed by the ethno-nationalists. The two Command members leading this sector were Beker (from Harer and Ambaye (Haile Abay) from Tigray as stated earlier).

5. In the meantime, at the end of April, and beginning of May, the TPLF forces, deploying 4 divisions and moving from four directions, and assisted by the Sudanese regime, attacked EPRA's Northern Sector, and its base in Quarra/Matebia. The four directions were: from the Chilga/Metema side (Gonder); from the Achefer side/Agew midr/Yismala/Dangila (Gojjam); from the direction of Pawi; and the main force with heavy trucks and heavy guns, from Sudan.

Two weeks before this massive assault, and during the assault, several EPRP members had been kidnapped by Sudanese soldiers from border towns and turned in to TPLF. The Sudanese soldiers themselves killed a few of the EPRP members. 8 were killed, and 22 handed over to TPLF from the border cities of Fazra, Tiha and Basonda. Others, especially farm laborers and Amharic speakers, were summarily executed in the bushes.

In the first battle at Mehedid (on the way from Sudan to Quarra), the two hayls and department members that were in the area, along with the local Gumuz people, fought gallantly most of the day, and later were forced back by the massive TPLF army. The EPRA organizer that was organizing the Gumuz for the fight, Ibrahim, and a few EPRA members and Gumuz peasants were martyred. The TPLF forces overpowered the resistance along different sites, and entered Quarra, putting under their control the *Finote Democracy* radio broadcast center, the logistics and supply center, the training center, and the central medical offices (the *Finote Democracy* radio broadcast to Ethiopia was re-launched only when EPRP moved its center to the Diaspora. Along with *Hibret* radio in DC managed by the

CHAPTER FIVE: THE SUN SETS ON EPRP'S GOLDEN AGE

indefatigable Mesfin Tefera, and targeting the Washington DC Metro area Diaspora, it continued to serve as EPRP's link to Ethiopians).

As much as TPLF deployed massive forces, the loss on the part of EPRA was limited. As earlier preparations had taken place, all sick and wounded comrades and others were in a safe place. The main fighting forces were in the Southern Sector, and although notified to come for the counter-attack, they were only able to arrive as the TPLF forces were leaving. However, the TPLF forces managed to take property, including EPRA's cars and trucks, which were transported into Sudan.

The TPLF forces, after evacuating Quarra, moved still in the Northern Sector, around Gazgei, Pawi and Chilga, and continued to harass EPRA units and the local militia. This kept EPRA and the militia engaged in counter-attacks in and around Delghi, Gomengei, Tenkel and Dembia in Gondar.

6. In the Southern Sector, at the end of May/start of June, EPRA units planned and executed a successful raid against TPLF forces in Gimjabet town, in Agew midr awraja. The raid was undertaken to boost the morale of the local people, and raise the fighting experience of the army. As usual, the town residents and the locals fully supported EPRA units in the annihilation of TPLF forces. Again, the EPRA units hoisted the Ethiopian flag to the utter joy of the residents.

In both Sectors, students, teachers, ex-soldiers and officers, continued to join the ranks of EPRA. While this increased the number of the army, the numerical strength was not matched by quality. It was simply difficult to politically and militarily train new recruits while at the same time fighting a war of survival, and not a war of choice. Therefore, EPRA was faced with various challenges the most serious of which was the loose morals of the new recruits that resulted in drunkenness, sexual assault, and improper behavior towards the local people.

Because there was a temporary respite in the fight, the EPRA Command decided to offer seminars on discipline and related ethics. The first seminar took a week and was held in the Southern Sector. While preparation was underway to offer a second seminar for those that did not attend the first, the battalion commander trusted with bringing them to the seminar deserted his units and gave himself up in Chagni to TPLF forces, and the army units had to be quickly pulled out of a danger zone. To add insult to injury, the same traitor was a scout to TPLF forces who came out the next day to attack and capture the EPRA units the traitor led a day earlier (more on treason and the details in the next chapter). The EPRA forces, however, managed to fight their way out of this treason with heavy machine gun shots behind them, perhaps coming from the same "comrades" they had a day earlier.

7. In the Northern Sector, a similar treason also took place. The column that was operating in Alefa and Gazgie was directed to travel from the highlands of Alefa to the lowland area in Seraqo. However, the commander (Gashaw or gurezaw), despite the objection of the commissar and his deputy, ordered the column members to camp near Delghi on a flatland, and engaged the members of one of the battalion in gymnastics. Later, he took two hayl commanders with him to Delghi town, and soon after TPLF forces descended upon the column members who were still camped on a flat land. The commissar and deputy commander organized an encirclement breakout, and most managed to break, except those hayls who sustained losses and whose leaders went to Delghi. The commander again gave himself up to TPLF forces.

These continuous treasonous acts added to the already strained relationship among EPRA units. Even the local militia did not know if they should trust any more the EPRA army commanders. Unfortunately, the treason was to go on unabated.

8. As the rainy season started, the TPLF forces started a new attack with massive force in the Southern Sector. The areas of attack included Agew midr, Metekel, and Chagni. The targets were the Command center (although this was always mobile, and not stationery), the supply and logistics and the medical offices. The rivers in the area, Beles, Dura, and Abay were overflowing their banks, restricting EPRA's mobility.

This lack of mobility forced operating in small units to break the encirclement, and also to get supplies. The Wombera area was particularly prone to food deficits during the rainy season among the Shinasha, Gumuz, and Shankila ethnic groups. At the end of June/start of July, these groups got to the lowlands of Wombera after much trouble.

CHAPTER FIVE: THE SUN SETS ON EPRP'S GOLDEN AGE

Falling in Enemy Hands

It was not difficult to predict based on internal and external conditions that it was a matter of time that EPRP/A was going to face annihilation by a determined TPLF force that had EPLF's and the Sudanese regime's assistance. Although the local people's support was solid and the army was growing astronomically, there was no time to train the fresh recruits, and get them ready for the hard battles that were being fought incessantly. Added to the EPRA Command's woes were the treason factor by senior commanders and rank and file. The suspicions and frustrations were not helpful in an army that was engaged in a fight that was to determine whether or not it continued as a fighting, independent political and military force. The TPLF was determined to have no incipient guerrilla army fighting it as it took power in Addis Abeba. The other fighting force with a semblance of independence, OLF, was bought off, and was now being groomed as part of TPLF's transitional government. The only independent force left as a thorn on the side of the TPLF/EPLF project was EPRP/A. Therefore, defeating it, and ensuring its annihilation was the major goal for the TPLF/EPLF duo. On its part, the EPRA command sensing the danger it was in had earlier decided to decentralize the army and move from area to area in smaller units. This was particularly common in the Southern Sector where the army's movement was restricted by the overflowing rivers, and the non-stop attacks by the TPLF.

As the TPLF attacks increased in the Southern Sector in the rainy season, two members of the Command (Gayyim and Beker) decided to take two battalions to the Northern Sector. The remaining Command members in the Sector were also directed to join the single Northern Command center before the rains swelled the rivers and mobility was limited. After spending the night at Bullen in Eastern Wombera with members the Army Leadership there, they set out to continue on their trip when they were attacked in a surprise attack by a TPLF force. A member of the Leadership Committee was wounded, while another member disappeared for a long while after the war before he finally re-joined.

The following were the main Leadership members losses through martyrdom and capture that created the chain of cascading events that eventually sealed the fate of EPRA in Quarra:

EPRP

1. In June 1991, a member of the Army Leadership committee by the name of Abera (nick name key zeb/red guard) fell in the hands of TPLF forces at Zigem while coming from the Ayehu mechanized farm to attend the second seminar. There was a brief skirmish. Conditions started deteriorating for EPRA units.
2. Two days later, another EPRP CC member and a member of the Leadership committee, Yishaq Debretsion (nick name Abebe Bariaw, and Eritrean by heritage) that was with the forces moving in Dibati, also fell in the hands of TPLF after trying to retreat following an engagement with TPLF forces at Berber.
3. A week later, while waiting to meet with the Quarra Leadership Committee members at Jebai, the forces that were on route to the Northern Sector learned that the Quarra Leadership members were delayed because they were attacked by the TPLF. As a result, another EPRP CC member and deputy commissar of the army, the Eritrean Geleb Dafla (Eshete), along with Dereje, a medic, were martyred.

Three members of the EPRP CC were captured along with Ayalnesh. The three included Tsegaye Gebremedhin (nick name Debteraw), Sitotaw Hussien (Tadelle) and Amha Belette (Gebrei). Although EPRA units were sent out to intercept the TPLF forces and retrieve their comrades, TPLF's fresh reinforcements would not allow that and TPLF quickly made away with their war prisoners.

This was a major blow to the EPRP/A. This incident took place at Ayma Dar, long the medical center of EPRA. The Sankissa area in which Ayma Dar is located is at the crossroads of trader routes coming from Belaya and Pawi. Enemy forces coming from Pawi or Dangur could also reach it by traveling through the lowlands without being seen. Thus, the area was vulnerable. Knowing that EPRA units were under incessant attacks, the members of the Leadership stayed at Ayma Dar for 4 days, thus exposing themselves to danger and enemy espionage. The EPRA Command later learned that the TPLF forces made the decision to attack at the last minute, changing their plan to pass the night farther afield, and traveling all night to make the surprise attack and net their human trophies.

This raised the issue of radio communication, both EPRA's and TPLF's, and who possibly could have alerted TPLF to help them

CHAPTER FIVE: THE SUN SETS ON EPRP'S GOLDEN AGE

change their plans. First the failure of EPRA's system of radio communication surrounding the incident: To its credit, a few days before this sad event, the Command had deployed a hayl in the Bakussa area to serve as a scout for the Leadership at Sankissa. Accordingly, learning about the TPLF movements, the night before the raid, the hayl dutifully dialed the radio center at Dagngei. Unfortunately, due to a broken communication radio, or some other unexplained reason, the Dagngei radio center did not pick up the warning message. Curiously, in the morning, the Dagngei center picked up the message just before the attack and dialed the warning message to Sankissa. In the middle of a war, unfortunately, the Sankissa radio center has not turned on the radio, and could not receive the message. Another radio 2 hours away, at Jebai, picked up the message meant for Sankissa, and dialed to Sankissa, to no avail. Soon after the TPLF forces overwhelmed the EPRA units.

Be that as it may, EPRA's communication failure still does not answer the question who it was that alerted TPLF to change its plan and attack Ayma Dar. Although it is not a consensus, most now agree in their suspicion that an EPRA spy/mole by the name of Gebre Hiwot who knew the location of the Leadership, and assigned in the trade sector of the army, may have radioed his TPLF counterpart, thus alerting TPLF for the raid. Lending credence to this suspicion, after the army gathered solid evidence of espionage against him and as it was about to bring him to justice, Gebre Hiwot smelled the danger and escaped to a nearby TPLF force in April 1992.

Another equally credible explanation was the fact that the EPRA units had been lax at times changing their radio codes, and TPLF could have easily picked up their messages, or/and the various traitors could have supplied it with the codes, thus enabling it to attack.

The two battalions that came from the Southern Sector were assigned to ambush the TPLF units taking the EPRA POWs. While on their way, they accidentally met with another TPLF force and a skirmish ensued at Mugechet. Although no major losses occurred, the two battalions lost communication with each other. A search was underway for the lost battalion when it was discovered, once again, that a commander had deserted his troops and went over to TPLF.

At this time, the decentralized EPRA forces in the Southern Sector were still under constant pressure, a radio communication was not established between them and the Northern Sector, and the locals were despairing and wondering out loud if EPRA/P had any future in their areas. Some of the ethnic groups, especially the Shankilla, turned on the EPRA small units to kill and arm themselves following their traditions.

Sensing this bleak situation, the two Command members who just arrived in the Northern Sector, along with 3 others who were already there (Gayyim, Beker, Matewos, Meskerem (Chakaw) and Maaza) decided that all the units in the Southern Sector have to be folded and brought into the Northern Sector in Quarra. Other forces in faraway areas in the Northern Sector, such as Seraqo and Gazgei, had also to be pulled into Quarra. Supplying the army would not be difficult, as EPRA still had farms and cattle out of the reach of TPLF forces. While 3 of the Command members were assigned to implement these decisions, the remaining two were assigned to establish radio contact with the South and advise them of the new decision.

While this was launched, a TPLF force entered that area of Bambaho through Murgen, near Quarra. The army Command taking into account that it was necessary to lift the local morale, and dispel the news that EPRA was about to crumble, decided to engage the TPLF forces rather than retreat. The battle took place in mid-July 1991 (while the TPLF was plotting in Addis to hold the July conference of ethnic groups to establish the Transitional Government of Ethiopia). The hayl commander of TPLF was killed in the battle, and a few were captured, and weapons obtained. EPRA's wounded were taken to Ayema/Arenkuk and the units retreated as TPLF's reinforcements arrived. The new force just picked up its wounded and did not even bury its dead. This momentary victory gave EPRA a fresh lease on life and was a moment to celebrate.

Obviously, this victory did not last long. Perhaps learning that the EPRA units were now to converge in Quarra, the TPLF forces descended upon Quarra from different directions. The Command warned its forces to avoid direct confrontations, and most did that. However, one battalion came face to face with TPLF units at Alti, and was heavily decimated impacting the morale of the tense EPRA army.

4. From mid-July to early August 1991, successive losses were incurred by EPRA/P, especially the martyrdom and capture of senior members. Ambaye (Haile Abay) was killed by a member of a

CHAPTER FIVE: THE SUN SETS ON EPRP'S GOLDEN AGE

Shankilla ethnic group, and two Army Leadership committee members (Berhe, who was also a Command member, and Alula) were captured by TPLF at a war in the Southern Sector.

5. In the same war in the Southern Sector, a member of the Army Leadership committee of the Southern Sector (Amberbir) was martyred, a senior female comrade, and Gayim's sister (Ayelech - other names Birkti, Mebrhat) was wounded and being cared for in a cave when a peasant betrayed her to TPLF forces.

Although earlier the Northern Sector Command members had planned to fold the Southern Sector, these wars and events appear to have sealed the fate of the Southern Sector. The remaining units managed to make the long trip back, crossing rivers, and avoiding the enemy and rejoined their comrades in Quarra. There were/and still are after two decades, unconfirmed reports that there are small units of EPRA units left behind and operating in the Southern Sector. The Command tried to verify and establish contact with them by sending out scouting teams, but no verifiable information was obtained.

As soon as the fate of the Southern Sector was known at the end of July 1991, seven members of the Army Leadership committee (Gayim, Beker, Jabbir, Matewos, Meskerem, Maaza and Gebremichael) held a meeting and reviewed the grim situation.

They made the following decisions:

1. Although EPRA had sustained heavy losses at the hands of TPLF, until the party's CC decides on the fate of the armed struggle, EPRA units should not evacuate the field and should operate in small, and mobile units.
2. The sick, wounded and physically weak should be taken to Sudan. Although the Sudanese regime is TPLF's ally, attempts must be made to move them there in a clandestine manner, or/and by enlisting the help of humanitarian NGOs.
3. Those members willing and capable should be approached secretly and deployed to urban areas to do underground organizational work.
4. If pushed and pressed by TPLF, we should plan ahead, and prepare supplies to retreat into the border areas with Sudan.

On the last decision, there were some nuances of differences among the Leadership members. While some explicitly wanted the bulk of the army (leaving squads behind) to enter into Sudan if

TPLF's push becomes unbearable, others did not want to leave Ethiopia and get inside Sudan no matter the cost. This difference, however, was glossed over for now and focus made on the common tasks at hand. The difference was, however, to occupy EPRP/A for the following few months until its final days in the fields.

According to the decisions, they divided tasks and started implementing the decisions. As they were gathering EPRA forces, a battalion commander with 20 armed members pretending that they had an assignment marched into Seraqo to give themselves up to TPLF, thus unnerving the edgy EPRA units. Emboldened by the number of the increasing desertions coming over to its side, and as part of its long strategy, TPLF knew it was a matter of time before it completely evicted EPRA from the field. Thus, in August, it launched two wars in a week's time against the beleaguered forces of the EPRA. The army's fighting spirit had sapped at this time, and at the slightest provocations, fleeing in every direction became common. The TPLF took more EPRA property, and supplies that were being prepared for the retreat.

As to the implementation of the plans, talks and arrangements were underway with cross-border traders to take with them the wounded and sick EPRA members. Similarly, agreements were made with these traders to buy EPRA cattle and sell them in Sudan to help reduce the party's logistical burdens. As a result of these agreements, two wounded Army Leadership committee members, Gebremichael and Maaza, and a few other members were sent to Sudan in mid-September. Over 100 cattle were sold as part of the preparation for the retreat.

In the meantime, TPLF was busy implementing its divisive ethnic policy by organizing the Gumuz feudal lords, who previously were Dirgue's tools, as Tahrir Guba -Liberation front for Guba, and importing Beni Shangul supporters from Sudan, as a counter-weight and placeholders in place of EPRA. However, other than being political tools of TPLF, these forces were never engaged with EPRA forces on their own.

In mid-October, a senior comrade by the name of Mulugeta who was a responsible cadre for the Metekel area went to the TPLF side, and brought with him TPLF forces to attack EPRA units. While no harm was done on EPRA units, the TPLF invading forces took control of the Gumuz cowherd and the 400 heads of cattle that the party was going to sell.

CHAPTER FIVE: THE SUN SETS ON EPRP'S GOLDEN AGE

The Fate of the Armed Struggle

We have indicated above the differences among the Army Leadership when at the end of July 1991 it took up the issue of the armed struggle. The difference was between those who did not believe that the armed struggle should be folded, and those who argued EPRP/A had sustained huge losses, and its current situation does not support an armed struggle. At the end of September 1992, a CC member who came to Sudan (Samuel Alemayehu) sent a letter of position on the issue that purportedly expressed his and the position of the EPRP members in Sudan. He sent the letter to leadership members in Metekel and Quarra at the same time. The position in the letter supported the folding of the armed struggle, and the necessity of saving the remaining EPRA units into Sudan. The Leadership in Metekel following the request of the Sudanese letter, gathered all the members in the Metekel area, and read the letter. They all thought this was now the position of the EPRP CC, and just not one member. To that effect, they started burying weapons, expediting property placement and distribution among the locals, and preparing to go into Sudan. They then traversed the Alatish lowland with a guide going into Sudan. Suddenly, they established radio contact with an EPRA team that was caring for the cattle, that told them that no such decision has been made by the CC, and suggested they come and rejoin them. The Metekel group soon came and joined.

In November 1992, after pulling all EPRA units into the border area (leaving a small force in the hinterlands to monitor TPLF's movements), the party and army held a seminar that lasted five days at a place called Jebbra, near Mehadid. The seminar was two-phased. First, the 5-man Army Leadership committee deliberated on the issue of whether or not to continue the armed struggle and the related issues. After voting on the issues, the second phase took place. Here, all 15 party members discussed the issue with the Army Leadership committee in attendance, but the leadership without saying a word, and without letting the members know their decisions lest they unduly influence the members decisions.

It is not clear if non-party members of the army did deliberate and vote. In the first phase for the Leadership, the first motion was the following;

> "Although we have sustained heavy losses, there is no choice but to continue the armed struggle, and to launch other activities, such as urban organizational work as activities supporting the armed struggle".

A vote was taken on the motion, and this motion had 3 supporters, 1 objection, and one abstention. The second motion was the following:

> "We have sustained heavy damages, thus, the priority activities of the party henceforth should be organizational and political activities. The armed struggle should be done by small -armed propaganda units, thus saving most of the fighting force for the future strategic struggle. In addition, we have also to hold a conference to evaluate the changed national situations and come up with new tactics and strategy".

The voting on this second motion was 1 support, 1 abstention, and 3 objections- the exact inverse of the first motion of the first motion. Hence the decision to continue the armed struggle carried the day, and now it was up to the party members to vote in the second phase. Here, unlike at the Leadership committee, the motions were three instead of two. The first motion appears to have been injected to agitate the members and solidify their anger against the TPLF and make them inclined to vote the way the Leadership committee voted. The motions were framed as follows:

1. " To fold the armed struggle, kneel down, and turn over our weapons to the Woyannie"
2. "Fold the armed struggle, retreat into Sudan (clandestinely, and openly when convenient; contact human rights organizations to get support, and deploy members to urban centers for politico-organizational work".
3. "Continue the armed struggle regardless of the bleak circumstances".

Obviously, the third motion was supported by party members with only one objection. At this seminar, the members also elected two additional Army Leadership committee members to increase the

CHAPTER FIVE: THE SUN SETS ON EPRP'S GOLDEN AGE

number from 5 to 7. The two newly elected members were Sendek and Anteneh. The 7 elected a three-man provisional Command that consisted of Jabbir (CC), Gayyim (commissar), and Beker (commander).

In accordance with the decision, the Leadership re-structured the army in smaller guerrilla units, prepared new by-laws reflecting current conditions, and decided to operate in the Northern Sector.

EPRP/A appears to let anger and the urge for vendetta get the best of it when confronted by critical situations. As we saw in Chapter 1, in the late 1970s, some party CC members pushed the urban struggle to the limit when preparations for rural deployment, or other means should have been earnestly searched. Here again some 15 years later, knowing full well that the chances of an armed struggle succeeding were next to zero, most of the Leadership and membership voted to continue it in what can only be explained as out of anger, and frustration at the capture and martyrdom of members. One quality of leadership is to know when to retreat, and focus on other tasks until objective situations change. This was not to be, and the second biggest mistake in the party's history was made. In this decision, 3 of the EPRP CC members who were in the US and Europe had also expressed their support for the armed struggle to continue, or to support the decision made by the majority (Mersha, Mohammed and Fassika). In the next paragraphs, we will see the cost of such ill-considered and inadequately thought-out decision and judgment.

With the re-launching of the Northern Sector in smaller units, the locals were hesitant initially to give EPRA units full support, afraid that they might be victims of TPLF's wrath. Additionally, some rogue EPRA units that eventually went over to TPLF have been abusing them in the name of the party, thus sullying the good name of the party and the army.

Starting in February 1992, the TPLF forces overwhelmed the Northern Sector from many directions, occupying all the towns, villages, and even the water holes. They were ruthless and meted out punishment on those peasants they suspected to be EPRA sympathizers, and forced others to be their informants.

In April, a senior comrade by the name of Tesfaye Eju, operating among the people in highland Quarra was surrounded by TPLF forces and gallantly fought before he took his own life. Similarly, near

Mehadid, another senior comrade by the name of Wassihun was killed during a fight.

Indeed, the decentralized EPRA forces from time to time had scored victories against the bigger TPLF units. In March, they used explosives to blow an army lorry killing and wounding over 30 soldiers. In April there was an ambush at a place called Lemant where a TPLF hayl was decimated. However, what the Army Leadership did not seem to realize was the subsequent massive retaliation by the TPLF and the inability of the smaller EPRA units to withstand and continue for long. Following this defeat, the TPLF forces came out hunting the smaller forces, and in the ensuing battled decimated 2 units out of three, and most senior and experienced comrades were martyred. The Army Leadership committee met in November after the Jebbra seminar, and again for the second time met in April. Here the lone voice that objected to the continuation of the armed struggle, the commander Beker, raised again his objection, and stated that he was no longer in a position to continue in an operation he no longer believed in. He also mentioned his poor health as an additional reason to separate from the army. At the end of June, after some unsuccessful attempts to get him to change his mind, Beker was sent to Sudan.

It is not clear how soon after Beker left the formal operation of EPRA field forces ceased. Prior to Beker, the army's commissar, Gayyim, came to Sudan to discuss with the CC member who was there about a month or so before him (Samuel Alemayehu). After completing the first round of discussion at the end of May 1992 on a Friday, plans were made to continue the discussion the next Tuesday. However, on Monday, with help from Sudanese security forces, TPLF blatantly kidnapped 24 party and army members, most of whom were sick and receiving medical assistance. The details follow below.

Thus, the heroic struggle of the EPRP/A inside rural Ethiopia was concluded leaving its imprint on Ethiopian history as an inspirational struggle for future generations for Ethiopian democracy, rule of law, and prosperity.

Once again, just like in 1978 where the party was criticized for not deploying its forces in the countryside to avoid a head-on clash with the much stronger Dirgue, and more importantly to rely on a protracted rural armed struggle, the party was now in 1992 criticized for not doing the opposite but for the same self-preservation reason:

critics stated that the party/army should have avoided a head -on clash with the much stronger TPLF, and instead deployed its forces to other areas, such as Wolkayit, and/or deploy more of its cadres into urban areas in the wake of Dirgue's slow death, to repair old and ruined organizational networks. It seems again and again EPRP/A was instinctively bewitched by the daring of Ethiopian patriotism that at times did not leave room for self-preservation for later days, but instead laid it all out at once......

The West's and the Sudanese regimes' convergence to destroy the Dirgue regime was also at the same time a convergence to destroy Ethiopian nationalism. During the planned encirclement, the Sudanese army was covering Tiha, Fazra, Demazine and into Metekel. George H. Bush was in Sudan coordinating and consolidating the anti-Ethiopian forces under the cover of cross-border food relief program. Thousands of trucks were ferrying back and forth weapons into Ethiopia, and vandalized properties of the Ethiopian people into Sudan.

The Kiddnaping in Ghedariff

The kidnapping of 22 party and army members and 2 hired female cooks from where they were sheltered in a foreign country was the first by an Ethiopian regime - even the much-maligned Dirgue never dared to commit such a crime. (the author of the Amharic book "Neber" talks about the Dirgue's security launching an anti-EPLF commando in West Germany in the 1980s, an act even if true, pales in comparison)[1].

One of the victims was Beyene Gur'aa. Beyene was born in Gulomakda woreda in Tigrai in a village called Se'biya. He completed his elementary school at a Catholic school in Alitena, and continued his secondary and junior college education at a Catholic school and a seminary in Adigrat. During his junior year, the "edget behibret

---

1. ibid., p. 58. the Dirgue sent to Germany a 2-man team consisting of Shambel Basha Tedla Samuel, an explosives instructor at the Air Borne, and corporal Getu, to secretly murder an anti-Dirgue opposition element, probably an EPLF partisan. The mission goes awry when the explosive meant for the EPLF man kills the corporal and permanently maims the Shambel Basha.

zemecha" campaign was in full swing, and he was assigned in Kilteawlalo awraja. When he joined the EPRA that same year, it coincided with the fact that he was going to be one of the replacements to the depleted beginning army that suffered its first defections. He was going to be one of the 15 or so local EPRA members that joined the army as the second batch of EPRA (the first batch being the group that came through Eritrea and was the starting unit). He was one of the volunteers later in 1980 in Tselemt who stayed behind in a squad while the army went to Bertya to re-organize itself (Chapter 2).

According to Beyene Gura'a, one of the captured from Sudan, the scenario unfolded in the following manner. He was in deep sleep in a house he shared with his wife, a maid, and a relative. It was around midnight on June 1st, 1992. Security members of the Sudanese regime forced their way into his bedroom. They blindfolded him, and ordered him to climb onto a truck. Despite his blindfold, he was able to hear the moans and painful sighing of other compatriots. Among those kidnapped, there was a wife of a party member who was a mother of two infants, although she was 2 months later released when those kidnapped arrived in Azezo. The captured were at first taken to Metema. The Sudanese security forces in league with TPLF forces drove past the town of Metema into the nearby woods where the detainees stayed in the woods for 2 hours before they were driven back to the town in a make-believe drama to give the impression that they were captured from within Ethiopia, and not from a neighboring country.

At Azezo, the kidnapped were jailed near the airport in one of the military dwellings called "kebero beit", due to their hemispheric design. They were made to sleep on the cold cement floor without adequate mattress, and used their jackets and mats as mattresses (they were kidnapped in their night clothes, and some of the TPLF fighters had to give some of them their own spare clothes). The kidnapped were being interviewed by various TPLF investigators. The interrogations focused on documents TPLF obtained from the martyred, or documents captured from EPRA Leadership members. At Azezo, TPLF added a few more prisoners captured from the fields. One of the newly jailed befriended Beyene, and later managed to escape from jail through his ingenuity. After their stay in Azezo, the kidnapped were taken to Makelle, Endayesus.

CHAPTER FIVE: THE SUN SETS ON EPRP'S GOLDEN AGE

At least in Makelle, for members like Beyene who were born in the region of Tigrai, it was relatively easier to get visitors and be visited by family members, and Catholic priests. Until their arrival in Makelle, the kidnapping incident was a well-kept secret by Sudanese security forces and TPLF. Of course, EPRP released press reports about the incident, but no meaningful action was taken by any of the humanitarian and international agencies. Finally, the Catholic priests, friends and family members notified the Red Cross about the kidnapped EPRP members, and that agency's representatives were allowed visits.

While in prison, the kidnapped heard rumors that there were other EPRP prisoners, including captured members of EPRP's leadership committee at Quiha, near Makelle. This was important news because, other than the fate of a few mid or low-level prisoners of war TPLF captured, the fate of captured members of the EPRP/A Leadership, such as Debteraw (Tsegaye Geberemedhin), Sitotaw Hussein (Tadelle), Abebe Bariaw (Yishaq Debretsion), and Amha Belette (Gebre), to this date is unknown. It is a shame that ex-TPLF leaders like Siye Abrha and Gebru Asrat who should be in a position to know the fate of these fighters have not to this day publicly revealed what they know about their condition. The captured members of the EPRP leadership committee, all without exception, have struggled against Haileselassie's feudal rule, the Dirgue's brutality, and TPLF's narrow nationalism, and should have deserved a more honorable treatment at the hands of TPLF than their case being totally shrouded in secrecy.

The interrogations that started in Azezo continued in Makelle. The kidnapped got information from a TPLF fighter/prisoner who stayed overnight that they were in the notorious TPLF jail called 06. Other subjects of their interrogation included: 1. pressing Beyene to confirm that he was in the party's leadership (he was not), and to share with them all relevant information; 2. to provide to TPLF the names of senior party members and their residence addresses in the various cities in Sudan; 3. to help direct them to where they can find the party's money and property; 4. to provide them with the urban organizational structure of the party; and 5. to share with them information about the guerrilla units still in Quarra.

After two months of "re-education", and anti-EPRP political education, most of the kidnapped were released at Makelle, and each went to their desired destinations. However, Beyene and 5 others were detained for 6 more months in Makelle, and then transferred to Ba'ata prison in Gonder. At the Baa'ta jail, they were told they would appear before a court for sentencing. Their jail master at Baa'ta was an ANDM member by the name of Captain Abdu. While in jail, the kidnapped established secret contacts with EPRP, and the party sent them money at least once. At Baa'ta jail, there was an open market outside of the jail where prisoners could buy tea and other snacks from private vendors. The kidnapped made at least 14 trips to court. The means of transportation was a horse-drawn *garri*, paid by the captured themselves.

Finally, after 4 years in jail, the kidnapped were released in 1996. And because Beyene's wife was given a refugee resettlement in Denmark, he was allowed to emigrate there under a family re-union plan. The immediate result of the kidnapping by TPLF forces from within the borders of Sudan was the fact that for the United Nations High Commissioner for Refugees (UNHCR) to unwaveringly understand that there was no peaceful future for EPRP/A members in Sudan to live as refugees in that country. To that effect, it facilitated their re-settlement in other countries, and Denmark, New Zealand and Australia were the first to step up and were the resettlement destinations.

Gayyim

Gayyim (Gebreegziabher Woldemichael) was a member of the CC that was elected during the 2nd Party Congress in Quarra in 1984. Prior to that, as we saw in Chapter 2 , he was one of those that volunteered to stay behind as a member of a squad when the army retreated to Bertya to re-organize itself. At that time (1981), he was captured by the TPLF where in captivity he helped them translate some Russian documents (he was educated in the former USSR), and also helped them with the military plan of the attack on Mai Tsebri because he was so familiar with the area's topography (It is said that Gayyim was not really captured by the TPLF; but because he was severely injured as a squad member, and as the squad did not have medical equipment to help him, it was decided for him to go over to TPLF as a captured EPRA fighter to receive medical help). During the post-raid celebration and euphoria following the successful attack by the TPLF forces, Gayyim slipped out of captivity, and escaped to

CHAPTER FIVE: THE SUN SETS ON EPRP'S GOLDEN AGE

the Waldba monastery where he secretly stayed for 3 months until he established contact with his EPRP comrades.

Around May 1992, Gayyim came to Sudan to discuss with the area comrades about the future of the armed struggle. Another CC member, Samuel Alemayehu, who has been in the field helping with the Finote Democracy radio also arrived in Sudan a month or so before Gayyim. They were the two CC members in Sudan (Other CC members, such as, Jabbir were still in the field, and Mohammed had to leave Khartoum a year earlier as the new alliance between Sudan and EPRDF resulted in the closure of EPRP's office there, and subsequent tragedies)

As discussed earlier in this chapter, Samuel had sent a personal note to the field leadership (intercepted by members who read it and decided to leave the field based on the notes) advocating the folding of the armed struggle. Gayyim seemed not to share that idea, and the manner in which the decision was being made (his position seemed inconsequential as the events on the ground gave no chance to the continuation of EPRA's armed struggle). A few days later, the kidnapping discussed above took place.

According to Mersha, a collective CC decision was made to deploy Gayyim to Addis to lead the laying of the urban organizational network. Why Gayyim, a man already familiar to TPLF more than any other senior comrade, was chosen for the task is baffling. Gayyim seemed to have been successful in his assignment where he stayed in Addis in clandestine for a little over a year. He seemed to have noticed that he was running out of time, as advised by close family members and other comrades in Addis. In his letter to Iyassu which he sent from Addis to Nairobi, he seemed to indicate that he was expecting a replacement and for other comrades to take over the work. However, before this was consummated, in late 1993, Gayyim was involved in a shootout with his TPLF attackers, and died during the shootout at his shelter. There is a report that one of the members of EPRP that was deployed from Quarra to Addis for organizational work met Gayyim, and reported him to the TPLF secret agents. The party "member", a teacher by the name of Abrham Getu, initially came to Bahir Dar on his way to Addis, where he might have been recruited by the TPLF as a mole. After facilitating the murder of Gayyim, he was sent back to the Bahir Dar area as an educator where a member of the EPRP avenged Gayyim's death by killing him. Despite offers by EPRP for a safe passage to Kenya, the avenger refused to leave his area, and was subsequently hunted down by the TPLF and killed.

Based on documents TPLF obtained at Gayyim's residence, cadres and senior cadres were captured in Addis and Bahir Dar, such as Me'aza (a female comrade who was helping with the radio broadcast in Quarra and sent to Addis as part of the infrastructure, and with an injured eye as a result of shrapnel at the Mai Tsebri raid). Other victims included Tesfaye (from Wollaita), Abahoy and Haile in Addis, Dilu, Tsegaye and Abrham in Bahir Dar.

CHAPTER FIVE: THE SUN SETS ON EPRP'S GOLDEN AGE

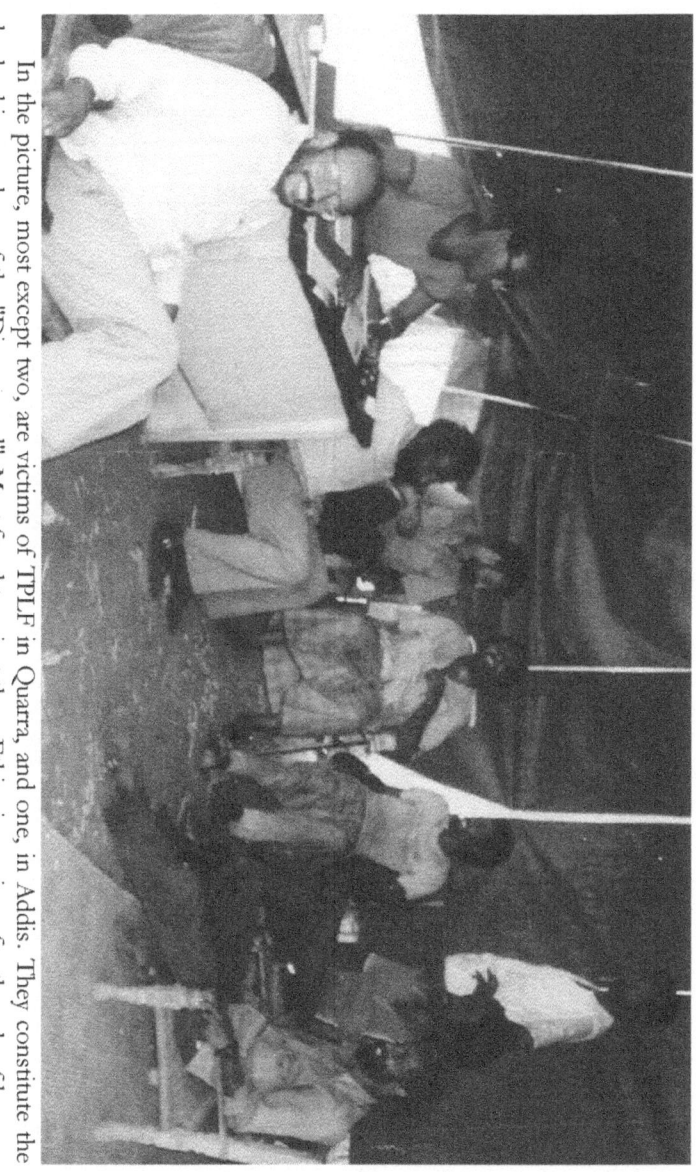

In the picture, most except two, are victims of TPLF in Quarra, and one, in Addis. They constitute the leadership members of the "Disappeared". Most fought against three Ethiopian regimes for the rule of law. From the left, Mersha Yosef, Gayyim, Abebe Colombo, Sitotaw Hussein, Mohammed Ahmed, Gebre, Abebe Debteraw (standing), Jabbir and Geleb Dafla.

Chapter Six: The Role of Major Defections in EPRP/A

Pre-Quarra Defections

EPRP/A has had a long -standing provision in its bylaws affirming the right of any member to separate from the organization at any time (for instance Article 26 of Members Rights in EPRA's bylaws, codified after the 1977 army rectification movement). Indeed hundreds of fighters and party members took advantage of this right, and the party/army honored their wishes. However, curiously, the right seemed inadequate to prevent and resolve group dissatisfactions at major junctures.

We have seen in Chapter 1 how the "anjas" in the urban areas created a separate group and how some of them turned against the party by allying with the Dirgue. Then, in the infant EPRA, eight of the first army volunteers defected to Adigrat following the Land to the Tiller Awaj. Those who received military training by the Palestinians and deployed through Eritrea to start EPRA include Binyam Adane (died en route), Mahmood Mahfuz (died en route), Abdissa Ayana, Haileyesus Woldesenbet, Adugna Mengistu, Abebe Beyene, Abdurahman Ahimed, Wubshet Retta (Wollo martyr), Tefera Berhane (Wollo martyr), Zer'abruk Abebe (Wollo martyr), Mehari Gebre Egziabher/Tsehaye, Semere-Ab, Siyum Kebede (the only one deployed to Addis for organizational work where he was killed). All came to Palestine from the US, USSR, Algeria and Holland. Tesfaye Mekonnen also was with the original group.

Those who were already in Eritrea and left Ethiopia through Somalia include Eskinder/Girmay (martyred at Ebinat/Gondar),

Abiyu Berlie, Dawit Assefa, Zekaryas Mohammed, Gashaw Mengistu, Ayalew Kebede, Hailu Woldegiorgis. All these, along with Berhanemeskel Redda formed the first unit of EPRA. Soon after the declaration of the Land to the Tiller Awaj, and after many skirmishes with Berhanemeskel and the rest of the group, the following 8 marked the first major defection from the EPRA, and went to Adigrat to the Dirgue: Tesfaye Mekonnen, Dawit Assefa, Abebe Beyene, Haileyesuss Woldesenbet, Zekaryas Mohammed, Gashaw Mengistu, Ayalew Kebede and Hailu Woldegiorgis.

At the time of their defection, Dr. Tesfaye Debessay and Berhanemeskel Redda were en route to Addis for a central committee meeting, and at a stopover in Adigrat. When the defections were known, after the initial shock, the army had to scramble to get the two CC members out of Adigrat, out of harm's way.

The Proclamation of the Land to the Tiller Awaj in March 1975, and the subsequent defection of half of the EPRA should have sent a strong signal to the EPRP CC, and should have triggered a series of discussions at the CC level on where the struggle was going to go in light of the drastically changed circumstances. One possible outcome of such a discussion could have been pulling out most urban structures and members into rural areas for the fight for the formation of a democratic people's government. Instead, the party was caught in a haze, on the one hand rightly complimenting the Dirgue for issuing the Awaj, and on the other organizing its own demonstration in support of the Awaj after the massive outpour of support to the Awaj by Ethiopians.

The next major defection cum desertion was 4 years later in 1980 during the turmoil in each of the four regions.

The internal turmoil in the 4 regions displayed in equal parts voluntary separation and defection. In Tselemt, as a region-wide meeting was being called to try to resolve the issues, members of hayls and departments gathered near Mai Tsebri and declared " all are free to go where they wished", and the majority went to the Dirgue. This act created a chain reaction and panic. While peasant comrades in general rallied around the Leadership, most urbanites fled to the Dirgue. The meeting that was planned to be held at Gilbena was then moved to Ternasha to be held with what was left of the army and cadres. At this time, peasant representatives from Belessa arrived in

CHAPTER SIX: THE ROLE OF MAJOR DEFECTIONS IN EPRP/A

Ternasha and pleaded with the army not to leave their areas and made a futile effort to stem the tide of defeat and defection.

One of the worst crisis- replicating act is for members in responsible position to defect. The day after the Ternasha meeting was over, two members of the regional army leadership, Messelu and Jemal, defected to Sudan. They were not the last members of the leadership to do so. Sensing it needs to re-organize its remaining forces, the party and army leadership decided to go to Bertya.

At Bertya, we have seen how the situation was fluid (Chapter 2). The single incident of shooting and killing blew the fissures. Trust among comrades was a commodity in short supply. 14 members defected to the Sudan, and those close to them were the next day put under arrest. According to ABS, the 14 were: Semere, Tekeste, Aklog, Demmelash, Kelbessa, Fitsum, Fassil, Hiwot, Simret, and "three others".

After the army re-organization at Bertya, the major defection that was costly for the army was the defection of the 11 at Gichew, who later ambushed Bitweded Adane and his traveling party as they were returning from Sudan. This resulted as we saw in Chapter 2 with a full-blown war between EPRA and the people of Armachiho, and for the army to never set foot again in Armachiho, an area it had heretofore so heavily invested in.

The Defections in Quarra: Mistrust and Instability

When TPLF was a stone's throw away from Addis, and a month before it entered the capital, the first mortal blow was thrown by it at EPRA. After forcibly evicting the TPLF's army from a town called Maksegnit (Chara Woreda, in the environs of Dangila - an EPRA stronghold), a column with 2 of EPRA's best battalions hovered around the town for two full days -despite incessant warnings from the army command, and from the members of the column itself to leave the area and confuse the enemy. In the meantime, TPLF brought several relief units and surrounded the column, and attacked it from many sides. The battle-tested EPRA column members fought gallantly, but they were no match to the TPLF that was bringing in fresh reinforcements. The column commissar, Alemayehu, committed suicide, and the commander, Dembelo, was wounded and captured. The whereabouts of the deputy commander, Chaklie, was not immediately known (chapter 5).

The remaining forces eventually retreated, and realized the magnitude of the loss. The two best battalions were nearly decimated, and the psychological impact of this defeat was not lost on the rest of the army. Many wondered how it was possible to commit such a silly mistake by a veteran column leadership. Distrust among the EPRA members was slowly creeping in. Suspicion of senior commanders was at all-time high.

Then, a week after TPLF came into power, an attempt was made to offer a seminar to those EPRA forces that did not participate in the second army seminar. However, the column commander entrusted to lead the two battalions to the seminar, Gebremeskel, camped the battalions strangely on a flat land called Menta Wuha, turned off his communication radio possibly to make himself unreachable, and fled to the town of Chagni to the enemy taking with him documents and thousands of birr collected for the army by the people.

What made this particular defection more painful for the EPRA was the fact that Gebremeskel had his roots in the working class, and when he joined the army he was illiterate, and was a beneficiary of Article 22 of EPRA's bylaws that made it a right for any member to learn to read and write. After 11 years in the EPRA, the party and the army had bestowed upon him the highest honor by making him the commander of a column.

Learning that he had defected at night, the remaining commanders pulled the army to high ground and while anticipating an attack, they were surrounded by enemy forces led by none other than Gebremeskel. He had a couple of commanders who had conspired with him, and they created problems while the army was gallantly fighting its way out of the encirclement. The EPRA forces successfully retreated while being shot at in their backs by their own one-time comrades. Undoubtedly, this further exacerbated the tension between commanders and other fighters, and the EPRA forces were at their wits' end.

Soon after this incident, a similar treason took place in one of the columns assigned in the Northern Sector. The army senior Command had directed the column at the end of May to go to the lowlands of Serako leaving the highlands of Alefa Takusa. Instead,

CHAPTER SIX: THE ROLE OF MAJOR DEFECTIONS IN EPRP/A

the commander (Gashaw or Gurezaw), despite objections from his deputy commander and the commissar, ordered the two battalions (a column) to stay in the flatlands around Delgi doing physical exercises. Following this, he instructed the hayl commanders to join him in Delgi, to make sure the absolute encirclement and annihilation of the column. The enemy advanced from Chilga and Metema and attacked the column at Delgi.

The commissar and the deputy commander displayed exceptional bravery to rescue their troops, and after a successful counter-attack against the enemy, orderly retreated. However, the TPLF forces using information readily supplied by the defectors, looted the army's property, attacked the people's militia and their property, and adversely affected the feelings of the locals. Again, within the army, mistrust and suspicions were growing by leaps and bounds.

In Chapter 5, we have seen how senior army and party CC members were captured by the TPLF. The question of how TPLF was able to know their whereabouts to this day remains a mystery; however, the most plausible explanation of all was the fact that a guy called Gebrehiwot who was assigned in the foreign trade/self-reliance office of EPRA at Mehadid near the border was considered to be a TPLF spy who secretly supplied his handlers with crucial information. Lending credit to this hypothesis is the fact that EPRA units had been closely following his actions after the event, and had conclusively proven that he was serving the TPLF. Just as the EPRA was about to bring him to justice, he fled the army and joined a nearby TPLF force that subsequently left the area altogether with their spy.

The month of Senei (end of May to June) was not a particularly good month for EPRA. Losses and defections were rampant. The defections were not limited to the Northern Sector. Just as well, the Southern Sector too had its misfortunes.

Two battalions of the Southern Sector were assigned to intercept the TPLF forces that kidnapped the CC members, and given the mission of rescuing the CC members. While en route, they accidentally fell upon other TPLF forces and were engaged in fighting. Although the number of casualties was minimal, the two battalions separated and establishing communication was not possible. The deputy commander had one battalion plus a heavy machinery unit, while the commander led the other battalion. The commander was able to establish contact with headquarters, but was still unable contacting his deputy and his troops. Their whereabouts was unknown.

While purportedly looking for the missing troops, the EPRA commander of the battalion (the column commander), along with two of his friends, went over and gave himself to TPLF forces, taking with him the usual - money, documents, communication radio, and arms. The troops managed to find their way back to Quarra after some trial and tribulations. Later it was learned that the deputy commander and the missing battalion too had suffered defections and had disintegrated.

At this critical juncture, the rate of defection in Quarra almost paralleled that of Regions 1 and 3 ten years ago. The Quarra army was gripped by a contradiction: on one hand, there were hundreds and thousands of new recruits under training, and on the other battle-tested and veteran army members were defecting, creating a sense of confusion in the minds of the new recruits.

At this time, as we saw in Chapter 5, the Southern Sector was folded, and the Northern Sector was under directions to operate in small, decentralized units and squads. As preparations were underway to implement these new directives, the battalion commander of a force that came from Seraqo, armed and organized about 20 of his troops under the guise of going on a mission, and went over to the enemy in Seraqo. Again, this threw the remaining EPRA forces in a tailspin, and the question of whether or not EPRA could continue as a fighting force became increasingly the question of the day.

The final major defection took place on October 6, 1992. A veteran EPRA cadre of the Metekel area, Mulugeta, who knew everything about the area and its surroundings (list of members, army property, people's militia names, etc) went over to TPLF unexpectedly. Subsequently, he came back leading a TPLF force and they raided EPRA's cattle and took about 400 cattle along with the EPRA (a Gumuz) cattle custodian.

*

Defining the nature and cause of defections is a complex task. One may be tempted to simply dismiss the defectors as opportunists and weaklings. This may be true in some cases. However, the underlying causes also need to be scrutinized, not to justify the defections, but to fully grasp the challenges.

Indeed the nature of the first major defection by the 8 from the beginning army is drastically different from the defections in the

CHAPTER SIX: THE ROLE OF MAJOR DEFECTIONS IN EPRP/A

Gondar regions and in Quarra/Gojjam some 14 years later. Also, adding to the complexity is the fact that members in leadership positions and those who have gallantly fought earlier were now among the defectors.

The Ethiopian army too suffered huge defections to both TPLF and especially to EPLF. While to a large degree that could be ascribed to inept and incompetent Dirgue leadership (Mengistu murdering able generals, some commanders engaging in corruption, others selling the nation's secrets, the soldiers being forcibly conscripted, etc, etc.), none of these applied to EPRP/A.

A whole set of new dynamics appeared to be in motion with respect to EPRP/A. The overarching cause appeared to be a daunting task....to be between a rock and a hard place for a long while, and now even the hard place itself appearing to be harder than ever and creating a feeling of hopelessness and average human limitation setting in....

Chapter Seven: Notable Foreign Relations

EPRP had made significant efforts to make foreign friends in order to secure diplomatic, financial, and material aid. Of these, the most significant ones might be its relations with China and Sudan.

Relations with China

The EPRP Foreign Office had a good relationship with some countries, and China was one of the chief ones- a relationship established long before the party held its First Congress in 1972[1]. Meison, too, claims that around this time through its relationship with the CCP, an agreement was reached between it and the CCP to send 10 Ethiopian revolutionaries to China for military training, and that this information was shared with the Algerian Group, but somehow did not materialize. It is therefore not clear whether EPRP and Meison separately had contacts with the CCP at that time[2]. Delegates consisting of senior party members had gone to Beijing twice, in 1977 and 1979. It appears the period was when Chairman Mao died at the end of 1976, and the colorless Hua Guofeng had taken over. Gua Feng was known for his February 1977 promulgation of the "The Whatever Theory": It meant that the Chinese would resolutely uphold whatever policy decision Mao made, and unswervingly follow whatever instructions Mao gave[3],

---

1. Kiflu Tadesse, part ii, p. 310
2. Andargatchew Assegid, p. 78
3. Henry Kissinger. On China. Penguin Books, 2011, p. 32

reminiscent of what most Ethiopians say about the current Ethiopian Prime Minister and his alleged worship of the former Prime Minister, Meles.

One of the agreements EPRP concluded with the Chinese Communist Party was to help with the training of a core group of cadres, whom upon return, would train others and make the EPRP self-sufficient and expert in the use of heavy machine guns, explosives, and general sabotage. A group of 8 EPRA members under the leadership of TA were sent to Nanking for the training in early 1979. Chinese assigned to the South Yemen diplomatic post also helped train EPRA fighters about to enter the field, such as GB, with the skills of acupuncture (Mersha).

Around the same time, Mengistu himself including delegation members Tesfaye Gebrekidan, Berhanu Bayeh, Mogus Woldemichael (Dirgue members), Berhanu Dinka from Ministry of Foreign Affairs and Dr. Negede Gobeze from POMOA were secretly in China to ask for armaments. This was a time when Mao was recently deceased, and the Gang of Four were being harassed by state media. According to Mengistu, the Chinese leadership was condemning the USSR leadership as social imperialist, and expected the Ethiopian delegation to echo the same line. Instead, Mengistu says the delegation emphasized the need for the unity of Marxist forces. The Chinese leadership gave Mengistu and his delegation what they wanted in terms of arms. But at the same time, they gave them some advice which Mengistu impugns as "smelling" of EPRP and which had the "footprints" of EPRP. But Mengistu does not tell us what the advice was. He says that Captain Mogus (an EPRP member) having traveled once or twice to China before must have represented EPRP's line instead of the Dirgue's[4]. During one such trip where the Ethiopian delegation included Captain Mogus, Dr. Senay Likke, the Chinese recommended to the delegation to resolve the nationalities question through granting regional autonomy based on their own experience[5]. This, however, was to be a divisive policy among the progressive forces that were represented in POMOA.

We can only surmise what the Chinese leadership could have told Mengistu and the delegation: make peace with EPRP, and form a

---

4. Mengistu Hailemariam. Tigilachin (in Amharic), Tsehay Publishers, 2011, p.350-351
5. Andargachew Assegid, p. 313

CHAPTER SEVEN: NOTABLE FOREIGN RELATIONS

united front of all the leftist forces in the country. This is based on what they have been telling EPRP itself as we will see below.

In the meantime, about the same time in Addis, the 2-man EPRP CC had initiated contact with the Chinese. Mogus was recently murdered by Mengistu and when the Chinese were told that he was an EPRP member, the news gave additional weight to the relationship[6]. There was one-to-one contact. Just as they might have told the Dirgue delegation back in Beijing, the Chinese in Addis had been insisting that EPRP should make some kind of alliance with the Dirgue. They were more emphatic about it following the land proclamation in 1975. But when the USSR sided with the Dirgue in 1977, this insistence was dropped.

Just as they demanded of the Mengistu delegation in Beijing, the Chinese in Addis demanded that the EPRP condemn Soviet social imperialism. The Chinese contact was told that the EPRP had condemned Soviet involvement in Ethiopia. The issue of social-imperialism has been raised at the 1972 founding congress, but that Congress deferred characterizing the Soviet Union as social-imperialistic. The labeling was to be done in mid-1977, and the Chinese delegate was happy to learn that[7].

One interesting aspect was the strong objection of the Chinese to EPRP's urban warfare. They based their disapproval on their own disastrous 1920 experience. Instead of taking to heart the advice of the Chinese even at this late hour (mid-1977), Kiflu tragically tells us how the EPRP contact was "educated" and instructed to pass along to the Chinese " the differences and salient features of the Chinese and the Ethiopian revolutionary struggles!". Thankfully, Kiflu says that "even after a repeated effort, the Chinese could accept neither the assessment nor the conclusion EPRP had reached" [8].

Despite their reservations about EPRP's tactics, the Chinese gave some funds to the party in 1978, and military training in 1979. Another EPRP delegation visited Beijing in 1979, after the 4th Plenum. The delegation told the Chinese that EPRP had criticized its military activities (which was true), then in another breath lied to the Chinese by saying that X (Zer'u) was the main proponent of the urban warfare and that he has been dismissed. Because X was the

---

6. Kiflu Tadesse, p. 311
7. ibid.
8. ibid.

delegation leader in the first meeting when EPRP vehemently disagreed with the Chinese on urban warfare, the Chinese seemed to believe the story[9]. But by 1979, EPRP was on the wane, and whatever the party told the Chinese, it did not seem to matter.

The 8- man military trainees reflected EPRP's multi-national foundation, and included Tolossa (Oromo), Ishmael (Saho), Aya Kurate (Tselemt), Paulos (A.A.), BekureTsion (Eritrea), Yilkal (Gojjam), and one Tigrean chap who upon return went over to TPLF in Khartoum. The Chinese trainers included a military attaché and a political commissar. The training included parade formation, explosives, target practice and the like. On the 7th anniversary of the party's formation, the group leader TA notified the authorities, and they took the trainees to a supermarket to buy party supplies for the celebration. The shoppers who never saw black people, attired in Chinese military attire to boot, were shocked and surprised.

The Chinese were very rank-conscious, and always deferred to the team leader. The group was well-fed, and well trained. A couple of them received medical training. The Chinese were so disciplined that they effectively hid the training schedule of other liberation fronts from each other, possibly trainees from fronts like the EPLF.

When the trainees arrived in Khartoum after a 6-month training, the army, particularly those in Region 2, was leaving en masse to Sudan. The trainees were only able to come down to River Shinfa, a river that demarcated the border with Sudan and where the Region 2 army was waiting impatiently to bury its weapons and continue onto Sudan. It is not difficult to imagine how shell-shocked these trainees were, and their understanding that the skills they spent months training for were not going to be used.

It is a shame to see China, a country that was a beacon of hope for humanity at one point, today aiding and abetting Third World dictatorships.

Sudan

Unlike China, in Sudan the party not only had party-to-state relations, it had also its own organizational structure, party committees and cells. Following the 1969 student unrest triggered by

---

9. ibid.

CHAPTER SEVEN: NOTABLE FOREIGN RELATIONS

the murder of Tilahun Gizaw, university student activists had started fleeing the country. According to one of those who fled the university to Sudan at the time, Solomon Workneh, there were about two dozen activist Ethiopians who were there. They included Fisseha GM, the late Kedir Mohammed, Haile Gebreselasse, Tariku Debretsion, the late Dr. Worku, Yohannes Kassahun, Mekonnen Bayissa (a youth activist who was killed in the course of the urban struggle), Mohammed and Ahimed-two youth activists, Mulugeta Kebede, and Tesfaye Tadesse who later moved onto Lebanon. Others, such as Yohannes Kifle and Abrham Gebreegziabher (who wrote books in the 1980's on the Ethiopian revolution using a pen name *Addis Hiwot*. One of his books was *From Feudal Autocracy to Revolution)*, and who went to Europe from Sudan after a short stay. Solomon Workneh and his then friend Haile Gebreselasse were aided to come to Sudan by Netsanet Mengistu and her late husband, Yirga Tessema. The couple lived in Assosa at the time as University National Service teachers and where Netsanet's father was a municipal official of the city. After staying in Assosa for some time, Solomon and Haile were sent to Kurmuk, and from there onto Khartoum.

While most of these were associated with the World Wide Federation of Ethiopian students that later supported EPRP as the split crystallized in 1973, there were other students loyal to Ethiopian Students Union in Europe which later sided with Meison. These included Berhanu Dibaba, Hailu Gerbaba and a Dr. Ahmed. As a branch of the WWESF, the students sent delegates to the student congresses, and the last delegate to the 1973 congress in Berlin was Tariku Debretsion. Most were affiliated with the University of Khartoum. When the 1974 revolution broke, most of these student activists went back to Ethiopia where they played prominent roles. The student union continued to function with diminished vigor with those few that stayed behind. But as the Red Terror intensified within 2 years, a large number of youth refugees started streaming into Sudan.

The EPRP leadership in Ethiopia understood the significance of Sudan to the party's operation. Mohammed Ahimed Jemil, a Gurage and a Moslem, who was studying in Germany on a scholarship was assigned to be the lead organizer and EPRP man in Khartoum. According to Mohammed, as a result of his assignment, in mid-1975, he came to Sudan. As there was no party infrastructure (we saw earlier how nearly all the student activists returned to Ethiopia after the outbreak of the Ethiopian Revolution), he had to rely on his own resources to build things up from the ground. Iyassu, a CC member was in Italy, and Mersha, a senior comrade, was in Yemen, and these two were Mohammed's closest contacts and report recipients.

After he stayed in a hotel for a few days, he had to move to a less cheaper and permanent lodging in a student hostel where he shared a room with a member of Meison, Abdurahman. His identity and officially assumed title was a "researcher" at the University. He immersed himself among the Sudanese to learn Arabic as soon as possible, and for that purpose did not mingle with fellow Ethiopians as much. Later, he started socializing and met future EPRP men such as Belete/Amha (disappeared by TPLF), and Ghelawdewos Araya, Getachew Midekssa, an EPRA fighter who was later killed and beheaded by a peasant. Similarly, he introduced himself to Eritrean representatives, who at that time were falling over each other to curry favor with EPRP as it was the biggest, and most famous opposition party fighting against the Dirgue. The representatives of the two organizations were more than willing to introduce Mohammed to the Sudanese government as EPRP's representative. However, because they were rivals, Mohammed could not choose one over the other. Besides, because his status in Sudan was illegal, questions might have arisen about his status during the introductions. So, he chose a different route. Through them, he had met the Palestinian representative there, and the guy was willing to introduce EPRP to the Sudanese security chiefs. Still, the legal status question was not addressed, and Mohammed did not want to start things on a wrong path. He discussed the issue with Iyassu and because Iyassu was known to the security chiefs during the airplane hijacking in 1969 when the plane landed there before the hijackers were packed to Algeria, Iyassu came to Khartoum from Rome, and met General Kalifah Kerar, a Sudanese security chief. Iyassou mentioned to the security chief that EPRP's representative would be sent and soon visit him. Iyassu left, and Mohammed shortly met the General who was too happy to receive an EPRP representative.

General Kalifah soon after contacted the Eritrean representatives and barked at them why they had not told him about the EPRP man. They in turn were mad that EPRP had met the chief without them playing a role, and they started attacking Mohammed by calling him "Kebede" - their derogatory description of an Ethiopian....an Amara

CHAPTER SEVEN: NOTABLE FOREIGN RELATIONS

and a non-Moslem. They were often to resort to this "decertifying" of Mohammed whenever they felt threatened by EPRP.

In the meantime, organizational structures of EPRP were being incrementally laid in Khartoum, and later, Ghedarif. A year or so later, Oumar, an Adere/Hareri, and a founding member of the EPRA after his military training in Palestine and deployment through Yemen to Assimba, joined Mohammed and partnered in the diplomatic work. Oumar eventually left the party. EPRA was actively operational at this time, and one of Mohammed's duties was to escort recruits from Europe, to Sudan, and eventually to the field (he had been in the field 3 or 4 times for leadership meetings and other reasons). Other accomplishments included approaching embassies stationed in Khartoum and introducing EPRP, soliciting aid, procuring arms from the Sudanese government (about 1,000 guns were obtained); launching delegations to Somalia to get the release of Ethiopian political prisoners and to start diplomatic relations. In addition to General Kalifah, EPRP had also an ally in General Tirefi who was deputy chief of military intelligence. His boss was ardently anti-EPRP and a TPLF supporter, and perhaps a CIA mole.

While other Ethiopian opposition organizations, such as EPLF, ELF and TPLF bribed their way through unethical means to reach the high echelons of Sudanese power, what EPRP had it going was forming a family bondage with the few friendly Sudanese officials, what the Sudanese call "aqua'n" -brotherhood. Mohammed visited the General's house, played with the kids, and took small gifts for holidays.

The TPLF was introduced to the Sudanese and other Arab countries through the established offices of the Eritrean fronts. While spreading misinformation about EPRP to prevent it from having a foothold by saying such things as "EPRP are Amara Ethiopians, they want a stronger Ethiopia, and they don't support the Eritrean cause", the Eritreans facilitated for TPLF the diplomatic outreach. Yemane Jamaica, Fisseha, and Siyum Mesfin alternated as TPLF representatives in Khartoum.

Starting in 1984/85, EPRP had an official office in Khartoum. 5 years later, the Dirgue regime was crumbling, and Sudan unveiled a transitional plan for Ethiopia's opposition for OLF, TPLF, and EPRP to form a coalition transitional government. OLF's representative, Dr. Tadesse Eba and EPRP agreed to the plan. The TPLF representative told the Sudanese that there were other efforts by the Americans and the West, and that he would rather wait to see the progress of those efforts. Shortly, the London Conference was scheduled and TPLF officially responded to the Sudanese that they would not work with EPRP. Situations changed fast, and the Sudanese security allied with TPLF security and started hunting down EPRP members. The kidnapping of EPRP members from Ghedarif we discussed in Chapter 5 took place around this time.

EPRP members in Khartoum discussed the grim situation and resolved that Mohammed had to leave Sudan immediately. Getting a visa was difficult. While one or two friendly embassies in Khartoum agreed, but when they checked with their capitals, it was unambiguously denied. Finally, the Italian government agreed, but still there was concern Sudanese security might intercept the representative at the airport. EPRP had credible information that Meles himself en route to Ethiopia from the London Conference had asked the Sudanese to hand over to him the EPRP representative. General Tirefi sent a message to Mohammed that he should under no circumstances give himself up to Sudanese security, and that he should not stay in the same house, and had to keep moving. The French helped the EPRP representative at the airport in making sure that there was no foul play by the Sudanese and TPLF security duo, and the representative safely left Khartoum for Rome.

In the meantime, the EPRP office in Khartoum was overflowing daily with TPLF supporters singing and chanting at their capture of power in Addis, and harassing EPRP members and supporters.

Before he left Khartoum, In the late 70's, the EPRP representative in Khartoum was invited by a pro-Iraq Baathist Eritrean party to attend a congress in the Eritrean field. While Baathist party representatives were warmly treated, the EPRP representative and a Saudi Arabia representative were shabbily treated. They were both assigned to sleep on the floor while beds were arranged for others. This brought the two together and had many discussions. The Saudi representative, Abdalla Bahbari, had lived in Ethiopia in the 1960s, and as a result knew prominent Ethiopian Moslem leaders, one of whom was the father of the EPRP representative. During the discussion, this came up, and the bondage was more cemented. The unceasing propaganda of the Eritreans against EPRP as "Kebede", Amhara, and non-Moslem was exposed. After leaving Eritrea, Abdalla invited Mohammed to visit Saudi Arabia, and Mohammed did. The Sudanese security tried hard to

CHAPTER SEVEN: NOTABLE FOREIGN RELATIONS

prevent Mohammed from going to Saudi, but due to Abdalla's insistence, they had to relent. In Jeddah, the EPRP representative was treated as a state guest, and stayed in a posh hotel.

When Abdalla held a session with Mohammed, he was surrounded by Eritreans who have been misinforming him. Sensing that Abdalla had no ears for them, the Eritreans appealed to his boss, Saudi security Chief Al-Turk who died recently. Turk overruled Abdalla, and EPRP was not to get any aid from the Saudi government.

Despite the presence of various antagonistic Ethiopian forces and their various spheres of influence, the Sudanese people and government have helped the Ethiopian people's struggle for democracy and unity. They have hosted hundreds of thousands of our refugees, and allowed us to live in their midst despite our cultural contamination of their Islamic puritanism. In turn, EPRP had also facilitated the passage of many Southern Sudanese to SPLA areas of operation through Galabat when the occasional pogroms took place in Sudan proper against them. One hopes South Sudan today would be grateful for this action prompted merely by the love of justice.

On the other hand, Sudan had been a center of counter-revolution where Americans and Israelis conspired with corrupt Sudanese officials to export our Bete Israel citizens to Israel. A Sudanese vice president to Nimieri, Omar Tayyib, had solicited EPRP to be part of this conspiracy, a demand EPRP quickly rejected which earned their wrath. EPRP was also asked to be part of the tragedy in which TPLF took part: parading thousands of hungry Northern Ethiopians in Kassala for the benefit of propaganda and to discredit the Ethiopian regime using our people as propaganda tools. To that too EPRP said no. There were also other counter-revolutionary and anti-Ethiopian national interest schemes in which EPRP was coaxed to play a part, and which the nationalist and Ethiopianist EPRP rejected. For these brave acts, history will remember the patriotic responses of the EPRP.

Chapter Eight: How Democratic Was EPRP?

Background

This is a very tricky question that has many sides to it, and we should be able to see it from many angles to get the full appreciation for our inquiry. As an illustration, let's pose the following questions: how democratic was Atse Tewodros or Atse Yohannes? How are their reigns evaluated? by what yardsticks? Let's also pose the same question about their contemporaries, or near-contemporaries: how democratic was Thomas Jefferson, commonly known as the father of American democracy so much so the brand of American democracy is named after him - Jeffersonian democracy. But was it not the same Jefferson who owned hundreds of slaves to work on his plantations? and wasn't it the same Jefferson who did not bother to recognize the equality and humanity of women?

From the above, it seems reasonable men and women would agree that each ruler, party or empire, should be measured by the reigning standards, so to speak. If there is agreement on this, no rational person would fault Atse Yohannes for not having a formal cabinet of ministers and a parliament. Granted, still there may be some basic values that cut across ages which hold every one accountable regardless of their century. This may be a difficult proposition. But let's explore it further in more detail. Take for instance the value of treating one's enemies with kindness or leniency. Animals almost always have no such compunction, but there have been instances where there were exceptions to this rule. Humans, despite their century, must always on the average be a bit above animals in their judgments. Whether it is due to religion, culture, or superstition, different rulers have treated their enemies differently although most commonly have treated their enemies without mercy. During wars, captives have been either summarily executed, or taken as slaves, or allowed to assimilate and live a dignified life. The modern world tried to legislate the behavior of nations during wars by codifying the Geneva Conventions related to the treatment of war prisoners after the WWI.

Revolutions and rebellions have self-arrogated impunity as the cost of freedom. The motto has been the end justifies the means. There might be not only collateral damage, but targeted damage as long as at the end of the exercise a society is promised peace and prosperity. So much so, isn't it an oft-heard refrain that a revolution consumes its children first?

Starting with the French revolution of 1789, and going through the Russian and Chinese revolutions, the Reign of Terror has been the modus operandi. Such notions as the rule of law and civic and human rights be damned.

Now when discussing the democratic credentials of EPRP we have to look at the issue in its proper context: the international situation from which the party emerged; its avowed affiliation; its record vis-a-vis its contemporaries, and its unique situation.

If we start with its party program, there is almost nothing to criticize and everything to applaud....fighting to grant land to the masses, political rights to oppressed nationalities and jobs, education, healthcare and social services to any one that wanted them. These are the most democratic ideals. When the party declared its existence and went public in August 1975, the program was what initially endeared it to millions. Soon, the romance was to sour as the party transitioned into attempting to implement its program. That was because the rules of the game between opposition and regime was not predicated on peaceful competition. Knowing in advance that this was indeed the case, the party trained abroad a fighting force numbering some two dozen fighters and brought them in through Eritrea. Now, the institution of an army has different and more serious rules of engagement that mostly are anathema to democratic practice. The prerequisites for an efficient fighting force inherently demand that both the soldiers and the people willingly or by coercion give up some of their basic rights.

CHAPTER EIGHT: HOW DEMOCRATIC WAS EPRP?

Historically, organized fighting outside of individual shiftas and rebels was the domain of government. The Eritrean situation changed that starting in the 1960s. So, for good or ill, and mostly for ill, the Eritrean struggle and experience affected EPRP's trajectory. In the urban areas, after a year and half of relatively peaceful political work that did not impact in a significant way the party's democratic praxis, the party was thrown into a head-on clash with the regime, and soon after, with its own members (the anjas). So, although the party was the aggrieved party and the party sustained the most losses in this conflict, no one can say with certainty that the party itself was blameless (see chapters 1-4).

The Case of "Ha" and "Le"

One such example was the case of Getachew Maru (Ha), a CC member. He and Berhanemeskel (Le) were stripped of their CC membership at the Third CC Plenum in November 1976 for factional activities and for violating the party's constitution. By the party's decision, Getachew was detained in March 1977. Getachew had been insistent on his case to be resolved as soon as possible, and the A.A. IZ entrusted with detaining him was indignant because they had no jail of their own to continuously detain Getachew. As the Dirgue was closing in on the 13 or so safe houses the IZ was using, according to Kiflu, one day Getachew overpowered the assigned EPRP guard to escape, and imperiled his life, his description for the cause that triggered the end of Getachew's life[1] In *Tower in the Sky*, narrators to Hiwot talk about a "benevolent killing" of Getachew by squads to protect him from Dirgue identification of his body[2].

Similarly, Berhanemeskel and his comrades were rounded up in Shoa by Dirgue forces and murdered in cold-blood by Mengistu Hailemariam. His party, EPRP, as Ghelawdewos Araya correctly notes, instead of mourning him, celebrated and officially declared "Death of a Renegade" in *Abyot*, a journal published by its foreign section[3]. Berhanemeskel was admired both by opponents and friends. One apolitical Ethiopian who happened to meet him in Bahirdar in the late 60's when Berhanemeskel was temporarily working for the

---

1. Kiflu Tadesse, part ii, p. 322
2. Hiwot Teffera. Tower in the Sky, p.173
3. Ghelawdewos Araya, p. 123

Ethiopian Herald paper during one of his college boycotts remembers a dedicated patriot who, after his Assosa national service days, built a library there and was fundraising and book collecting for the library. A year and half later, he was to hijack an airplane to leave the country to Algeria[4].

Based on available documents, Hiwot's *Tower in the Sky (1)*, Kiflu's *The Generation (2)*, and Berhanemeskel's *On The Mass Line (3)*, the following describe the genesis, emergence, and positions of the Opposition inside EPRP, commonly called the faction:

- The formation of the faction within the EPRP can be categorized into two phases. The first phase from September 1976 until April 1977, and the second phase began when some members began collaborating with the Dirgue (1); p.180
- Members of the faction never tried to hide their factional activities from the party. Two members, Nebiyu Aynalem and Mesfin Shiferaw, told the CC -the former about a detailed discussion, including submitting a report in writing as the Party demanded, and for which he was expelled, and the latter, to his CC contact, Kiflu Tefera, about his knowledge and opposition to the planned attempt on Mengistu's life (2) p.249-251
- Berhanemeskel never thought he was involved in factional activities; but considered his group as members of a "Rectification Movement" (1) (3)
- The faction lead members wanted to negotiate with the party by retreating to a safe place, such as Wolaita (Abiyu Ersamo's idea), and were determined not to turn in the arms under their control(2) p.276-279;
- The faction members were adamantly opposed to the staging of urban armed struggle by the Party (1) (2) (3);
- Bothe Berhanemeskel and Getachew opposed taking action against Mengistu (1)p.327
- In March 1977 the CC decided to arrest both Ha and Le for factional activities, including their extra-structural activities

---

4. Siyum Wolde Ramsie. Kurfiya Yeshefenew Fegegita (in Amharic). Artistic Printing Press, 2003, p.

CHAPTER EIGHT: HOW DEMOCRATIC WAS EPRP?

and disruptions of the urban armed struggle; Le was detained, and Ha had already left for Shoa (1) p.182
- The Opposition said they had differences with 3 policies: on forming a UF with the Dirgue; on urban armed struggle, and describing the Dirgue as Fascist, and demanded for a Party Congress to deliberate on the issues (2) p. 249-251
- Some members of the faction had been collaborating with the regime. When the EPRP began retaliating, some of the Anjas, esp. those that belonged to the party or youth defense units, joined the regime and were organized into government assassination squads(1)p.325
- The Party received a report that appears to contradict Berhanemeskel's position on what he meant by a UF with the Dirgue; the informant reports without the nuances and conditions described below (1) p.180)
- Berhanemeskel states that the UF is only under limited conditions and for certain objectives. He further stated that this was adopted in 1975 by party members and the Youth League, and accused what he calls the "Clique" (his name for the CC that expelled him and Getachew) for subverting the members' position in an ultra-leftist adventure (3) p.4-5
- Berhanemeskel's group who had moved with his group to Merhabete in March 1977 probably could not have taken a direct role in factional activities in Addis (1) p.328

As can be seen, the time period between April 1976 and April 1977 was a critical time for EPRP's leaders when political differences emerged regarding the course and nature of the struggle. Had the party been allowed to legally operate, things would have turned out much differently. Instead, on September 11, 1976, the Dirgue publicly announced that EPRP, ELF, and EDU were its enemies and that they would be brutally suppressed. EPRP then tried to eliminate this threat by making an unsuccessful attempt on the life of the Dirgue's head, Mengistu Hailemariam, on September 23, 1976. Had the peaceful path been taken, the party could have called its Second Congress at the beginning of 1977 (instead of waiting nearly a decade), summon delegates from all party branches and provinces, and discuss the issues raised by Berhanemeskel and Getachew in a deliberative manner. This was not to be. Alternatively, had the Abyot group whose main leader was Getachew Maru demanded equal representation in the makeup of the EPRP CC when the merger took place, it was very likely the "Ha" and "Le" position of objecting to the urban armed defense might have had the majority vote. Although Abyot brought a significant amount of structures and resources to EPRP, only Getachew was a full CC member. The next one from Abyot was ZB, an alternate CC member. Youthful idealism of the early 1970s had no room at the time for bargaining positions in a committee as long as everyone thought they were all in it to give their lives for the people's emancipation.

Left to fend for itself, a messy and fractured decision making system threw the party and its structures into their eventual urban demise.

Re-Evaluating Berhanemeskel Redda

Berhanemeskel Redda Wolde Rufael was a hero of the Ethiopian Student Movement and the EPRP. We have seen how he was a leading student activist who boycotted classes protesting the imperial regime's oppression. Back in Addis from Assosa where he was stationed for the National Service, we have read how he was prodding acquaintances and others to contribute books and money for the school library there. Then in 1968, along with 6 other radicals, they hijacked a plane and ended up in Algiers. Following that, under the pen name Tilahun Takele, he wrote a trail blazing paper on the national question with Marxist overtones. Finally, in April 1972 in Berlin, he played a leading role in the formation of what would later be EPRP, and was the first secretary of the party.

Surrounding the loss of some party founding documents, we have read according to a few how Berhanemeskel held Zer'u Khishen responsible, and how the fallout between the two started. When the initial armed group was trained by the Palestinians, and ready to go to Ethiopia in 1973, through Yemen, and via Eritrea, Berhanemeskel was assigned to go with the group. The group was delayed in Eritrea for nearly two years. No sooner had the group finally arrived in Assimba when half of those who came with them defected to the Dirgue. Although the main reason appears to be disillusionment about the future of EPRP's armed struggle, especially after the March 1975 Land to the Tiller *Awaj* by the Dirgue, some blamed Berhanemeskel's dictatorial way of doing things for their flight. Some

CHAPTER EIGHT: HOW DEMOCRATIC WAS EPRP?

believe that Zer'u and others still nursing a vendetta, used this complaint to strip Berhanemeskel of his secretary position, and eventually his membership in the politburo.

Berhanemeskel did not take kindly to losing his secretarial position. It is hard to say that his subsequent differences with the party leadership were not colored by this slight. Soon after the party was declared in August 1975, differences started creeping up between him and Getachew Maru on the one hand, and the party leadership on the other. The differences were both procedural and substantive. The main issues revolved around characterizing the Dirgue as a fascist regime, and the intensification by the party leadership of the urban armed struggle. He described his political rivals in the leadership as the "clique", and named who they were: Kiflu Tadesse, Tesfaye Debesay, Zer'u Khishen, Tselote Hizkyas and Yosef Adane. According to him, the party in turn made 7 allegations against him:

1. Meeting members outside of organizational structure; 2. Objecting to the assignments of urban defense squads and rescinding their orders; 3. Claiming that the decisions made by the party who to kill was made without solid evidence; 4. Misleading the leadership by planting an editorial in Addis Zemen by consulting with the then editor, Berhanu Zerihun, and thus claiming that the Dirgue was ready to work with all progressives, including EPRP; 5. Maligning the politburo by accusing it of usurping the central committee's power and duties; 6. Falsely claiming that he was a prisoner of the EPRP leadership; and 7. Arguing that *Meison* should not be considered the enemy when it is a M-L party like EPRP with international support (Abera Wakjira, a CC member who did not seem to have played a meaningful role in EPRP CC due to illness and who might be in Europe, might be a person who could shed light on the disputes between Berhanemeskel and his accusers. Berhane said that when he was without cause demoted from the PB he was assigned at the founding congress, Abera offered to resign so Berhane could take his place). Berhanemeskel had incessantly argued that EPRP was wrong in characterizing the Dirgue as fascist. He claimed that the party had not studied the subject of fascism in earnest, and should not confuse brutality with a system of capitalist rule. While this argument by him may have a grain of truth, he unfortunately breaks his own dictum when he used the adjective fascistic in describing EPRP's actions taken against him (p. 34 of his Forced Confessions dated July 1979). As stated above, he was also harshly criticizing the party's

involvement in urban armed struggle. He says at a party leadership meeting in August 1976, after debating the issue for 10 hours, the CC was divided equally into two between those supporting urban defense actions and those opposed (p.23). While Kiflu Tadesse says that the party had agreed on a mechanism to take actions only on approved targets, Berhanemeskel does not agree, and said instead, the compromise agreements of the divided leadership were *not to take any action against Dirgue or POMOA members,* and for those party structures itching to take actions, they could do so on their own volition, and the party should instruct them that it had not made a decision on the issue (p.22).

Then Berhane says that his informant, an Interzone member who was later killed by the party, Abiyu Ersamo, told him that a member of the PB had instructed the A.A. IZ that they could take actions, but needed to notify the party secretariat 15 days ahead of the planned action. Berhanemeskel says he told Abiyu that was not the decision. Abiyu then reportedly sought unsuccessfully to get clarification from the PB. Thus the party started to plunge into a crisis.

In the meantime, Tesfaye Debessay tipped Berhanemeskel that Captain Mogus was EPRP's member, and that he had suggested that the party needed to "hit *Meison* from below, while, they in the Dirgue, would do it from above (p.28). Berhane shared this information with Getachew, and the two were worried about the party's path towards a coup d'état and decided to do whatever they could to stop it.

At the November 1976 CC meeting, the two were dismissed from their leadership positions, and in March it was decided to arrest them for violating party principles as outlined in the 7 allegations above. While Getachew was arrested, Berhanemeskel severs all relationship with the party by moving out from the shelter they provided, and in March 1977, went with his group to Merhabete/Menz.

The Sojourn in Merhabete/Menz

In Addis, Berhanemeskel seemed to have Zone 1 party structure in his support with a smattering of support elsewhere in the structures. Through this, his group was able to procure money and arms to start an armed struggle in Shoa. According to Kiflu, Berhanemeskel just took over an area that he knew the party was studying to launch its own armed struggle (p. 179). Two members that knew the area well, Ayalew Kibret, and Demisse Hailemariam,

CHAPTER EIGHT: HOW DEMOCRATIC WAS EPRP?

offered the sanctuary and made the settlement relatively easier. The group appeared to have enough arms and did not exceed in number more than 30. They had to traverse swaths of land to obtain food, and to also hide from Dirgue forces and its militia. There were two groups of shiftas operating in the general area with significant following: one was a feudal remnant by the name of Mengiste Defar, and the other, a Colonel Belihu Wolde who led an organization with a fanciful name, but unknown. Although both EPRP and Berhanemeskel's group in their history allied with feudal lords, EPRP's was from a position of strength, and always almost called the shots, and when the love/hate relationship soured, it annihilated the feudal forces. This happened in Gichew and Quarra as we will see later in the book. However, this was not the case for the out-numbered forces of Berhanemeskel. In Merhabete, they were the hostages of the Mengiste Defar shifta group. They had no choice but to avoid a fight with them, and for protection, they had to provide the shiftas various arms, and a promised payment of $1,000 a month. Because the group had contacts with their members in urban areas, they occasionally got supplies of medicine, arms, and money, out of which they paid their feudal protectors. One of their members, Lieutenant Abebe Jemma decided to switch sides and went over to join the feudal forces of Mengiste Defar. According to Kiflu, the lieutenant was not a willing member of the group to begin with (p. 316).

The group called itself APOG: Armed Propaganda and Organizing Group, while their urban comrades were called "the Rectification Movement". They tried to teach the shiftas and their peasant followers on elementary rules of democracy and governance, such as not to burn huts and houses during wars, not to pillage, etc. To that effect, Berhanemeskel drafted bylaws for them, and a minimum united front platform for the two groups (p. 52, 53, 65).

Obviously, APOG was in a dire situation: they were literally the prisoners of Mengiste Defar. If they opted to break away, they were afraid that he might wipe them out.

Berhanemeskel's group, APOG, was like EPRP, caught between a rock and a hard place.

Berhanemeskel says they were working on 3 options:

1. They had instructed their urban representatives to contact the government to discuss on ways of working together. The

messenger was Melikte Yohannes, a bright high school student, who instead of being an intermediary, was thrown in jail thus sealing the fate of this avenue;
2. If that were not possible, they directed their urban structures to send them more weapons and people so that they can fight their way out if needed, and assert their independence. This was not easily forthcoming;
3. If both fail, to disband the group, and for the urban structures, to send them money for members' transportation to their destinations (p.62). In May, Berhanemeskel's wife, Tadelech H. Michael arrived and told them they might get some money if a few plans succeed.

Finally, 2 years after they came to Merhabete, they were surrounded by half a dozen militia peasants and ordered to surrender. Instead of fighting out a force inferior to them in both number and weapons, they gave themselves up. The peasants led them to the regular army where they were disarmed, and all their property that included the following confiscated: 12 guns with several ammunition, 3 grenades and 2 binoculars, other buried guns and pistols were uncovered and confiscated, watches and gold rings, medicine, medical equipment and cash in the amount of $16,200 (p, 85).

The legendary Berhanemeskel was taken prisoner and faced the merciless thugs of Mengistu, none of whom were his equals by any standard. He was asked to write his autobiography, using for outline 6 allegations the Dirgue made against him:

1. That he was responsible as member of the EPRP leadership for all the "havoc the party created and the destruction of life and property"; 2. Although separated from the EPRP leadership, he still did not decide to surrender to the Dirgue, but instead went to Menz/Merhabete to resurrect EPRP; 3. Although he claimed to be a revolutionary, in practice, he sided with feudals and signed agreements to fight the government; 4. Coordinated the vandalism and robbery of banks and money through his urban members; 5. Encouraged and assisted members of other organizations to abandon their cadre posts and join him (ABOG may have succeeded to win over some EMALEDH members due to their internal friction); and 6. For supporting the military capability of Mengite Defar by supplying him with stolen weapons.

CHAPTER EIGHT: HOW DEMOCRATIC WAS EPRP?

In his autobiography-cum response to the allegations, Berhanemeskel seemed to show some low points unexpected of a heroic leader. For instance, he tried to recant and retract his solid positions he formerly outlined in his paper, "the Mass Line". He tried to put all blame for what went wrong in the Ethiopian Revolution, on the EPRP leadership. He could not defend the democratic bylaws he prepared for the shiftas and instead tried to backpedal, hoping perhaps that might save his life. Worst of all, he tried to convince the murderous Dirgue that by giving up without a fight, he was showing that he was a man of peace. Such rational arguments work only with reciprocating minds, and not with the vindictive and blood thirsty Dirgue. He was talking to a Mengistu Hailemariam, a thug and coward that did not spare even the life of his friend and mentor Haile Fida - a man both foe and friend admire as one of the more civil men among the notables of that revolutionary era.

On the other hand, Berhanemeskel had also glorious moments where he flashed courage and was true to the ideals of EPRP: He told the dictator and his minions that he still believed the Dirgue was responsible for giving rise to unnecessary bloodshed by denying democratic rights to Ethiopians. He was to the last adamant about the right of nations to self-determination, and in principle to secession. At last, one of the greatest revolutionaries who dedicated his life to the cause of the Ethiopian masses for over 2 decades was murdered in cold blood. He was 35 years old.

In the Army

For over a year since its launch, one may say without erring that it was an army that was neglected. Although it was the army of a self-professed proletarian party, it had few systemic study guides and curricula for its members and cadres, it had scant bylaws, and it had no institution of ombudsman. Some have described this situation and attributed the cause, with a few grains of truth, as the design of a leadership bent on capturing power through the urban armed struggle. Still, there were democratic moments in EPRA where military justice was in full display, such as the judicial proceedings in trying and sentencing those leaders found to be guilty following the Hayl 3 debacle in Arbaya/Ebinat raid of February 1977. As a result of a legal defense put forth by his "attorney" Selamawit, one of the three accused, Ammanuel, was acquitted, while the other two defendants responsible for the debacle were sentenced to a 1-year and 6-month, respectively, debarment from elections and holding offices and bearing arms. The army did not always have a tradition of critically evaluating each engagement to draw lessons. Had that been the case, the Arbaya/Ebnat incident might not have taken place in the wake of the first major disaster that took place in Wollo 8 months earlier in July 1976 where peasants overwhelmed EPRA units.

One of the darkest stains on the army was the existence of a ganta called 44 and whose assignments were not known to the majority of the members. Its existence and job description was only officially revealed during the Rectification Movement, as discussed elsewhere.

Undoubtedly, ganta 44 was modeled after the Eritrean *halwa sawra,* an intelligence unit whose tasks include the torture of suspected members and peasants. Two recent books by former EPRA members and victims of ganta 44 have shed some light on the dirty work of this unit.

Asmamaw Hailu, in his Amharic book, titled simply, *"EPRA", Part 1,* describes frugally what happened to him. Ayalew Yimam, in his book *"Yankee Go Home"*[5]*,* describes bitterly in large detail what happened to him and other prisoners there.

Asmamaw tells us while he was in jail with Ganta 44, the following also were his jail mates:

1. Getahun Sisay (a CC member representing Red Banner sent to Assimba from Addis due to suspicions of leaks. He was not legally represented even after the Rectification Movement, and was finally killed along with those other anjas when the army evacuated Tigrai)
2. Habtom (came from Yemen, later released, and re-joined the army. Died during a battle with TPLF. Even TPLFites admire his heroism; when ordered to surrender, he emphatically told TPLF units "he is the son of EPRP, and would never surrender)
3. Ayalew Yimam (the author we mentioned above)
4. Ayalew Mergiya (Saed). Joined EPRA from ESUNA.

---

5. Ayalew Yimam. Yankee, Go Home! The Life of an Ethiopian Revolutionary and the Fall of Assimba, EPRP's Red Base, 1969-80, Signature Book Printing, 2011

CHAPTER EIGHT: HOW DEMOCRATIC WAS EPRP?

5. Addis Alem (a member of Woldiya's EPRYL; died in battle with TPLF after his release)
6. Lieutenant Berihun (a graduate of HSI Harer Military Academy; released and went to ELF, but died there due to malaria)[6].

Although Asmamaw does not tell us why he was jailed, it is probably because he joined the army without the proper paperwork, and thus was suspected of being a spy.

Ayalew too joined EPRA without coming through the proper channels. He was a senior University education major at AAU when the revolution erupted, and according to him, with enough credentials as a USUAA activist. After an incomplete rendezvous with the Red Banner's Assefa Endeshaw, Ayalew was exposed and without security in Addis. Thus he decided to go to Eritrea where he was a national service teacher at Agordat. Ayalew's many Eritrean friends helped him link up with EPRA, and later after his fallout with EPRA, took him back and brought him to Sudan safely.

Ayalew joined EPRA in September 1975 and was a free man for a year until he was jailed (an innocent letter he exchanged with a Swedish pro-Eritrean supporter and intercepted in Sudan helped make him a suspect).

He accuses Woldeleul Kassa (Kesete) and Gerra who are no longer with the party as the coordinators of his harsh and cruel treatment. He could not know the three actual torturers. He says he was tortured for 8 months before he escaped to Eritrea.

However, the two books are works in contrast.

For Asmamaw, he devotes merely 4 pages out of his 324-page book, and barely makes a reference to what type of torture he underwent. Asmamaw seems to have overcome his resentment, and understood the torture within the larger context of what EPRP/A were. The same cannot be said about Ayalew. Ayalew has adopted some extremist positions such as an all-out support for the TPLF regime, perhaps not out of conviction but more so out of spite. One would not find a single positive attribute of EPRA/EPRP (even about the rank and file ex-comrades of his who had nothing to do with his torture) in his 366-page book.

Another stain on the party was the summary execution of jailed anja members described elsewhere. While about 8 of them were

---

6. Asmamaw Hailu, p. 155-156

released[7], 14 of them, including the most senior party member among them Yirga Tessema, were executed as the army was retreating into Eritrea. Despite the convening of a military tribunal to try the suspected anja members (the tribunal members were Geleb, Grum, Mulualem Wassihun (Yohannes), Ambaye, and the prosecutor for the plaintiff was Indrias), the TPLF push did not allow the consummation of the process. The correct procedure could have been to expel the accused from the party and spare their lives (by precedent) as one of the decision makers, the late Col. Alemayehu Asfaw advised. This was not to be. In fact, the party had a precedent for leniency.

When the 8 army starters deserted Assimba following the Land Proclamation and went to Addis, Berhanemeskel had decided that they had to be executed for the offense, and to that effect had established a tribunal in the army from the remaining members who passed the decision. Although Tesfaye Debessay was in the area at the time, it did not seem he was part of the decision and did not share Berhanemeskel's enthusiasm. According to Kiflu Tadesse as quoted in Asmamaw, some of the party leaders in Addis talked to some of the deserters directly and indirectly, and were convinced that their offence did not merit execution, and Berhanemeskel's push was rebuffed. This may have been related to the party's extraordinary meeting held in July 1974, when Birhane Meskel lost his Politburo position, while retaining his seat in the CC[8].

As stated earlier, Zer'u Kishen had the chance to commute the deaths, but did not, and instead was the first to get to Sudan as the EPRA was being pummeled by TPLF and the army leadership made these rash, life-and-death decisions.

In mid-1976, the Rectification Movement was initiated in the army structures in Tigrai (several months later, in Gondar). Although a few of the side effects of the Movement were to have adversely impacted the army (such as resulting in loose military discipline), the Movement made important strides in terms of advancing the democratic rights of army members and the people. EPRP/A was the only fighting force that enshrined as a right that any member could request dismissal without fear of rejection or retaliation. In fact, the army gave the resigning comrade a modest sum for

---

7. ibid., p.205
8. In Bahru Zewde, ed., Melaku Tegegne, p.151

CHAPTER EIGHT: HOW DEMOCRATIC WAS EPRP?

provisions on his route, usually to the Sudan. For the first time, there was a Members' Rights Ombudsman Committee. As indicated earlier, they had some success in getting some of the suspected anjas to be released. Members were allowed to elect part of the leadership committee at various echelons. Even in the urban structures where secrecy was the modus operandi, instead of the CC appointing zonal committee members, the IZ appointed them, and each Zonal Committee in turn selected its representative to serve in the IZ[9]. The previous tradition in the army was the appointment of the leadership by the party. And this had given rise, with credible evidence, that those in higher echelons appointed and assigned positions not based on merit, but sometimes on acquaintance and friendship. Despite these democratic gains, even after the Rectification Movement, there were problems in the armies in Tigrai and Gondar in tolerating dissident views, or views differing from the mainstream and party conventional wisdom. The hayl 58 incident surrounding the deputy commissar, Gideon (Haddis Bitew), the anjas, and others are proof that the army came short in upholding the rights of dissident views. This in turn contributed to a climate of fear by those inclined to speak their minds to withhold and self-censure themselves.

EPRA/P women were treated largely with respect by their male comrades, and the leadership. This does not mean that there were no chauvinistic attitudes, or any problems. But by and large, the army gave the Woman Question its due place as we shall see in the next chapter.

Similarly, comrades from minority ethnic groups and their cultures were respected. From disseminating in 1975 its party programs and later some Democracia issues in many Ethiopian languages, to centerpiece the multi-national mosaic culture of Ethiopia in shows and holidays was routine. Many of EPRA comrades spoke the local languages, such as Tigrigna, languages they did not know before, and the peasants enjoyed hearing these comrades talk to them in broken local tongues. Many comrades in EPRA Tigrai enjoyed and joined the uniquely Tigrean/highland Eritrean dance called *Guayla,* where peasants and comrades danced in circles and drummers spiced up the song and dance. "*Biattiaga*", a

---

9.   Kiflu Tadesse, part i, p. 146

Wolaita cultural song, was one of the most popular songs among the EPRA, taught to the army by comrades from Wollaita, such as Tesfu.

In its relations with the people, EPRP/A has always been respectful and deferential. This was a totally new thing, especially for peasants who suffered at the hands of officialdom in their previous lives. Even the other liberation movements treated the peasants harshly and extracted their labor and supply needs often by force. For instance, in the 1980's, the EPLF army was mostly composed of helpless peasants abducted from their villages. This forced conscription, called *giffa* in Tigrigna, , imposed dire consequences on the peasant population. The International Crisis Group, in its March 2013 report[10], sums up the *giffa:* "in its scope, it involved tens of thousands of peasants; in its duration, it lasted for about a decade and a half; and in its consequences, it ravaged entire rural areas".

In some areas, especially in Armachiho, however, the respectful attitude by EPRA was met with disdain and contempt by the peasants where lawlessness and rebellious behavior was held in high esteem.

In fact, such respectful behavior had cost lives of comrades in some war zones. The comrades sent to Sidamo to start an armed propaganda unit in late 1976 were surrounded by the local peasants who did not know who the strangers in their midst were. Resolving not to shoot at the revolutionary allies of the proletariat, the comrades were overwhelmed by the peasants who captured them and gave them up to Dirgue officials for their eventual murder and drowning. A few months earlier in the same year, units sent to Wollo from Assimba were also surrounded by peasants, and when there was a good chance of escape by shooting their way out, some of them refused and were captured. This was to repeat itself intermittently in future years. (The first Wollo expedition of the army in July 1976 is faulted by some as an operation undertaken without adequate study and political work between Assimba and Wollo. As a result, such comrades as Zer'abruk Abebe, Woubshet Retta, Teferi Berhane were martyred).

Dr. Tesfaye Debessay, implementing the decision of the CC and the Military Commission, is said to be the one that gave the orders to the EPRA Command to embark on this tragic operation despite the

---

10. International Crisis Group. Eritrea: Scenarios For Future Transition, March 2013

CHAPTER EIGHT: HOW DEMOCRATIC WAS EPRP?

Command's protest. Dr. Tesfaye Debessay was perhaps the leading party leader almost everyone acknowledges as being the most democratic, perceptive and tolerant. In that vein, one wonders why Tesfaye did not seem to ponder through a couple of issues that sealed the fate of this party, and why he did not urge his comrades in the leadership to change course: 1. why Tesfaye failed to see that resolving the differences among Ethiopia's leftist forces most of whom were abroad in the early 1970's and failure to realize that the issue was a sine qua non to stump out sectarianism before party formation and coming into Ethiopia; 2. why he failed to see the EPRA Command's protest in June 1976 and insisted on to simply carry out a "party decision" to send units to uncharted areas of Wollo; 3. why he did not intervene when Berhanemeskel ordered the army to be confined, and not take initiatives unless in self-defense (and later Tesfaye demurring that this was a policy given to the EPRA Command); and 4. why he failed to see that the urban folly was going to lead to an irreversible disaster. One dynamic party leader that was a victim of EPRA's benevolence towards peasants was Berhane Iyyasu, who survived the Wollo incident, but fell victim in Sidamo. EPRA members had a culture of challenging the leadership and were fond of openly complaining at perceived shortcomings. So much so, even Debteraw, a long time membership of the CC and the General Command quipped once that he, too, had a question for the Leadership!

From the foregoing, the purpose of evaluating the democratic credentials of EPRP/A should be in the proper historical context for a fuller understanding.

Chapter Nine: The Woman Question

"The poorest of the poor in Ethiopia are women. Not all Ethiopian women may be poor; but among the poorest, the women are worst off. Many women are considered and treated as inferior in the family and mistreated by their husbands and male partners. They suffer injustice and maltreatment by various agents and mechanisms, such as tradition, culture, religion, justice administration bodies, police, prosecutors, judges, and family arbitration tribunals". Original Woldegiorgis, *"Democratic Process and Gender"*[1]

The Early Days

As the democratic awakening started in Ethiopia, primarily among students in the 1950s and 60s, one of the first questions that was on the agenda was the rights and conditions of women. At that time, women's education which came about as the result of the nation's modernization was being challenged by traditionalists that included even fellow male students [Yonas Admassu recounts in an essay, a university college debate where a college woman affirmed her right to be educated along with her male compatriots[2]]. The place of the woman was thought to be in the home, as in any patriarchal society. *"Melkam Set Lebalua Zeud Nat"*, roughly translated as "a fine woman

---

1. Original Woldegiorgis. Democratic Process and Gender, in Ethiopia: The Challenge of Democracy from Below, ed. Bahru Zewde, Siegfried Pauseway, Elander Gotab, 2002, p. 169
2. Yonas Admassu. In Project Muse, Callaaloo, v.33,#1, winter 2010, p. 64-81. What were they writing anyway: Tradition and Modernization in Amharic Literature

is one that is a crown to her husband", was a decorative plaque hung in the living rooms of urban couples. In rural Ethiopia, women were/are overworked, accounting according to UN studies for two thirds of the work, but making 10% of the income men bring in.

On top of that, women and girls were abducted, abused, married off at an early age, and generally treated as second class citizens. Although there have been some improvements over the years on their lot, in Ethiopia, the oppression of women has by and large remained unchanged.

In the course of the Ethiopian Student Movement, there were notable women students inside the country and abroad who fought for justice in general and women's equality in particular. Martha Mebrhatu, Tadelech Kidanemariam, Dr. Hanna Gobeze, Genet Zewde, Abebech Bekele, the late Tsehay Yeshitila, and Zenebework Tadesse abroad can be cited as the veterans of the movement. Later, when political parties emerged out of the student movement, women like Genet Girma, Nigist Tefera, Fikrte Gebremariam, Selamawit Dawit, and Mezgebnesh Abayu on EPRP's side, and Nigist Adane and Atnaf Yimam on the *Meison* side were the more known examples.

Even the supposedly bastions of progress and the two democratic institutions in the 1960's in Ethiopia, the Haile Selassie University and the Confederation of Ethiopian Labor Union, were not immune from ignorance and chauvinism. In the early 1960's one Miss USUAA, selected every year at the welcoming ceremony of freshmen, died by falling from a building while fleeing a would-be student rapist. As a result, the student union USUAA was banned, and campus was temporarily closed[3].

According to Netsanet Mengistu, university girls were not embraced even by the radicals and the student leadership. They were the butt of their cruel jokes. They derided a heavy-built girl as "*Wondimagegne*", a supposedly unattractive one, as "*Wolidew Ayitilu*", one who walked unevenly as a "tragic sight"[4].

USUAA'S main journal, *Struggle,* had a cartoonist by the name of Zewde Hailu who caricatured women as items of beauty, interested only in mini-skirts and partying. During College Day, where popular poetry contests of the 1950's and 60s were attended by the Emperor

---

3. In Bahru Zewde, Netsanet Mengistu, ch. 7, The Gender Question, p. 117
4. ibid., p. 118

CHAPTER NINE: THE WOMAN QUESTION

for many years until students were asked and refused pre-screening of their poems, it is not clear if there were any notable women poets that won any prizes. The winning poems were uniformly attributed to male students, such as Abebe Workie, Hailu Gebre Yohannes, Yohannes Admasu, Melaku Tegegne, Ibssa Gutema, Yilma Kebede, Waleligne Mekonnen, and Tamiru Feyissa[5]. The last poet, Tamiru Feyissa, had a poem titled "*Dehaw Yinageral*", which Bahru Zewde, used as a cover for his book, *Documenting the Ethiopian Student Movement*.

During March 1968, organized by the University Women's Club and some Peace Corps volunteers, a cultural show was staged at the university. Ethiopian women students wearing European attire were modeling the latest fashion of mini-skirts. Under the instigation of radicals, students protested the show describing it as 'cultural imperialism' promoted by aristocratic Ethiopian women and American imperialism[6]. Ironically, at the same time, Western feminists and radicals were fighting for their rights to wear the very same fashion Ethiopian radicals abhorred. Male students condescendingly described women students "our sisters heads have been washed by Western soaps"[7].

There were of course student radicals who tried, and modestly succeeded, in embracing and welcoming women. The late USUAA president Tilahun Gizaw and the late EPRP CC member Yohannes Berhane and IZ member Girmachew Lemma are cited as examples (for Tilahun, this must have been an epiphany. When he lost out to Mekonnen Bishaw USUAA's presidency in 1968, the swing voters tilting for Mekonnen were thought to be women, according to Balsvik)[8]. As a result of these efforts, women started slowly participating in student activities, such as organizing help during boycotts for poor and rural students, participating in Congress elections, and in demonstrations (at least one high school female student died during the melee following Tilahun's murder in 1969). One woman correctly bemoaned the fact that although this student activism later translated into EPRP activism, where women were

---

5. Kiflu Tadesse, part i, p. 36
6. Ghelawdewos Araya, p. 62
7. Randi Balsvik, p. 216
8. ibid., p. 487

accepted as leaders of squads and party units, to this day the documentation of their struggle is scant[9].

Perhaps the class of 1972 at Addis Ababa University might have been the class that showed the greatest increase in women enrollment at the university. The numerical strength led to other cultural changes, such as dressing -"wearing bell bottoms, mini-skirts, windbreakers, bandanas, sneakers, platform shoes and flip-flops"[10]. Cigarette smoking, and romance by the kissing pool also flourished with the class. Still, male chauvinism was not beating a retreat. Hiwot talks about a male law student and his friends disparaging her about why she would not wear a skirt was it not because she did not have "the legs", forcing her to oblige and show off her legs[11].

That same year, on December 8, 1972, two young women took part in an unsuccessful airplane hijacking along with male comrades. While one of the young women, Martha Mebrhatu, a medical student, lost her life, the other, Tadellech Kidanemariam, survived the ordeal.

In 1973, when a student rally was growing at 6 Kilo campus to make various demands, police interrupted the rally and started beating on the students. They took IDs and suspended 15 students, two of whom were women: Hiwot, and Azeb Girma. They were involved in such activities as fund raising when the cafeteria was closed to punish protesting students, and later when their suspension was lifted, Meles Tekle was instrumental in recruiting them to count ballots for the unbanned USUAA elections[12]. It is to be recalled that that was the last university union in the annals of the Ethiopian student movement, and the President and Secretary of that union were Getachew Begashaw and Aboma Mitiku, respectively.

Abroad, while university women were taking baby steps about their rights in the 1960s, some women around ESUNA were engaged in studies about women, and were trying to organize Ethiopian women students in the US and Europe. The leading woman student in this effort was Abebech Bekele. She visited local Black Panther offices in the New York area to borrow books about women, and

---

9. In Bahru Zewde, ed., Original W/Giorgis, p. 125
10. Hiwot Teffera. Tower in the Sky, p.12
11. Ibid., p. 55
12. Ibid., p.69

CHAPTER NINE: THE WOMAN QUESTION

participated in local discussions with them on gender issues and other social justice issues[13].

According to another activist, ESUNA was a male-dominated organization all the way to the 1970's. The presence of women was acknowledged only during fund raising events when their skills were sought in cooking and dancing. ESUNA seldom considered giving leadership roles to women[14]. But there was a sea change in attitude after 1969 when many militants immigrated to the US and the composition of ESUNA changed.

According to Abebech, activists like her fanned out on their own to initiate discussions around gender issues, and to organize women locality by locality. Her lone ally during that period was the late Tsehay Yeshitila, and later in the 1970's Zenebework joined them. The first seminar they put together succeeded in bringing together about 16 women. Trying to link up with women in Europe, she turned to her ESUNA comrades, and they gave her the name of a "Negede". Thinking that this was a woman's name, she was elated, and the response she got later from "Negede" did not clarify matters. Persisting in contacting women, she sent a message through a woman called Yeshi Mihretu who was visiting a sick sister in Moscow to facilitate contacts with women in the USSR, such as FGM, and Nigist Adane. This led to the formation of World Wide Ethiopian Women Study Group that used to hold its meeting around the same time as the World Wide Ethiopian Students Federation. However, the need for forming a separate women's organization was not readily recognized even by progressives at the time.

In the early 1970s, Genet Zewde was in Boston, and linked up with Abebech. Abebech was elated to find a link inside Ethiopia, and once Genet went back, Abebech started sending her and Martha Mebrhatu study materials on gender issues. A journal Abebech used to send a few copies to Ethiopia was a journal she published called "*Teneshi Ethiopiawit*"- "*Rise up Ethiopian Woman*". She sent a copy to each of the two women she had contact with, Genet Zewde and Martha Mebrhatu. Genet used to put a copy in the university library. One copy made it to a high school girl in rural Ethiopia, and the girl, to Abebech's joy, responded back after reading the journal.

---

13. personnal communication with Abebech Bekele
14. In Bharu Zewde, ed., Zenebework Tadesse, p.122-123

Abebech initially named the journal *"Teneshi Labaderit", "Rise up Ethiopian female proletariat"*. When she shared the proposal with the late Binyam Adane who was in Algeria at the time, he advised that the name proletariat implied a sectarian focus and a narrow group, and hence suggested the *'Teneshi Ethiopiawit"* name which Abebech promptly accepted. Binyam was later to die of an asthma attack in the lowlands of Eritrea while traveling among the first EPRA fighters trained in Palestine.

In 1973, at a Worldwide Ethiopian Students Federation meeting, Berhanemeskel Redda nominated Abebech Bekele to be its first president. Unopposed, she took the position. That same year the Federation received invitation to send a delegate to an International Youth Forum holding its meeting in East Berlin. Abebech delegated Tadellech Hailemichael to be the delegate. As a memorabilia, Tadelech was given a fine ring by the Forum. Tadelech offered the ring to Abebech who refused taking it by saying that the ring was a gift from the Forum to the delegate who attended. But Tadelech too refused to take the ring and sneaked at night and put the ring on Abebech's finger. Abebech wore that ring up till Assimba, and parted with it when Mulu (mother) asked for it when she came out to Sudan and gave it to her.

Perhaps the student Federation's contribution in its short-lived life was in soliciting and sending famine aid when the 1973 Wollo Famine struck. The late Samuel Alemayehu was in Addis Abeba and sent back pictures showing the victims of the Famine that were used for fundraising. Abebech, in her capacity as the President of the Federation, wrote a letter to the UN for that agency's help to aid the Ethiopian famine victims. The late Abdul Majid Hussein was instrumental in approaching BBC and facilitating the deployment of Jonathan Dimbleby to cover the famine and expose Haileselassie's secret. Dimbleby's film clip was obtained and distributed to all student chapters to help in fundraising. Siyum Wolde, in his autobiographical book talks about an art drawing he made for the Federation's fundraising effort and titled, *rehabu yadeqeqew*. Sadly he tells us the picture mysteriously disappeared in the hall where students were gathered, but the tickets sold as part of a lottery to win the drawing raised some funds and were turned in[15]. The Federation was very strict in making sure that the funds raised for the Famine

---

15. Siyum Wolde, p.139

CHAPTER NINE: THE WOMAN QUESTION

were directly distributed to the victims, and to ensure that, it had a close working relationship with the famine fund distribution committee established at Addis Abeba University. The University at Addis had formed a Famine Relief and Rehabilitation Committee, with teachers giving 10% of their salary, and students giving up their breakfast for a semester.

Likewise, the other democratic organization in Ethiopia in the 1960s, CELU, did not fare better when it came to respecting women's rights. At the Baratollo Cotton Factory in Asmara in the 1960s, the majority of the workers were females. However, as organizing for a union started, the 3 Eritrean workers chosen by management to attend CELU training in Addis were all males. Their leader, Berhane Andom, however, articulated the women's oppression at the Factory[16]. Further, in the CELU branch of Asmara, there were no female labor officers.

The CELU in Addis was no different. Through its independent existence and beyond, no female officers were elected. Even when 2 prominent EPRP members were at the helm in the June 1975 provisional election -Markos Hagos the President, and Tessema Deressa the General Secretary, all 13 provisional officers were male. Later when CELU was transformed to the Dirgue's AETU -All Ethiopian Trade Union in 1976, again, all 12 officers were male. However, to CELU's credit, with financial assistance from the International Union of Petroleum, Oil and Chemical Workers, it organized a seminar exclusively for women workers. It was conducted at the Augusta Shirt Factory where a large number of females worked. 60 women participated (6 of the 60 did not finish due to lack of spousal support). The topic of the seminar was the Labor Relations Decree issued in 1962[17].

Women workers, in addition to suffering oppression as workers, suffered also humiliation and pain as a result of their gender. A case in point is a woman called Yeshi working at the Fiber Company whose *idir*/union was under the leadership of Abera Gemu, a legend and pioneer in Ethiopia's labor history. The general manager at the company was a British citizen named Nash. Although a lot of complaints were being leveled against this man, and the complaints officially known to the government, the government did not care and

---

16. Beyene Solomon, p. 92
17. ibid., p. 188

did not take action. One of Nash's crimes was raping Yeshi and impregnating her while her husband worked there[18].

Women, EPRP, and the Yekatit Revolution

When the Yekatit Revolution erupted in 1974, and students in the US and Europe started coming back home, Abebech was asked by the EPRP CC to come home and help in organizing women. At the end of 1974, a Women's Coordinating Committee was set up under the tutelage of the Dirgue, with Major Fisseha Desta as the liaison. The initial members solicited representatives from major companies in Addis, and they included FGM, Nigist Tefera, Selamawit Dawit, Daro Negash, Mulu Hadera (mother), Mezgebnesh Abayu, Nigist Adane, Gerawork G/Egziabher, Atnaf Yimam and Alemtsehay Wodajo. The Committee members included both Meison and EPRP supporters. They held regular meetings in the compound of the Ethiopian Parliament. One of its achievements was the convening of a meeting in April lasting 3 days at which 360 women were present. Col. Fisseha Desta gave the key note speech (this is the Fisseha Desta, Gebru Tareke, in his book, "The Ethiopian Revolution", quotes and ridicules for saying, "...a weak husband does not kick his wife out, rather he leaves with the luggage, instead of confiscating everything and throwing his partner out empty-handed")[19]. At the end of the seminar, a 16-strong coordinating committee was established and was instrumental in preparing and celebrating the first Women's Day in Ethiopia, on March 8, 1975. Hiwot Tefera, in her book, *Tower in the Sky,* says Mengistu H/M, and not Fisseha Desta, was the one that gave the opening speech. Hiwot participated in the conference as one of three women representing the Addis Ababa *ediget behibret zemachoch*. The other two representatives were Amsale Tamrat and Azeb Girma, a militant youth leader that was killed by the Dirgue[20].

At the extended conference of EPRP held just a month before the party was officially declared, Mezgebnesh Abayu reported to the

---

18. ibid., p.54
19. Gebru Tareke. The Ethiopian Revolution: War in the Horn of Africa, Yale University Press, 2009, p. 379
20. Hiwot Teffera. Tower in the Sky, p.131

CHAPTER NINE: THE WOMAN QUESTION

Conference on the activities of the Women's Committee[21]. Mezgebnesh contributed immensely to the intellectual enrichment of learned Ethiopians of the late 1970's in her capacity as an editor of the magazine Goh. The publication's articles by her and others on Stalin, Tilahun Gizaw, the Palestinian Leila Khalid, the American Angela Davis, the Chinese general Chu Teh, and its interviews with Ethiopian literati, such as Tsegaye Gebremedhin and artist Afework Tekle were readers' favorites. The poems of Goh were beautiful, and particularly its short story titled "Tulu Forza" are memorable. Mezgebnesh was sadly stabbed to death in 1988 in her home in Philadelphia, and her murderer(s) still unknown.

From 1975-77, both internal and external factors may have subsumed the women's movement. As a result, the movement did not seem to be able to form a solid, sustained and structured movement such as EPRYL as a branch of EPRP, or as an independent entity (the issue of the relationship of a pro-EPRP woman's organization to the party was hotly debated by EPRP women without any resolution). This does not mean, however, that the contribution and sacrifice of women in the struggle EPRP waged is not a huge marker in Ethiopian political history, and that the movement did not help to bring into the struggle many women. The internal factor was the fact that the struggle of young women submerged in the youth league's movement, and externally, the split between Meison and EPRP could not hold together a single women's movement, and later the Red Terror claimed the lives of thousands of young women and mothers.

Mothers, in particular, saw in horror as their sons and daughters were being murdered in wanton violence; and their dead bodies desecrated with placards affixed calling out "Let The Red Terror Intensify"; and being forced to pay $250 per body for the cost of a bullet to claim the bodies of the dead from morgues; and denied the right even to mourn their losses. These inhuman acts by the Dirgue and its violent machinery, that had no precedence in our history, galvanized mothers to form, particularly in Addis Abeba, what were called "Ou Ou Ta Committees". These mothers engaged in resistance against the Dirgue by engaging in such activities as turning off lights at night in their homes to obstruct the Dirgue killers rampage. They also screamed in unison with "ou ou ta" and banged pots and pans to

---

21. Kiflu Tadesse, The Generation, part i, p.239

disrupt the Dirgue's campaign of rounding up youth. The mothers occasionally demonstrated in public protest. Women also were members of Family Councils that the party and youth league encouraged their members to form as discussion and resistance forums.

The leading women figures in Addis were Mezgebnesh Abayu and Nigist Tefera (the former publishing a pro-EPRP popular journal called *Goh*, the latter was tasked with the creation of a nation-wide Ethiopian women organization, possibly by collaborating with pro-*Meison* women, such as Nigist Adane and Tiruwork Waqeyo). While Mezgebnesh was able to join the struggle in Assimba, Nigist was a victim of the Red Terror. Many women were assigned in various party tasks as described elsewhere, including notable squad commanders such as Tsehay Solomon who came from Jimma and died in a shootout at American Gibi in Mercato; Askale Nega (Berhaun Nega's sister) who was assigned in the waning days of the UDF to exchange experience with the squads of ELAMA, and who was killed soon after[22]. (Another sister, Adanech Nega, after time in the EPRA, lost her life tragically in a car accident in DC).

The other leading women, such as Abebech Bekele, FGM, Selamawit Dawit, Tirsit/Konjit continued the struggle in Assimba. There in EPRA, they got a firsthand opportunity to work with peasant army members and peasant women. In EPRA, the army had to contend with contradictions between peasant and local army members on one hand, and those who came from the urban areas. In addition, there was also male chauvinism in the army that the EPRA had to deal with rules, regulations and education (these are problems the EPRA faced on top of the pressures from TPLF (to force it to leave Tigrai), from EPLF (to accept its colonial thesis), and internally (an army whose ranks swelled from those who narrowly escaped the Red Terror, and some of whom were now challenging, or questioning the validity of the party's political line).

Soon after the rectification movement was completed in the army, the women of EPRA held a conference in a place called Assefat near Assimba. The conference is hence known as the "Assefat Guba'e". There were about 40-50 EPRA women in attendance. The agenda of the conference was to lay bare the underlying causes of male

---

22. personal communication with GT

CHAPTER NINE: THE WOMAN QUESTION

chauvinism, and to find solutions to it in the army. To that effect, the 5-day conference started with analyzing the historical causes of male chauvinism, the various ways of its manifestations, consciousness raising undertakings and how EPRA women should ascertain their rights and relate with their male comrades. The discussion naturally transformed from the theoretical to the personal.[23]

Many women fighters started sharing boldly their personal agonies and attempted rapes. It was particularly encouraging to see peasant comrades overcome cultural oppression and internalizing personal problems pouring it out. It was a woman-to-woman moment, and a group therapy. The women comrades were urged to report any perceived and real violations on themselves, and also to counsel male comrades who attempt to violate them. At the conclusion of the conference, their decisions were enumerated and distributed to all army members for discussion, and through the chair who was Abebech Bekele, the decisions of the conference were submitted to the EPRA High Command. The least popular decision was the women's recommendation that smoking comrades quit smoking for health reasons, and also to help the party and army save money.

Although the Assefat Guba'e was an eye-opener, and made aware both male and female fighters about what is right and what is not, problems between the genders persisted. Because the army was not at a stage to allow marriages, fraternizing between the sexes in a sexual way was prohibited. Article 24 of EPRA's Rules and Regulations accepted the legality of pre-existing marriages- couples married before they joined EPRA, and Article 49 prohibited all manifestations of male chauvinism[24]. Popular male commanders of EPRA in Gondar were dismissed from the army for alleged violation of women's rights.

EPRA strove to respect the rights of its women fighters, and the rights of peasant women in areas where it operated. Peasant women fighters learned literacy and numeracy in the army. They also learned not to accept as natural male domination. Some bloomed in the army, and achieved prominent positions as commanders, commissars, or medics. The late Dilay, perhaps a high school student from Woldiya, rose up in the ranks to become a deputy commander

---

23. Asmamaw Hailu, p. 196-199
24. ibid., p.284,290

of a Hayl before she lost her life in a battle. Eletai, Ayalnesh, Masresha, Fisseha Manjus, Tirsit, Meritsa, the late Jamilla and the disappeared Aberash Berta were other examples of women who accomplished great achievements in the EPRA. As we saw in Chapter 5, Aberash and Tirsit/Konjit Teklu, were members of the General Command in Quarra. A few EPRA women, such as Mother, FGM, Mezgebnesh, Alemnesh and other young mothers, left behind with relatives toddlers and infants to join the rural struggle. Only a parent can fully understand the depth of their commitment.

Similarly, in the rural cadre structure, the oppression of women cadres was no better. Because their unique assignment facilitated their co-habitation with a male cadre, or in a family setting, sexual activity among them was reported at a much higher rate than in the disciplined and group-living army. As a result, unwanted pregnancies among female cadres, either through consensual or forced sex/rape, was considerable. In that regard for those located in the Armachiho area, Nurse Alemnesh played a crucial role in performing abortions, counseling women on health issues, and generally as a source of support.

In terms of women's specific needs, the party did not have resources to supply its fighters and cadres with feminine sanitary items during their periods. Fortunately, perhaps due to the strenuous physical activity, and the little food available, the periods of almost all women disappeared, and nature took care of the issue.

We have heard and read over and over again that Judge Bertukan Midekssa was the first female leader of a political party. That is somehow erroneous. EPRP/A has had at least 3 that were members of the collective leadership of the party at various time periods: Abebech Bekele, 1978-1980; Mezgebnesh Abayu (for a brief period in 1979 until the 4th plenum), and Genet Girma in 1995. TPLF too had the lone CC member for a long time in Aregash Adane. The description may be qualified by saying that Bertukan is the first head of a party without a collective leadership (co-leaders).

The Woman Question in Ethiopia is today as bleak as yesterday. Even the self-professed revolutionary, and "I -am-holier-than-every one-else" former head of state Mengistu Hailemariam still wallows in male chauvinism. In complimenting his onetime deputy, who was among this murderer's countless victims, Mengistu says "in my observations, and through the testing times Dirgue was faced with, I have not seen Col. Atnafu in fear in situations that tested

CHAPTER NINE: THE WOMAN QUESTION

masculinity!" (sic)[25]. Even democratic and progressive nationalists in Ethiopia dominantly address their audience in their literary style talking directly to the reader as a second person male. This has to be corrected and is unacceptable.

There is the heroism of three Ethiopian women who were tortured during the Red Terror by Kelbesa Negewo, a *keftegna kebelle* chairman. The three women, Hirut Abebe Jiri, Ejigayehu Taye and Elizabeth Demisse, identified Kelbesa in Atlanta, US, where he was working at a hotel. They sued him in a US court and won their case. The Ethiopian special prosecutor subsequently requested for his extradition, and he is currently serving a life sentence there.

Similarly, women in TPLF faced the same male chauvinist tribulations. In one of their conferences in 1988, they sent a messenger from the field inviting Abebech to participate, undoubtedly to hear and share her experience. However, Abebech was about to immigrate to the US and did not accept their offer[26].

The TPLF leadership did not appear to have a history of accommodating an independent, democratic women's movement both in the field and since it took power, as one woman activist tells us. The leadership demeaned the women activists for being inspired by feminism that looked down on men as the enemy rather than the system. The Tigrean army women vehemently denied this accusation. The activists were condemned because they demanded that men use condoms for sexual activity rather than women use pills -because of the pills' health complicating effects (this was after marriage was allowed in the army); and for suggesting husbands help their wives in collecting firewood[27].

Further aggravating the women's organization, during the Women's 2nd Conference in 1988, the leadership of the meeting was taken over by the male-dominated TPLF politburo. The politburo decreed which of the women could be elected and which could not. For instance, Aregash Adane, the lone CC member was prevented from running for women's leadership position under the pretext of being overworked[28]. After TPLF's victory over the Dirgue, its domination and the division it created within the women's leadership

---

25. Mengistu Hailemariam, p. 239
26. personal communication with Abebech Bekele
27. Yewubmar Asfaw, p. 116
28. ibid., p.121

team worsened by dividing them into "old blood" and "new blood" despite election results by women themselves, and fits EPRDF/TPLF control model of independent organizations including women's[29].

The Ethiopian women's struggle, unlike its contemporaries elsewhere, never veered to extremist feminist positions, and was always anchored in the most basic social justice demands of its constituency.

During the revolutionary years of 1974-1978, EPRP was undoubtedly the first party that organized and mobilized women in their tens of thousands throughout the country to fight for democracy and their genuine rights.

When Ethiopian women make significant strides in terms of access to health, education, and job opportunities, then that is when the "Woman Question" could be said to have found its answer.

---

29. ibid., p. 174

Chapter Ten: EPRP in the Diaspora: the Fulcrum of United Fronts in the Era of Multy-Partyism

COEDF: Preparation, Formation and Activities

As the existence of the army was made precarious by the new alignment of forces that were on the rise, TPLF, and EPLF, aided by the Sudanese regime, EPRP/A literally ran out of operational space inside Ethiopia. As the once powerful EPRA that was organized by battalions faced defeat after defeat, the last remnant units were trying to cover a large swath of land through decentralized movements.

Fassika was assigned to travel to the US for the new phase of diplomatic and united front work among Ethiopianist forces. Mersha too was deployed to the US, but stayed in Europe to solidify organizational work there. This was early in 1990. The late Kahsay and Genet Girma were assigned to lead the work in Europe. During this time, perhaps copying the successes of EPLF's relief agency and TPLF's REST, to garner financial aid from the West in the name of relief for their regions, EPRP set up a relief organization called ROFE: relief organization for Ethiopia. Asgedom now residing in Australia and Biru in Berlin were the leads on this effort. However, while ethnic-based veteran relief groups such as REST, and relatively newer ones, such as ORA (Oromo Relief Association) persevered,

ROFE was unable to get off the ground due largely to staunch overt sabotage by Western interests.

Starting in April 1990, preparations were spearheaded by EPRP delegates to launch a coalition formation conference in Toronto as the danger of the TPLF and EPLF duo taking power and dividing the country became imminent.

Written invitations were mailed out to all Ethiopian forces of the time: EPRP, Meison, EPDA, DMTP, and EDU. The invitations were not limited to these; the ELF, EPLF, OLF and TPLF/EPRDF were also invited. However, due to the fact of the changed international situation that favored them in securing the West's backing, and their own internal strength, the latter group either ignored the call, or put up stiff conditions that diluted Ethiopiawinet as a condition of participation.

Notable individuals, such as Gomoraw, Yeshi Wondimeneh, and Khasay from Germany attended the Toronto Conference. The goal of the Toronto conference was to lay the foundation and facilitate the preparation for the convening of a conference for the formation of a United Front. The Toronto conference named the following individuals as the leads to facilitate the convocation: Professor Efrem Yishaq, Kassahun Bisrat (a former teachers' association secretary), Assefa Adefris, Dr. Yacob Haile Mariam (a vice-chair), and Dr. Gebru Tareke, who was the chairman of the committee. The Toronto Conference was held from July 12 through July 15, 1990, and laid the road map for the next UF formation conference to be convened within 3 months.

There were palpable obstructions to delay the convening of the conference and the formation of the United Front, most likely to ensure the taking of power by EPRDF and solidify the division of the country into two. In addition, concerted efforts were also noticeable to try to purge the influence of leftist organizations and lines. The UF formation that was slated to start within 3 months was delayed by a very long 9 months.

At about the 6th month of delay, Professor Efreim came with the idea of changing the name and theme of the conference from Ethiopia to that of the "Horn of Africa", and tried to sell the new idea by a promise of cash to be given by a Norwegian NGO to help cover the costs of the UF formation conference. Soon after, Dr. Efreim talked to the EPRP delegates on how they could peacefully operate inside Ethiopia once TPLF took power.

CHAPTER TEN: EPRP IN THE DIASPORA

The EPRP delegates were furious at the delaying tactics, and gave the committee a 15-day ultimatum saying that if the conference was not called within 15 days, EPRP by itself would organize the conference. At this time, Dr. Efreim, Dr. Yacob and Kassahun formed their own NGO in the name of a movement for Ethiopian peace.

A Canadian church-affiliated NGO provided a hostel to accommodate the participants, and money to cover the conference was obtained from a German NGO that had relations with Ras Mengesha Siyum.

The Toronto Conference made a call for the UF formation conference to start in April 1991 (a month before TPLF took power). The location was decided to be in Maryland at a city called New Windsor. EPRP was assigned to be responsible for the logistics of the conference (lodging, meals, etc.). The conference (held from April 17-21, 1991) was broadly representative, and the enthusiasm of the participants was high. EDU, EPRP, Meison were very enthusiastic, while EPDA's path was at the time uncertain (but later ended up as enthusiastic as the others). About 50 forums participated -groups not politically affiliated - and caucused to elect Abate Kassa as their leader. Because Col. Goshu was not elected in the caucus, the newly elected leadership co-opted him believing that he would play a constructive role.

Mersha Yosef was elected the chairman (after Ras Mengesha Siyum and Commander Tasew Desta declined), and Abera Yemane-ab was elected vice-chair and Head of foreign affairs. The new coalition was called Coalition of Ethiopian Democratic Forces (COEDF), and it had two leadership structures - a Council that has advisory and planning role, and an Executive Committee.

It is an understatement to say that the formation of COEDF is important. COEDF was a trail blazer in modern Ethiopian politics that brought diametrically opposed political views to find common ground in a coalition. As Abera Yemane-ab liked to say, it had members from monarchists to Marxists. It also brought together the two leftist political parties that fought pitched battles on the Ethiopian political field two decades earlier. COEDF was a powerful symbol of the potent force of Ethiopiawinet and Ethiopia that in the new political alignment, was being made superfluous and replaced by ethnic identities. While functional for about 4 years, it was a symbol of hope and inspiration around which Diaspora Ethiopians rallied.

Its supporters raised substantial amount of funds and turned out in tens of thousands when called out for demonstrations.

When Meles wrote to the UN to facilitate the unlawful Eritrean separation from Ethiopia, COEDF organized a protest demonstration at the UN's office in New York. It issued timely press releases. Because of its credible diplomatic work, COEDF had represented Ethiopia's interests at meetings and conferences convened by the Carter Center, and former congressman Harry Johnston's office.

This new experiment of working in coalition politics, unfortunately, was not free from any problems and hurdles. In what is suspected to be heavy American pressure, the first to drop out of COEDF was Ras Mengesha and his EDU contingent. Soon after, DMTP put out a press release disassociating itself from COEDF. Contrary to its expectations, this organization was denied entry into Ethiopia by the TPLF, and ended up in a political wilderness, unable to come back to COEDF's fold nor to operate inside Ethiopia.

The biggest damage to COEDF, however, came from Col. Goshu Wolde. He spent several months secretly agitating against the two former leftist parties, EPRP and Meison, as if he himself was not a member of a former worker's party, EWP. The organization that he formed, Medhin, was an important component of COEDF that was able to attract many intellectuals who were hesitant about belonging with former leftist parties. Col. Goshu was bellicose, confrontational and combative in his style. When he thought he was ready to split from COEDF, he took with him a good chunk of the coalition's human and leadership resources. Lij Seifu Zewde, Ato Cheru, Dr. Yonas (D.C.), Dr. Daniel Tefera (Michigan), Dr. Getachew Metaferia, Dr. Tsehay Birhanesellasie, and Fissehatsion Menghistu went with him. Soon after, General Taye Tilahun, a former ambassador and a Protestant faith follower joined him as a vice-chair of his organization.

With Col. Goshu's huge ego and combative style, his organization was not to last long. After severely weakening COEDF, Medhin did not even last a year, when its luminaries dropped out one after another, and finally the CEO himself completely retired from politics, never to be heard in the coming decades.

Ato Assefa Adefris who was an executive committee member since the Toronto conference was also another troublemaker. His forging of the chairman's seal and its posting on an Ethiopian

CHAPTER TEN: EPRP IN THE DIASPORA

magazine, and the fact that organizational secrets were being out in the streets created havoc inside COEDF. Assefa Chabo, after spending a decade in Dirgue's jail, and upon his release, came abroad when his honeymoon with the TPLF was over and was briefly the member of the executive office and a member of Hibre-Hizb, another organization inside COEDF. Assefa did not get along with his colleagues and a spat was created.

According to meto aleka Ayalsew Desse, a senior member of most coalitions in the Diaspora, and particularly a secretary of CAFPDE's North America branch, the following are the main accomplishments of COEDF:

- struggled for the establishment of an all-inclusive transitional government in Ethiopia;
- fought hard to ensure the infamous London Conference that crowned TPLF and EPLF to be inclusive, especially, inclusive of multi-ethnic Ethiopian forces;
- condemned the agenda of the July 1991 TPLF-led conference and its exclusive convention that led to the division of the country into two, and that consequently made Ethiopia landlocked;
- exposed the introduction of politicized ethnicity in Ethiopia, and EPRDF's fake transition from a provisional status to a non-provisional, dictatorial regime;
- set an example by its multi-ethnic composition, and the antidote against ethnicity.
- showed the futility and anti-Ethiopiawinet stances of EPRDF when it disbanded Ethiopia's national army, and when it fired 42 of AAU's able university professors and staff.
- defended and stood together with AAU students when they came out protesting the illegal separation of Eritrea in 1993;
- strongly condemned the ethnic cleansing and criminal activities of the regime when it harassed and killed citizens of the Amhara ethnic group living in Arba Gugu, Water and other southern Ethiopia areas;
- analyzed and critiqued in detail the substance of EPRDF's constitution and the manner in which it was dictatorially adopted;

- used various means of mass media, such as press releases, and a twice- weekly radio broadcast into Ethiopia, to defend democracy and the rule of law.

It is not an exaggeration to say that the tasks that COEDF accomplished would not have been possible without the support of EPRP's North America organizational structure, thanks to Fassika's leading role.

The reader should keep in mind that EPRP was better situated than any of the parties or fronts in the Diaspora to initiate and advance the practical implementation of a united front. This was because on the one hand, it had more members than any other party in almost every part of the Diaspora, most notably North America and Europe. Coupled with this, its members were experienced, daring and active. It is not a partisan statement to say that whoever wanted to break out of their shell, and take the stage of opposition as a leader, notables such as Col. Goshu, or Assefa Chebo, it is the EPRP foot soldiers that paved the way and took care of the logistics.

In that regard, EPRP activists were once again called to popularize and carry the tasks of a new coalition named after the city in which it met, Paris 1 (the number "1" indicates a second meeting later was to take place in this city, and to tell the meetings apart, a numbering sequence was used).

What was Paris 1?

While the formation of COEDF was a Diaspora affair, it was necessary to coalesce both the struggle inside the country and the one outside it. TPLF/EPRDF was not showing any inclination to resolve the outstanding issues of Ethiopia's political challenges in a peaceful way. To that effect, a meeting was held from March 11-13, 1993 in Paris of the main Ethiopi'a political organizations both from inside and outside the country. Organizations that were part of TPLF's transitional regime, such as representatives of the Hadiya Democratic Organization's like Dr. Beyene Petros, was one such participant. Dr. Beyene was also a vice minister for education. OLF, that was once part of the troika that took power in the London Conference, had now had a fallout with EPRDF, and elected to participate in Paris 1. The list of organizations that participated in Paris 1 included Southern Ethiopian Peoples Democratic Union, EPRP, Meison,

CHAPTER TEN: EPRP IN THE DIASPORA

OLF, Medhin, Hibre-Hizb, Congress Party, Tigray-Tigrigni party, and ARDUF (Afar).

Paris 1 was one of the few Ethiopian opposition conferences that was marked by the breadth and width of its touch of opposition parties. It brought together both ethnic-based opposition parties and multi-ethnic ones; it brought together home-based organizations and those in the diaspora; it brought together those that were part of the regime to be going forward part of the opposition. Ahead of the meeting, organizations were assigned to present well-researched position papers that would help in finding peaceful solutions and lead to national reconciliation. Its press releases and foreign affairs work immediately after the conclusion of the conference had earned it respect among foreign nations that were used to the squabbling among Ethiopia's opposition. On the third and last day, the conference decided to convene in the near future inside Ethiopia a Peace and Reconciliation Conference where EPRDF would be invited to participate, and assigned a coordinating committee for the task.

Perhaps for the first time since it took power in 2 years, TPLF/EPRDF was on the defensive. A large swath of representatives of the Ethiopian people was calling it to come to the negotiating table. Predictably, it rebuffed the conference's decisions, and had a negative view of the whole affair. Its immediate action was to expel Dr. Beyene Petros and his organization from the transitional government and fire him from his vice-minister position.

Following the decisions of Paris 1, In 1993, COEDF had worked hard along with the home-based opposition to organize a conference inside Ethiopia where EPRDF and the opposition, both Diasporic and home-based, were to hold a conference at Ghion Hotel and try to peacefully resolve the nation's problems. EPRDF had expressed a commitment to third parties not to disrupt the conference, and preparations were under way. The Americans insisted that this was a good opportunity for EPRP to engage in peaceful struggle, and that the leaders of COEDF that would participate in the conference should they opt to come back to the US could do so. At that time, the person entrusted to do COEDF's foreign affairs was Genenew Assefa, much later to turn to be an ideological bodyguard of Meles.

EPRP was fully sold on the Ghion peace and reconciliation conference. It included in COEDF's delegation its experienced members: the chairman of COEDF Mersha Yosef, and senior members Genet Girma, Mesfin Tefera (office manager), Muluken Muche, Berhaneselassie Assefa and Haimanot Lakew, COEDF branch activists. On Meison's side the vice chair and head of foreign relations Abera Yemane-ab was part of the delegation. Each delegate was responsible for their own plane tickets.

As soon as the first plane disembarked in Addis holding a part of COEDF's and other parties' delegations, they were rounded up and thrown in jail. Those jailed included OLF representatives, Medhin delegates, and of course COEDF delegates. The balance of COEDF's delegates was in Cairo en route to Addis Abeba. Their plane was delayed due to bad weather in New York and then in Frankfurt. When news broke that EPRDF had jailed the advance team, the coordinators in the DC office and in Europe (Dr. Negede Gobeze) warned the Cairo delegates to cancel their trip. The Addis Abeba conference preparatory committee too (Dr. Beyene Petros & Co.) advised the Cairo delegation to stay away. There were about 16 delegates in Cairo out of a total delegation of 23. All but Mersha returned to where they came from. The late Mulugeta Hailu of Meison stayed with Mersha the longest. Mersha was denied entry into the US, and staying in Cairo posed security and logistical problems. So, he went to Nairobi, and eventually settled underground in Kampala and embarked in organizational work that eventually culminated in Ethiopian Patriots' Front, the second and last chance to re-enter the Ethiopian countryside (more on this later). Meanwhile, the vice chair Aberra was among the jailed.

COEDF was feeling the pangs of defeat and organizational pain at losing two of its key leaders and many of its senior members. For the next 2 years, the leadership of COEDF rested on the shoulders of Dr. Mulugeta Siyum, who despite the gloomy conditions, admirably and honestly discharged his responsibilities.

The Scene at Bole and Going to Jail

Mesfin Tefera was the administrator of COEDF's main office in Washington DC. In that capacity, he handled all communications with branch offices, received and sent fax messages, dealt with other organizations, arranged executive office meetings, etc. His departure and jailing in Addis along other top officers, such as Aberra, coupled with the chairman's being stranded in Cairo, literally killed COEDF's

CHAPTER TEN: EPRP IN THE DIASPORA

lifeline. Here is a narration of the conditions there from Mesfin's perspective.

The plane with members of the advance team arrived at Bole International Airport at 10 p.m. Addis Abeba time, December 16, 1993. TPLF officials, the late Assefa Mamo and the late Kinfe Gebremedhin were waiting at the VIP in Bole, and therefore they were taken to the VIP lounge there. After the delegates and their luggage were searched, a young security officer started calling names and ordering delegates to line up. Security officers confiscated all conference documents, videos, cameras, and fax machines. They forced statements from delegates for future incrimination. Siyum Zenebe's name, a Medhin delegate, was not called. Suddenly, the person assigned by the Addis conference preparatory committee to receive and welcome the delegates started yelling, and protesting in broken English why the peace delegates are being detained. Perhaps the fact that he resorted to speaking in English was an effort to try to get the attention of foreigners.

In the mayhem, Siyum started to blend with the crowd, when suddenly Kinfe remembered Medhin's delegate and called out for him to join his colleagues.

They divided the delegates into two groups. The first group had Mesfin Tefera, Genenew Assefa, Alemayehu Deressa (a Meison member and a Swedish citizen), Genet, and Kebede Gebrai. Kebede was the lone delegate who came from Cairo to Addis because his father, who was a Dirgue major and a Tigrean, promised his son that he would not be jailed. Kebede was a US citizen. He was later to serve as the vice-chair of the Ghion Conference as a representative of COEDF (the chair was Beyene representing the Hadiya People's Democratic Organization, and the secretary was Dr. Taye Woldesemayat representing ETA).

The delegates captured at Bole were all taken to the 3rd Police Station where Mesfin Tefera again saw his high school friend at General Wingate school, Getachew Assefa, the current security chief (the first time he saw him was at Bole). It was a surprise for Mesfin. At 2 a.m., Getachew knocks on the cell door, and announced that Mesfin Tefera and Alemayehu Deressa were no longer wanted and were free to leave.

Alemayehu Deressa and Mesfin at dawn immediately contacted Negede in Europe and got authorization to represent COEDF. Mesfin relayed a message to Mersha through Negede that it was still unsafe to travel to Addis. Mesfin and Alemayehu then secured the services of two lawyers, Abebe Workie and Teshome Gebremariam to prepare to defend the jailed and fight for their freedom (Ato Mulu Mejja was also part of the legal team). In the meantime, the conference was going on at Ghion, and there was some media around the hotel to cover the event and the incidents surrounding the event. The two COEDF representatives gave press releases and interviews about their predicament and on EPRDF's failure to honor its word, and facilitate peaceful talks and national reconciliation.

Mesfin met his 16 year old daughter for the first time, a child he left back home when she was only 2. EPRDF/TPLF was not comfortable with the two freed delegates issuing press releases and playing activist roles. While the two were giving interviews to several journalists including the VOA, Alemayehu was called by someone and Mesfin noticed that he did not return. Mesfin suspected the worst and expressed his concern to the journalists, and that he too may be arrested. Indeed they took back Alemayehu to jail, and Mesfin too did not last long. They were both hauled back to their jail cells to be met with mocking laughter by their comrades. Their freedom lasted only 10 hours.

The security officers asked each delegate to write their biographies, and that was checked against security files. Every 14 days they were hauled for a court appearance. About 31 days after arrival in Addis, the delegates were transferred to Alem Bekagne prison (their arrival date was December 16, 1993). Alem Bekagne was less comfortable than the 3rd Police Station jail. They still had to do their routine court appearance.

Visitors were mostly family members. Genenew's visitors included Andreas Eshete, Dawit Yohannes, Kifle Wodajo, Abdul Mohammed, Genet Zewde, Yosef Tesfaye and President Girma WG (then a representative in parliament and most likely visiting his daughter, Genet).

TPLF prisoner guards admired Genet, among other things, for the fact that she came to Quarra from Europe for the 2nd Congress. She loved to discuss issues with them. Later TPLF changed the guards regularly. Meal delivery was by turns. Three weeks into Alem Bekagne, Mesfin's father suffered a stroke. The stressful situation of his son's incarceration must have made his situation worse and might have contributed to the onset of the stroke. Prior to that, Gayyim had stayed in his house anonymously for 3 months. Unbeknownst to

CHAPTER TEN: EPRP IN THE DIASPORA

Mesfin's father, it was arranged to rent a room to Gayyim at the house. Two months after Gayyim left the house and was killed by TPLF security forces in a shootout, his picture was made public. Later, after Gayyim's death, when his picture was made public, the neighbors of Mesfin's father were asking him "was it not the same guy you rented a room for a few months back? This by itself must have put on him a lot of stress. Getachew Assefa arranged for Mesfin to visit his father (in their high school days, Mesfin and Getachw spent some weekends at Mesfin's house after scout outings, so Getachew was no stranger to Mesfin's parents).

A US human rights officer and another embassy staff paid regular visits to the delegates. Aberra and Genet were the representatives of the delegates. Soon, the delegates were asked to sign a paper to secure their release. Genenew had earlier mentioned to Mesfin that Meles wanted to talk to him to sign the paper. The paper to be signed basically stated that each delegate would struggle through peaceful means only. The delegates discussed the issue, and finally decided to sign.

They appeared before a judge, and to their shock, learned that Abera was denied the right to be released. This dampened their spirits. Aberra was calm. He advised the delegates to take advantage of the situation and not stay behind for him. Every one cried uncontrollably, especially Genet who refused to leave, and was at last cajoled by Abera to leave and continue the struggle. The guards also wept along with the prisoners. Aberra said that he had a clean record and that he had nothing to fear. His saga was not to end until he left the country in 2012.

CAFPDE and the Chair Dr. Beyene gave a farewell party to the released delegates and family at Ethiopia Hotel, and most of the delegates flew out of Ethiopia in 4 days. Genenew stayed for 2 months, and Genet stayed for a month. While there, they visited Abera and consulted with his lawyers.

One of the jailed, an OLF veteran, Lencho Letta, within a week of his release , said unashamedly that he was unhappy in jail because he was jailed along with chauvinists! Imagine Abera Yemane-ab, Alemayehu Deressa and Genet Girma who have been at the forefront of the struggle being called chauvinists!

In the meantime, the Conference started on December 18 and continued for 5 days. About 45 organizations, both political parties and civic organizations had participated (Ayalsew). At the end of the

Conference, the participants passed a resolution. The highlight of the resolution called for the formation of a transitional government at the end of EPRDF's transitional tenure that would include the EPRDF and that would usher in a peaceful national reconciliation in the country. The conference formed CAFPDE. 32 member organizations were home-based, while 16 were in the Diaspora.

On the opening date, representatives of up to 30 countries stationed in Addis invited as guests were present. Mesfin Tefera's press release at Ghion on the condition of the jailed on the opening date must have rankled EPRDF as foreign diplomats got wind of its sabotage.

The residents of Addis had held a public demonstration to show their support for CAFPDE and for peace and reconciliation.

Paris 2

Opposition politics in a poor country like Ethiopia is prohibitively expensive. And we are not talking about the scarcity of money alone although that by itself is a big factor determining the reach and activities of any opposition party. In addition, in victory, everybody pretty much falls in line, and as the saying goes victory has many allies. In coalition opposition however, the following are common symptoms: fracturing, the impulse to go it alone, and not being accountable (there is no price to pay) are all too common. Exacerbating the situation is the fact that the coalition is made of forces and parties that do not command similar number of members and resources, or the coalitions so far formed do not account by giving bonuses with such things as voting privilege to those who have numerical and resource superiority. Moral sermons about "standing together" to defeat the enemy regardless of all these underlying factors have not been heeded. Making matters worse, the regime in power wreaks havoc within the coalition when opportunities present themselves.

Thus CAFPDE was tied in the course of the struggle with many ropes that would not let it move forward. Civic organizations assigned "associate" membership resented the political parties that have full membership. Most abandoned the work of the coalition, and the task rested on the backs of a few gallant fighters, such as Dr. Beyene. Even Dr. Beyene himself the chairman of CAFPDE attended a peace searching meeting in Washington DC initiated by

CHAPTER TEN: EPRP IN THE DIASPORA

American ex-congressman Harry Johnston representing not CAFPDE, but instead, representing the Southern Peoples Democratic Union. Slowly, the energy was sucked out of the coalition, and it was once again time to re-energize.

All the Paris 1 organizations minus the OLF attended Paris 2 held September 8 to 11, 1998 for three days. The OLF, despite the positive signs it showed at Paris 1 took back two steps and was a no show. New organizations not present at Paris 1, such as ONC were present. AAPO declined to attend Paris 2 saying "it finds it impossible to sit together with those who have picked up arms (sic!). The political back drop of the country was reeking of war with Eritrea.

After drafting the usual resolutions, Paris 2 established an executive committee to coordinate the struggle. Dr. Negede and Dr. Aregawi were elected chair and vice-chair respectively. Ato Mamo Yihunie of Medhin was elected the secretary, and Ato Kifle Tigneh was assigned to coordinate the home-based struggle in a capacity as a vice-chair.

Paris 2 was probably the coalition where EPRP members and supporters showed the least interest in coalition politics (it was hard enough to convince a sector of the membership that has not forgiven Meison and nursed grudges when COEDF was formed). Paris 1 led to the Ghion Conference, so there was reason to work hard for that. But Paris 2? Where was that going? For most, it was just not clear until election 2005 drew nearer and brought with it fresh hope of a meaningful struggle. And before the bustling activities around election 2005, there was an encouraging development that rekindled the hope of EPRP members to once again re-connect with Ethiopians in the countryside.

Some Ethiopians, including even those in the opposition ranks, are sometimes heard faulting the opposition parties and the coalitions for having no vision of their own for the country, and for often reacting to TPLF's initiatives.

This is largely an unfair criticism. In addition to having solid alternative political programs, most Ethiopian opposition parties and coalitions have prepared and distributed strategic papers on the key issues of Ethiopia's democratization. These include a peace and reconciliation blueprint, a transitional government charter, and a democratization and free election guidance. These are just but few examples.

EPRP's 25th Anniversary Symposium

EPRP members in the Diaspora celebrate the party's annual anniversary in most cities they reside in. The party's 25th anniversary was celebrated in Los Angeles at the Red Lion Hotel near Los Angeles International Airport in 1997. It was different from the other anniversaries in that the committee tasked with the preparations invited intellectuals and activists from across the spectrum of Ethiopian politics, and the attendance was a success. It was held From June 29th through July 1st. The theme of the Conference was honoring the Ethiopian Youth. One of the members of the preparatory committee, GB, was a key factor in meticulously planning the program and the celebrations. Also, the Los Angeles party committee members, such as Abune Biru, Mulugeta Alemu, Zewdu Mersha, Tafesse Woubshet, Alemu Endale, Daniel Kiddu and Danny Boy (Daniel Abebe), and the late Afework Belay and the late Endalkachew Yirgu (Chiqi) played exceptional roles in making the event a success. All conference sessions were well attended with an overflowing crowd.

The daily program was executed as follows:

June 29
9:00-11:00 -Registration
11:00-12:00 -Welcoming speech by the Los Angeles party committee representative; introducing the daily chairs and scribes; distribution of a booklet consisting the names of EPRP's martyrs; recognition of the sacrifices made by those who are/were wounded and injured in the struggle, commemorating those who were and still are jailed, and honoring the professional revolutionaries of EPRP; reading solidarity messages and a poem.
12:00-1:30-Lunch
1:30-1:45-Solidarity message from the European branch of EPRP
1:45-2:30-A message from EPRP
2:30-3:15-A call for struggle by senior party members
3:15-3:30- Reading of 2 poems
3:30-3:45- Coffee break
3:45-5:00- Video show: a) Message from Mersha Yosef (who was away on assignment with the Ethiopian Patriotic Front); (b) a video titled "From the Ethiopian Student Movement to EPRA"

CHAPTER TEN: EPRP IN THE DIASPORA

5:00-6:00-Posters and Informal discussions
6:00-7:00- Reception
June 30
9:00-9:30-Conference Opening; opening remarks -A Youth View, Hamrawit Tesfa; Conference Welcome -Getachew Begashaw; Honoring the martyrs
9:30-10:30-Session I, chair- Dr. Abrham Engida:
"Reflective Assessment of the Past, Present, and Future" -Gebru Gebrewold & Getachew Begashaw;
"Back casting for Gaining Foresight: Some Lessons on the Ethiopian Transition from the Student Movement to Party Political Movement Between 1972-74" -Prof. Mamo Muche
10:30-11:00 -Coffee Break
11:00-12:00 -Session II, chair-Dr. Solomon Gashaw
"The Political Status of Youthful Women: Prognosis for the 21st Century" -Prof. Tsehai Berhane Selassie
"Documented Sacrifice: The Experience of Young Ethiopians Now Seeking Political Asylum Abroad" -Prof. Theodore Vestal
12:30-1:45-Lunch break
1:45-2:15-Poetry reading; solidarity message/invited guest: Prof. Getachew Haile
2:15-3:15 -Session III, chair-Prof. Paulos Milkias
"The Youth and the Struggle of the Ethiopian People for Equality" -Kiflu Tadesse
"Differing Perspectives on the Structural Problems Hindering the Resolution of the Present Political Impasse in Ethiopia: The Tigrean Factor" - Dr. Assefa Negash
3:45-4:00 -Coffee break
4:00-5:30- Session IV, chair -Prof. Alemante Gebreselasse
"Are We Defeated?" -Iyassu Alemayehu
"When It Is Our Turn in History" -Dr. Mulugeta Siyum
July 1st
9:00-9:30- Poetry reading; solidarity message/invited guest: Prof. Habte Giorgis Churnet
9:30-11:00- Session V, chair-Prof. Tsehai Berhane Selassie
"A Reappraisal of the Political Role of the Ethiopian Youth" -Dr. Shumet Sishagne
"The Ethiopian Youth -Then and Now" - Dr. Solomon Gashaw
11:00-11:15-Coffee break
11:15-12:45- Session VI, chair: Dr. Shumet Sishagne

"The Survival of the Ethiopian Nation State and the Youth" - Prof. Alemante Gebreselasse

"The Sacrifices and Contributions of the Ethiopian Youth" -Prof. Paulos Milkias

12:45-2:00- Lunch break
2:00-2:15- Poetry reading
2:15-3:00- Open Forum: What is To Be Done?
3:00-3:30- Conference closing; closing remarks -Iyassu Alemayehu

Other contributed papers included the following:

"Global Ideologies and the Structuring of Identities: Ethiopian Intellectuals and Youth, 1960-1990"-Dr. Tsegaye Tegenu
"Reassessing Decentralization: The Case of Education in Ethiopia"-Dr. Minga Negash
On July 1, the last day of the conference there was a dinner party and dance, and the conference celebrating the 25th anniversary of EPRP's emergence was officially closed.

EPRP Political Work in Europe

Likewise, the 25th Anniversary of the Party was also observed in Europe in Frankfurt. In fact, we should say a few more things about EPRP's political work in Europe. Just like North America did, in Europe too, party committees, enlisted those willing to fight with the EPRA and facilitated their travel to the fields. As pressures intensified on the party in the late 70's through the work of the Anjas, and TPLF's pressure on the EPRA in Tigrai, this had an adverse effect on the student union in Europe. The foreign committee representatives, Melaku and Iyassou, tried to find solutions, and had some success in that regard. Those in Germany were probably ahead of everyone in Europe in terms of party activism. Emigrants from the USSR started flocking to Frankfurt and other cities and were organized as members and supporters. The party contact there was Chekene Eshete.

The asylum seekers from the USSR were assigned in various German cities, and the party tried to establish contacts for them in their new places. In 1980, a cell in Cologne notified the party that they would not be able to send a representative to the field for the 2nd Party Congress, but forwarded some questions through their contact Chekene, who in turn passed the questions to his contact, Genet Girma. Replies from the top leadership were slow in coming. When Chekene passed away as a result of a serious illness, party work in Cologne nearly froze.

After the Quarra 2nd Congress, at first Iyassou, following him Mersha and Fassika talked to ex-members in Germany, France, and Switzerland. Genet and Kahsai were assigned to build on the work the three senior members started. Both Kahsai and Genet had attended the 2nd Congress. Kahsai first went to London, then to Germany to follow up on the organizational tasks. He also attended the Toronto Conference held in 1990 and soon after passed away in Cologne.

Again, party work came nearly to a halt, and Genet repeatedly asked the party leadership for help. In 1993, the party leadership assigned Mohammed to take over and lead the European organizational work. By consulting and collaborating with Genet, party work was structured in many cities, and regional committees established within a year and a half in Switzerland, Holland, Germany, Sweden, Norway, Finland, England, Belgium and Italy. All committees in these areas, except for the ones in Belgium, Finland, and Italy, continued functioning until the party split into two in 2008. Also, the Sweden branch had a particularly grave problem of mistrust and inability to work together among comrades that lingered for far too long.

A European zonal committee was established to provide leadership and guidance. Some of its accomplishments include: member recruitment, holding meetings in various cities, fundraising activities, diplomatic and human rights work, hosting the 3rd Party Congress in Bonn, as stated above staging the Party's 25th Anniversary celebrations, establishing a minimum of 25 support committees in Germany alone- with a membership number ranging between 450 and 500; holding at least 7 membership conferences up to 2004, assigning members to participate in Ethiopian community social activities, and leading discussions on the new party program.

Ethiopian Patriotic Front/Army

The Ethiopian Patriotic Front, or as it is sometimes called the Ethiopian Patriotic Army was formed in 1997. It was formed by the decision of the following organizations: COEDF, The Beni Shangul

People's Liberation Movement, a faction of Kefagne. EPF should not be confused with the EPPF that is housed in Sha'abia's Eritrea.

It may not be entirely accurate to state that COEDF as a coalition was behind the formation of EPF. Meto Aleka Ayalsew Desse, in his serialized coalition narration, part 6 states that the formation of EPF was one issue COEDF constituent members did not fully endorse. To be fair, especially after the failure of the Ghion Peace and Reconciliation Conference by TPLF's intransigence, there have been on and off attempts to launch an armed struggle. EPRP leaders around East Africa were gathering and camping willing former army members now refugees. The cost of their maintenance was significant. One hope was to launch the armed struggle with the help of the South Sudanese. But with Rick Mechar's dissident group working closely with the TPLF, that plan failed.

From the available evidence, EPF seems to be the brain child of one of the members of COEDF, EPRP. Mersha Yosef was entrusted with the leadership of EPF.

The army was formed of former army officers that came to Sudan from Kenya and Uganda; university students that resided at the time in Kenya, and almost all of whom were EPRP members; refugees in various Sudanese cities most of whom once belonged to political parties, such as EDU, EPDM, etc.; and former members of EPRA. The three senior EPRP members in East Africa were responsible for the recruitment and maintenance -Iyassu, Mersha and Mohammed. EPF was formed in haste. The reason for that was Iyassu had received word from a Sudanese military attaché in Paris that Sudan might be able to help EPRP at that juncture because of a temporary spat with TPLF. For the experienced EPRP, things had to be done fast before the political winds changed direction. The Sudanese promised to arm up to 10,000 recruits. This promise had the undesirable effect of recruiting all sorts of available persons, even spies as it was discovered later.

The EPRP transported its dedicated members and supporters from East Africa to Sudan for the EPF project. Prior to that about 13 EPRP members were deployed to Borana to explore the feasibility of launching an armed struggle. However, they were all murdered by the OLF, and the party had protested this despicable and cowardly action.

The military training of the new recruits took place in Assosa with the help of the Benishangul Liberation partners. It was a four month

CHAPTER TEN: EPRP IN THE DIASPORA

training from August to November of 1997. The biggest problem at the training camps was shortage of food. The Benishanguls, whether members of EPF or just locals, would share the army's free food and planning to feed EPF recruits was difficult. As soon as the training was completed, the Benishangul leadership was not willing to guide the army into its operational area around Quarra. They wanted the food supply to continue, and they also wanted a joint operation with EPF to liberate one of their towns, Gizen. When they were asked to produce a military plan for the attack, they could not. Finally, the army decided to bribe some lower-level Benishanguli officials to serve as guides and left Assosa. After traveling for 21 days, the army arrived in Omedla. The guides were a 30-man strong group, and after arriving at Omedla, they went back.

From Omedla, the army traveled to a lowland area called Atish that is close to the Sudanese border towns of Fazra and Kershefil.

The first army leadership committee consisted of 5 persons: Tamrat- an EPRP member that was jailed by the Dirgue for 8 years, and who was a 5th year engineering student (close to graduation) before he left for Kenya. In Kenya, he was doing organizational work on behalf of EPRP and COEDF. He was coopted as a CC member in November 1995 by party members of the East African zone, assigned to be EPF's senior political officer; the second member was Major Negash Hailemariam, the EPF commander and a former officer who was among those the party recruited in Uganda to undertake armed struggle; the third was Dagmawi Awoke, a sociology graduate of AAU, and with work experience, strong and disciplined; the fourth was Faisel, a Kottebei Teachers College graduate, and who was a 3rd year AAU student when he was gang pressed by the Dirgue to the Blatei farm, and the fifth was Captain Denekew, a former officer assigned in EPF to be the deputy commander.

While the army trekked from Assosa to Omedla, the deputy commander was dispatched to Sudan to tell the party representatives of the march and to prepare them to provide the army with logistics. Unfortunately, the deputy commander was imprisoned by Sudan's security forces, and when the army reached its destination, there were no provisions. The beginning army was heavily demoralized, and some started deserting the army. Because of the pressing situation to feed the army, the leadership decided to go into the villages sooner than they had planned.

The people initially warmly received the army, and EPF disarmed some armed guards collecting about 27 guns. Based on this initial incursion, the army leadership decided to start a training camp and found a base camp. The army was divided into two, the commander leading the first batch, and the political officer the second. Perhaps burdening themselves with too much heavy stuff for a beginning army, such as carrying generators, a supply of medicine, books, and communication equipment, not to speak of camels and donkeys, the army's movement slowed down. Sadly, they encountered this time unlike their first incursion, Woyannie soldiers stationed in every village and on the lookout. There were a few skirmishes. Noting that their load was a burden, they buried most of the non-essential stuff and re-organized themselves in squads.

One of the biggest problems EPF faced was the turf war between those who were affiliated with EPRP/A, and those that hailed from the Dirgue's army. There was mutual recrimination and detest of each other's capacity to lead. This mistrust was simmering, and never resolved despite some attempts. At the end of the kremt rainy season, EPF forces attacked Salia (Tewodros Ketema), and netted some 200 arms and ample ammunition. Soon after this victory, the senior political officer of the army was canvassing the border area to purchase supplies for the army when he was suddenly ambushed by government forces.

TPLF, realizing that this force could grow in leaps and bounds, focused its attention on attacking and destroying it. Even as the war with Eritrea was in full swing, TPLF first attacked EPF and caused considerable damage. The desertion in the army, that had ceased for over 9 months, started afresh. A new clique that was supposed to set exemplary behavior for the younger fighters started exacerbating problems by its undisciplined actions and lack of subordination. By contrast, comrades like Dilu, who was the replacement leader after the leadership causalities, was a dedicated humanist who could have emigrated to the West had he wanted to. But regardless of his deteriorating eyesight, he put his country's and party's goals ahead of his, and provided important leadership in the critical period.

Despite the internal and external pressure, the people were still very warm towards the fighters. They had a good memory of the EPRA from 8 years back. The first question a peasant asked an armed unit was if they were EPRAites. A positive answer facilitated good relations. Even EPPF forces who happened to pass through the

CHAPTER TEN: EPRP IN THE DIASPORA

area lied to the people that EPRA was part of their movement. A few volunteers traveled from distant areas to join the army. Particularly, the Agew nationality youth were very fond of the army. TPLF could not brood this open show of love to EPF/EPRA. The punishment was swift and brutal. TPLF murdered an Agew family led by Ato Agidew simply because they exercised their right to like and support a party.

As feared, Sudan started warming up its relations with TPLF, and were looking for sacrificial lambs to show their friendship. Mersha had to evacuate Sudan immediately. The army could not transfer its sick and wounded, and TPLF's wars of annihilation were unceasing, thus after 2 years, the end of the final chapter of armed struggle in EPRP's 4 decades of existence became a reality.

EPF was saddled with many internal and external problems. Pretenders of all sorts used its name to raise funds for their own goals, or simply to sabotage the effort: Dr. Andualem Mulaw, Major Getachew Yerom, Tohat Paul, etc. created confusion and havoc.

UEDF

After the folding of the armed struggle perhaps for the last time in Ethiopia's political history, some patriotic groups were trying to bring together opposition forces. Two of the prominent ones are a committee called Gubae-Abew led by Colonel Asnake Engida and the Ethiopian National Congress (ENC). ENC has been trying to bring the Ethiopian opposition forces together for a long time, and it had once again its hand print on the formation of UEDF.

According to Meto Aleka Ayalsew Desse, organizations participating at ENC's urging which resolved to examine the unity formation experience and draw valuable lessons got together and started discussions. These organizations and their representatives were the following: EPRP (Ato Fassika Belete), Meison (the late Ato Mulugeta Hailu), Hibre-Hizb (Meto Aleka Ayalsew Desse), Southern Peoples (the late Ato Kedir Mohammed), CAFPDE (Ato Assefa Depaso), Tigrean Democratic Alliance (Ato Teshome Tsegaye). Although ONC was not represented by an individual, Dr. Merera Gudina's organization was a founding member. A representative of the OLF, Ato Ababiya Abajobir, sporadically attended the exploratory meetings[1]. This was in mid-2001.

To give more shape and continuity to the discussions, the exploratory meeting attendants decided to establish a 3-man executive committee and meet weekly. Accordingly, Dr. Desta Damtew from Hibre-Hizb was named the chair person, Ato Fassika Belete of EPRP was the secretary and the late Ato Kedir Mohammed of the Southern Peoples Democratic Organization was the deputy secretary[2].

It has to be noted that the facilities for these meetings were provided by EPRP by making its offices and supplies readily available. Two of the UEDF leaders have at various times acknowledged this contribution and expressed their appreciation. These are Dr. Beyene Petros and Meto Aleka Ayalsew Desse. The later goes back in history and notes EPRP's steadfast contribution over a 7-year period for the union formation, and encouraging all its branches and members to support the unity effort[3].

In addition to the 5 organizations that were engaged in the exploratory meetings, OLF as the seventh was on and off attending, as stated above. Soon after EDU, under the leadership of Major Iyassu Ayalkbet joined. Then, All Ethiopian Unity Party, despite the misgivings of some members, decided to join in October 2003. The same was true of EDP. The total number came close to 10. A year and a half after the efforts got underway, Medhin too, joined, and with that, most of the Ethiopian opposition appeared to be aligning together once again.

The executive committee soon started establishing branches and support committees. As in previous unity formation discussions, the two questions on the priority list were one where to hold the meeting and then when. Because school would be out abroad in the summer (kremit in Ethiopia), that was the consensus choice. As to the place, perhaps learning from the bad experience of the 1993 Ghion conference, it was decided to hold the meeting in Washington DC. Another issue needing a resolution was setting criteria for

---

1. see Meto Aleka Ayalsew Desse's serialized writings distributed on Ethiomedia on COEDF, subsequent UFs and UEDF formations, 2010; part 14
2. ibid.
3. ibid.

CHAPTER TEN: EPRP IN THE DIASPORA

determining the viability of political organizations that sought membership in the unity forming conference. Thus 8 criteria were agreed upon. At this time, OLF that has been participating irregularly requested if it could participate at the conference as an observer, and that question was quickly rejected[4].

In order to make the Conference as representative as possible, and as inclusive of the broad swaths of Ethiopian society, invitations were sent to the following: EHRCO, Ethiopian Independent Journalists Association, women's and youth groups, and renowned individuals. Some modest financial contributions was made to some of the invitees to facilitate their transport costs and lodging at the conference.

The Conference dates were decided to be July 27 through August 2, 2003. 17 organizations were registered to participate. Organizations were represented by 3 delegates each. 15 of the 17 were so represented, however, the Afar Democratic Union Organization, was able to be represented by one delegate as its two delegates could not get visas out of Africa[5].

On July 26, 2003, one day before the opening of the conference, there was a ceremony that brought together the community, and representatives. Although invitations were sent out to all religious leaders, only Abune Elias from the Ethiopian Orthodox Church attended and blessed the conference. A list of dignitaries, including the late Tsegaye Gebremedhin, poet extraordinaire, gave ringing speeches. The executive committee allowed each organization to introduce its party and its delegates. Later, there was a cocktail party given to foreign dignitaries and members of Congress.

The next day, the meeting was opened by Lij Michael Imiru, a former Prime Minister. There were 42 delegates (41 men and one woman), 9 members of the Conference preparatory committee, 3 note takers, two videographers, and 2 monitors (to attend to any needs of the participants). Security personnel were assigned by each organization and were posted outside. The first day passed with the discussion of past unity formation efforts.

At the end of the 7-day conference, the following decisions were made: 1. The new coalition that would have members abroad and inside the country was to be called Union of Ethiopian Democratic

---

4. ibid., part 15
5. ibid.

Forces, UEDF; 2. The coalitions formed over the past few years were nullified, with the exception of CAFPDE (this exception was afforded to CAFPDE because there were parliamentarians in the parliament that won hard-fought battles to get their seats, and these seats were not to be thrown to the wind after so much sacrifice)[6]; 3. The form of struggle chosen by the coalition was exclusively peaceful; 4.The coalition was to lead the struggle both inside the country and abroad, including waging a diplomatic struggle to force the EPRDF to accept open, democratic, fair and free elections. To that effect, UEDF formed structures to effectuate its plans.

EPRP was represented by Tegegne, Fassika and the newly arrived to the US, Mersha. EPRP had long resolved to engage in an all-embracing struggle. Although it dropped this strategy at times in deference to its coalition members (Paris 1, Ghion, Paris 2), and now for UEDF, it seemed to be another arena the all-embracing struggle was to be shelved. During the initial discussions on methods of struggle, those coming from inside Ethiopia naturally preferred a peaceful struggle. Others, such as the Gambella democratic organization, IBSO (an Oromo organization led by Olana Lemu), ARDUF and EPRP stated their preference for an all-embracing struggle (within the EPRP leadership, this issue has been a simmering pole of divisive issue as we will see below). Finally, as has been happening over the last decade, the peaceful -struggle- only plank won and was UEDF's strategy.

UEDF's position on participating in the elections was to some people vague and open to distortion. UEDF had never resolved to register and participate without any conditions. Rather, it decided to struggle for free and fair elections. As it stated repeatedly, if it decided the elections were not free and fair, it had the option to boycott the elections. As a result, when the 2005 national elections rolled around, UEDF did not have much time when it decided to participate and field candidates.

But before it even got to the elections, 2 of the founding members, EDP and AEUP, started making trouble. While the UEDF formation was underway in Rockville, Maryland, Dr. Berhanu Nega and Prof. Mesfin Woldemariam were in the US at the same time and in contact with the delegates of these two parties. According to Dr. Berhanu Nega, just before he and Prof. Mesfin left for the US (close

---

6. ibid.

CHAPTER TEN: EPRP IN THE DIASPORA

to the UEDF formation date), they had talked to AEUP in Addis about forming CUD, and AEUP has already agreed. So, Berhanu and Mesfin knew well ahead that they would be able to snatch AEUP and EDP away from UEDF, and thus continue the cycle of the lack of a single opposition center in Ethiopian opposition politics[7]. At the end of UEDF's formation Conference, Berhanu states that they contacted EDP's delegates, Dr. Admassu and Lidetu, who briefed the pair about the Conference and their decision right there not to continue in UEDF. The pair then asked them if they would join them in forming CUD, and they were reportedly elated[8]. Thus, the saga of coalition formation runs into hurdles repeatedly undermined by political intrigues and machinations.

AEUP, perhaps after realizing that its leader, Hailu Shawul, was not to be the first chairman of UEDF, and because of its prior deal with Berhanu and Mesfin, started withdrawing its name from other office slates. It gradually adopted an obstructionist position, and met only once for executive committee meetings. This obstructionist position by AEUP had internally damaged the organization, as reflected by the dissatisfaction of AEUP delegation's leader, the late Dr. Mekonnen Bishaw, and the disillusionment of AEUP's NA Branch leader Ato Wondayehu Kassa who has been instrumental in the conception and execution of the UEDF notion[9].

There were 3 issues AEUP raised as reasons for its problems with UEDF: 1. objecting to the structure of UEDF that had a shengo and executive committee structure, decisions AEUP itself wholeheartedly endorsed and voted for during the Conference; 2. objecting to the establishment of UEDF support committees (both EDP and AEUP supported only organizational support committee, and not a coalition support committee); 3. regarding elections both organizations objected to the coalition standing as one, since they argued that a coalition standing would undermine their organizational independence. EDP, after itself not carrying out its assigned tasks, blamed UEDF "for not doing anything on the ground a year after its formation".

---

7. Berhanu Nega. Yenetsanet Goh Siked (in Amharic). M.M. Publishing, Kampala, 2006, p. 215
8. ibid.
9. Meto Aleka Ayalsew Desse., part 18

EDP and AEUP were looking for pretexts to bolt out of UEDF, and form another coalition. That was proven a few months later when 4 organizations, including EDP and AEUP, formed CUD and contested the 2005 elections. UEDF's strategy of bringing all the opposition under one umbrella was dashed, and two coalitions (UEDF and CUD) squared off against TPLF, with disastrous results for all the opposition.

One of the decisions of UEDF at its Conference, and subsequently, was to open a dialogue with EPRDF, to find peaceful solutions to the differences between government and opposition. To that effect, UEDF had presented to EPRDF 29 ideas to make the 2005 election free and fair. EPRDF expressed its willingness to discuss these and other issues. UEDF had already assigned delegates in the event an opportunity arose to engage in a talk with regime representatives. The delegates were Dr. Beyene Petros, Dr. Merera Gudina, Dr. Admassu Gebeyehu and Ato Mulu Mejja. On February 4, 2004, a 2-hour talk took place in the Prime Minister's office. Meles used the forum to threaten and intimidate UEDF's delegates. He was dismissive about the key demands of UEDF for a free and fair election. For instance, the issue of a neutral election board was dismissed offhand, and Meles said it was not even a topic of discussion. He, however, added that logistics and election procedures could be discussed. Similarly, he underscored that foreign election monitors would not be allowed. He concluded the talks by stating that a team led by Bereket Simeon would continue the discussions, and the fruitless talks continued for almost a year without any tangible results.

When election 2005 finally came, some structural problems inside UEDF that were masked by "unity" came to surface. Indeed the pre-election work abroad by support committees was admirable. Funds were being raised to support candidates and their election efforts. Supporters were asked to sponsor a candidate with $250. Diplomatic struggles were underway to pressure EPRDF to hold free and fair elections.

During the debates with CUD/EPRDF officials, UEDF's performance was less than stellar. The home-based leadership's inability to marshall the help of intellectuals for the debates was a stark contrast to CUD's marvelous performance. Of course, EPRDF was its usual laughable self, and it exposed more its shallowness and vulnerability. UEDF was to contest the election not as a coalition,

CHAPTER TEN: EPRP IN THE DIASPORA

but mainly as Southern Peoples and ONC. This was again in contrast to CUD's image as an Ethiopian organization in juxtaposition to the hated tribalized politics of EPRDF that ONC/SEPDC were feared to reflect.

Many UEDF supporters were not sure whether they were funding the sectarian interests of Drs. Merera and Beyene. UEDF's finishing in the election as the junior party was not received well. Then things started unraveling. Drs. Merera and Beyene seemed to have calculated that their partners in UEDF located abroad were not to give them directions about the home-based struggle, and they were keen on keeping their organizations intact and legal in the face of EPRDF's fury after its electoral defeat when it declared an emergency and went after the legal opposition with vengeance. Without the endorsement of UEDF's executive committee, UEDF-A.A., decided to participate in the fake tri-partite post election irregularity investigation, consisting of EPRDF, CUD and UEDF. After this futile exercise, all the leaders of CUD went to jail after refusing to take their seats in parliament, and after EPRDF blamed them for the deaths of nearly 200 people whom it murdered in cold blood.

However, the leaders of UEDF in Addis decided to take their parliamentary seats despite UEDF's executive committee's decision, and despite the decision of UEDF's parliamentary candidates. Their decision to take up their seats in parliament created havoc inside UEDF, and worse, created resentment among CUD supporters whose leaders ended up in jail.

The conference for UEDF's parliamentary candidates took place in Addis at the end of July and beginning of August, 2005. This was 3 months after the May election. The candidates were asked to fill a form on issues such as what they thought of the election, process, and what UEDF needed to do in the future to ensure a peaceful and legal democratization. About 330 candidates participated[10]. Only 4.3% candidates (13) expressed entering parliament might help the struggle, while a solid 95% expressed their view that taking up parliamentary seats in the circumstances was not helpful.

Notwithstanding the survey, Drs. Merera and Beyene took up their seats by violating the decisions of their own constituents, in a body in which they made some noise for 5 years until they were

---

10. ibid., part 21

completely booted out of that rubber stamp institution in the 2010 election.

Perhaps one person that should not be forgotten in reference to the 2005 elections in Ethiopia is Ana Gomes. The Portuguese socialist and the then member of the European Parliament was the lone voice that defended Ethiopian democratization and rule of law for which she incurred the wrath of EPRDF.

Alliance for Freedom and Democracy (AFD)

Within a year after the May 2005 elections, and while the CUD leaders were languishing in jail, an effort was under way by opposition parties and fronts to form a new coalition. What made this effort unique was the fact that the endeavor brought together ethnonationalist forces that were avowedly seeking secession from Ethiopia and Ethiopianist forces in a scale unseen before. The initial partners in this effort were the Oromo Liberation Front, the Ogaden National Liberation Front, UEDF, the Sidama Liberation Front, the Ethiopian People's Patriotic Front, and CUD (CUD was represented by a faction of the NA Chapter).

While consultations were underway among the parties on how to prepare for the formation of the coalition, according to UEDF, an invitation dated May 12, 2006 was sent to it by OLF to be present in Utrecht, Holland, from May 19-22, for the signing ceremony of the new coalition[11].

Although this was a total surprise and undemocratic, UEDF elected to attend the front formation meeting where documents already prepared without the participation and agreement of all were distributed, and an effort made to form the AFD in an underhanded way. Needless to say, in the same press release discussed above, UEDF announced that it was not a founding member and part of the new coalition.

The AFD was formed by Abdulkadir Hirmooge, 2nd vice-chairman of the ONLF; by Meskerem Atalay, EPPF chairman; by Dawud Ibssa, chairman of OLF; by Yosef Yazew, CUD NA committee chairman; and by Galfato Feqa, chairman of the SLF[12].

---

11. UEDF Press Release dated May 22, 2006
12. BBC's post on the web dated May 23, 2006

CHAPTER TEN: EPRP IN THE DIASPORA

The AFD was gripped with crises as soon as its formation was made public. Although some gullible voices lauded its formation, and only saw it as the ticket to the dismantling of the TPLF, calmer minds steadily showed the programmatic, vision and democratic problems of the new alliance. Some of the prominent problems included: (1) in its bylaws, chapter 1, article 2, it said that those with separatist and secessionist agendas will maintain their positions; (2) in its item 8 in article 1, the statutes promise to promote good relations between Eritrea and Ethiopia (most of the signatories either reside in Eritrea or/and are financed by the Eritrean government); (3) in the "Understandings" part of the memorandum, it says that the AFD shall convene an inclusive conference to establish a workable arrangement on the basis of the present framework of the Ethiopian constitution (this when Article 39 of the constitution and its entire architecture built on ethnic federalism is a big issue for most Ethiopians).

Representatives of CUD in AFD were particularly under tremendous pressure to explain these anti-Ethiopia and anti-democratic stances, and their legitimacy to represent CUD in the Alliance was openly questioned.

UEDF had submitted several documents to the alliance partners to help lay the foundation of the Alliance on a solid ground. Unfortunately, these were not heeded, and in what can only be described as a sinister move, the OLF and its secessionist partners embarked to singularly own the alliance formation enterprise that eventually led to a disaster, and to the death of the AFD before it was even born. It crashed under the weight of the contradictions of its bylaws, statutes, and memorandum of understandings against the wishes and aspirations of most Ethiopians expressed at the polls not too long ago in May of 2005.

In conclusion, the struggles of the Ethiopian opposition to create a durable coalition, with EPRP often at the forefront, ebbed and flowed over the last 2 decades. One conventional wisdom is that the strength of EPRDF largely emanates from the disunity of its opposition. The formula for solid unity has so far been elusive. Currently, inside Ethiopia, there are some hopeful signs such as the coming together of most of the legitimate opposition under MEDREK. However, there are other opposition forces, such as AEUP, that are still outside. The pain of this reality hurts acutely during an election cycle when opposition candidates vie against each other.

These traditional unity forming forces, such as Meison, and EPRP (democratic) along with a few civic groups formed in May 2012 yet another coalition called *Shengo*.

As to EPRP, the fact that it had been nearly two decades since the party moved its center of operation from inside Ethiopia to the Diaspora bothered many of its members. Although formed abroad in 1972, EPRP flourished and expanded inside the country following the Yekatit Revolution. During those golden years, EPRP was indisputably the largest opposition party in Ethiopia. Following TPLF's coming to power, and the party's armed activities permanently dismantled, the center of operations moved abroad, and the party's role as the leading opposition party gradually diminished. Surely, the party has had cells and structures inside Ethiopia operating clandestinely, but nowhere near to describe the operations central to the party's activities.

Since the coming to power of TPLF, the party had genuinely tried to peacefully and legally operate inside Ethiopia. Giving the lame and contradictory excuses of at one time that party and its allies were not armed (therefore could not participate in the London Conference in 1991), and at other times accusing it of not renouncing violence (to deny it legal participation inside the country), the TPLF has shown that it was in no mood to slightly veer from the script of its autocratic rule.

During the prelude to the 2005 elections, Meles and EPRDF by their own admission took a calculated risk to open up the political space. One aspect of this was a promise to allow the Diaspora-based opposition to operate inside the country on the condition that the interested parties foreswear violence. This presented a narrow opportunity in the eyes of those members who were concerned with being shut off the country's day-to-day politics, and about their inability to live and work among their own people. This, however, was not shared by all members. Other members saw the opportunity as surrender and relished Diaspora politics. To EPRP's credit, a democratic mechanism was implemented to tally the votes, and the group that refused legally operating inside Ethiopia narrowly won in a 49-51 vote - but due to the sloppiness of those in the minority to get the votes of party members in Africa to be counted. These members later joined EPRP(d). Thus, a golden opportunity for the

CHAPTER TEN: EPRP IN THE DIASPORA

party to re-plant itself inside Ethiopia was squandered and disparaged as a "qorqoro" opportunity, and the party which could have played a critical role in the heady days of the 2005 election was still a Diaspora tiger, roaring from distance.

The last congress EPRP as a unitary party held was the fourth Congress that was held from April 8, 2006 through April 13 in Atlanta. The agendas included the land question and agricultural policy; social issues, the nationality question including the question of Eritrea (where unlike during the 3rd congress existing policy was affirmed and there was no heated discussion); federalism; social democracy as the party's guiding ideology and orientation; foreign affairs, methods of struggle, and on united front.

The differences and subtexts in the party simmered below the surface for several months, and exacerbated the additional concerns most members had about the leadership's accountability, transparency, and democratic practice. This boiled over in the summer of 2008 in DC where even holding the 5th Congress was impossible due to the acuteness of the differences, and led to the split and formation of EPRP (democratic). Within a year and half, EPRP (d) itself had another group split off of it. Ever since the split, initiatives and efforts have been underway to patch the split, and re-create EPRP as a whole unit again. The split has not appreciably helped either party; it has weakened the already struggling party in its quest to reclaim its once dominant opposition role.

As we have seen in this book, the members and ex-members who answered EPRP's call in August 1975 when the party was officially declared were from all over the country and its diverse ethnic groups. They were determined to give their lives for a noble cause. Many did. Others went to jail and served long sentences. Others were physically injured, and if alive, they are living with their physical and psychological pain and scars. Still others climbed the mountains, crossed the rivers, usually with little or nothing to eat for days.

Continuing this frugality and selflessness in their gray hair, those who are still in EPRP have amazingly continued marinating in the struggle sacrificing their time and money, for a struggle they started as brash youngsters. What makes this sacrifice unique and admirable is the fact that it is being paid when members fully well know that there is no return on their investment. Indisputably, it is truly a mark of altruistic cause. They were and still are convinced that no national problem is beyond solution as long as Ethiopians in their millions rally around national goals. History will show in the coming decades if their struggles and convictions were just utopian and idealist, or realizable.

Wherever EPRP set foot, today the refrain *Be EHAPA Gize* (meaning when EPRP was around, or during the period of EPRP's activism) is fondly recalled. In urban Ethiopia, it is a longing for the commitment and selflessness of the members. In rural Ethiopia, from Tigray to Quarra, it is the memory of the party's sense of justice, fairness, emphasis on gender equality, and above all, its humility.

Photo: EPRP celebrated its anniversaries with supporters and members. Here Hamrawit Tesfa, one of the guest speakers and daughter of Dr. Tesfaye Debessay, addressing the audience at the celebration of the 25th anniversary of the party's founding, July 1997, Los Angeles (see chapter 10 for details).

CHAPTER TEN: EPRP IN THE DIASPORA

Photo: Here a speaker addresses the audience at the 27th anniversary of the party celebrated in Washington DC in 1999.

Epilogue

The history of the last 30 years as documented here can be described in a number of ways: the partisans to the conflict may each claim that their side was struggling for many noble causes, such as democracy, equality and unity, and accuse their rivals for struggling to undermine these noble causes. As a result of the civil wars over the 3 decades, hundreds of thousands of lives have been lost, national resources squandered and destroyed, and communal enmity entrenched.

The fact that one of the protagonists ended up on the top, and is now a little over the last two decades the government, has not significantly diminished the entrenched inter-community suspicion and enmity, and the squandering of the nation's resources continues unabated if not on war materiel, on extensive and mind-boggling espionage and political incarceration of citizens. Only a genuine national reconciliation appears to be the fundamental solution. However, there are tangible hurdles that need to be overcome to implement a genuine national reconciliation. One, and perhaps the most important, is the asymmetry of power and strength between the government and the opposition and civil society. The ruling party commands the nation's resources, has international backing and legitimacy, and controls the security and repressive machinery of the state. Based on these assets, it may not have much motivation or desire to engage in a national dialogue that it considers might only result in the clipping and diminishing of its power and privileges. Compounding the problem, other forces arrayed against it are multi-variable, weak, and harassed. This dichotomy makes the notion of a genuine national reconciliation a pipe dream.

What to do?

Foreign friends and allies of the nation could be a neutral party to help bridge the gap. However, due to their operational procedures, they are perceived by each protagonist to have their own agendas and ulterior motives. For instance, human rights organizations and other non-governmental organizations are negatively seen by the regime as bent on undermining it and serving as a cover for sinister Western intentions. Similarly, Western governments are seen by the opposition and civil society as aiding and abetting a dictatorship, or supporting an autocratic system in the pursuit of their national interest dominant among which is the bi and multi-lateral politico-military engagement against radical Islam.

So, is anyone left to mediate?

Luckily, the current international situation does not favor a protracted armed struggle as in the 60's and 70's, thus obviating massive property and human life loss. However, it would be foolhardy for the regime and its supporters to bank on that and continue the business-as-usual marginalization and harassment of the opposition and civil society. History has shown in phases that urban mass upheaval could be as deadly and as destructive. Recall the Philippine revolution that drowned Markos in 1980, and then the anti-Communist uprisings of the mid-to-late 1980s in Eastern Europe, and the recent Arab Spring of the second decade of the new millennium.

So, the answer to fill the role of mediators has of necessity to look inwards to our tradition of the *shimgilina* culture. The institution of shimgilina is a time-honored, long running tradition of our people. A powerful, neutral, and national institution of shimaglewoch is badly needed. Attempts have been made since the last days of the Dirgue to appeal to regimes for a national dialogue. While Mengistu lived in his own dream world in his final days, and jettisoned any suggestion for a national dialogue, the current regime appears to have co-opted the institution and emptied it of its neutrality, and thus its trustworthiness. Recall its work around getting jailed citizens out of prison rather than dealing with the conditions that led in the first place for citizens' incarceration.

Ethiopia needs a powerful, neutral and indigenous *shimigellina* body. Its power emanates from its principled positions and the support it gets from citizens. Its challenges may be many, least of which, might be an overreaching regime that has the bad habit of

EPILOGUE

controlling all independent entities, and a populace impatient in its search for a neutral body. Its bylaws and constitution would be permeated by proposals of peace between political parties, religious communities, and regime and citizenry. Its success would depend on the support it gets from its constituency: the protagonists, and from the way it discharges its responsibilities.

With that institution in place and functional, the losses and deprivations narrated in the foregoing chapters, and other chapters of similarly-themed books, at long last, would be history, and all the people, hundred million-strong, would focus on economic development and cultural renaissance, and on defeating once and for all famine and poverty. Those of us old enough to have lived through the agonies of the stories of this book might be blessed to see the closing of a sad era, and the opening of a new one. If that is not the case for some of us, what more would be pleasing than knowing our progeny enjoy the fruits of trees planted by our *shimagelles*?

> *History says, Don't hope*
> *On this side of the grave.*
> *But then, once in a lifetime*
> *The longed for tidal wave*
> *Of justice can rise up,*
> *And Hope and History rhyme*

From *"The Cure at Troy"*, a translation of Sophocles by the Irish Nobel laureate, the recently deceased Seamus Heaney.

Selected Bibiography

Books

Abdulahi, Abdi. *Yaltadelew Tiwuld* (in Amharic). Negelle Borena, undated, most likely published between 1991-1995.

Abrha, Girmai. *Yemiyanebu Egroch* (in Amharic). Addis Abeba.

Aneme, Alemu-Girmachew, Schaefer, Charles, and Tronvoll, Kjetil, ed. *The Ethiopian Red Terror Trials*. Rochester, 2009.

Araya, Ghelawdewos. *Ethiopia: The Political Economy of Transition.* University of America, Inc., 1995

Araya Mekonnen. *Negotiating A Lion's Share of Freedom.* Lulu.com, 2011.

Asfaw, w. *Finixiwa Motam Tinesalech* (in Amharic): *The Uncrowned Struggle of Tigrean Women.* Addis Abeba: Far East Trading Publishers, 2009.

Assegid, Andargachew. *Bachir Yekerew Rejim Guzo* (in Amharic): *Meison inside the Ethiopian People's Struggle.* Addis Abeba: Central Printing Press, 2000.

Balsivik, Randi. *Haileselassie's Students: The Intellectual and Social Background to Revolution, 1952-77.* East Lansing: Michigan State University Press, 1985.

Berhan, Konjit. *Mirqogna* (in Amharic). Addis Abeba: Far East Trading Publishing, 2010.

Chambers, Whittaker. *Witness.* Regnery, 1987.

Clapham, Christopher. *Transformation and Continuity in Revolutionary Ethiopia.* New York: Cambridge University Press, 1988.

Deguefe, Tefera. *Minutes of An Ethiopian Century.* Addis Abeba: Shama Books, 2010.

Dinke, Berhanu. *Kesar and Abyot/Albo Zemed* (in Amharic).

Ethiopian Ministry of Justice. *Special Prosecutor's Charges Against Col. Mengistu Haile Mariam et al., and the Decisions of a Federal Higher Court* (in Amharic). Addis Abeba: September 2008.

Feleke Zenebe. *Neber, part ii* (in Amharic). Eleni Publishing, 2009.

Hailemariam, Mengistu. *Tigilachin* (in Amharic). Los Angeles: Tsehay Publishers, 2011.

Hailemariam, Yacob. *Asseb Yeman Nat?* (in Amharic).: *Question of Gateway to The Sea.* 2012.

Halliday, Fred. *The Ethiopian Transformation.* London: Verso Editors and NLB, 1983.

Hailu, Asmamaw. *EPRA.*(in Amharic), part i. Addis Abeba: 2010.

Harbeson, John. *The Ethiopian Transformation: The Quest for Post-imperial State.* Boulder: Westview Press, 1988.

Hareyo, Hareka. *KeNairobi Eske Jubilee Palace* (in Amharic). Addis Abeba, September 2004.

Henze, Paul. *Layers of Time: A History of Ethiopia.* New York: St. Martin's Press, 2000.

Kassa, Chanyalew. *Kedememelash Mekabir Afaf* (in Amharic). Addis Abeba.

Kebede, Messay. *Radicalism and Cultural Dislocation in Ethiopia, 1960-1974.* University of Rochester Press, 2008.

Keller, Edmund. *Revolutionary Ethiopia: From Empire to People's Republic.* Bloomington. Indiana University Press, 1988.

Kinde, Daniel. *The Five Dimensions of the Eritrean Conflict, 1941-2004: Deciphering the Geopolitical Puzzle.* Maryland: Signature Book Printing, 2005.

Kissi, Edward. *Revolution and Genocide in Ethiopia and Cambodia.* Lexington Books, 2006.

Kissinger, Henry. *On China.* Penguin Books, 2011.

Koesler, Arthur. *Darkness At Noon.* Scribner, 2006.

Koesler, Arthur, ed. *The God That Failed.* Columbia University Press, 2001.

Marcus, Harold. *A History of Ethiopia.* Berkley: UC Press, 2002.

Markakis, John & Nega Ayele. *Class and Revolution in Ethiopia.* Trenton, New Jersey: The Red Sea Press, 1986.

Moses, Wilson Jeremiah. *Black Messiahs and Uncle Toms: Social and Literary Manipulations of a Religious Myth.* Penn State University Press, 1993.

Nega, Berhanu. *Yenetsanet Goh Siked* (in Amharic). Kampala: M.M. Publishing, 2006.

SELECTED BIBIOGRAPHY

Ottaway, Marina & David. *Ethiopia: Empire in Revolution.* New York: African Publishing Co., 1978.

Sertsu, Berhanu. *Yederg Esir Betoch Tarik* (in Amharic).

Solomon, Beyene. *Fighter for Democracy: The Saga of an Ethiopian Labor Leader.* Baltimore: Publish America, 2010.

Tadesse, Kiflu. *The Generation, part i: The History of the Ethiopian People's Revolutionary Party.* Silver Spring: Independent Publishers, 1993; part ii. New York: University Press of America, 1998.

Tareke, Gebru. *The Ethiopian Revolution: War in the Horn of Africa.* New Haven: Yale University Press, 2009.

Teffera, Hiwot. *A Tower in the Sky.* Addis Abeba; Addis Abeba University Press, 2013.

Tola, Babile. *To Kill A Generation,* transl. by Tsegaye Gebremedhin, Free Ethiopia Press, 1997.

Vivo, Raul Valdez. *Ethiopia's Revolution.* New York: International Publishers, 1979.

Wolde, Ramsie, Siyum. *Kurifiya Yeshefenew Fegegita* (in Amharic). Addis Abeba: Artistic Printing Press, 2010.

Woldekirkos, Mersaehazen. *Tizitaye: Silerassie Yemastawusew* (in Amharic). Aster Nega Publishing, 2002.

Yimam, Ayalew. *Yankee Go Home!:The Life of An Ethiopian Revolutionary and the Fall of Assimba, EPRP's Red Base, 1969-1980.* Maryland: Signature Book Printing, 2011.

Young, John. *Peasant Revolution in Ethiopia: The TPLF, 1975-1991.* Cambridge University Press, 1997.

Zewde, Bahru. *Documenting the Ethiopian Student Movement: An Exercise In Oral History.* Addis Abeba. Addis Abeba University Press, 2010.

Articles, Videos & Websites

Admassu, Yonas. *What Were They Writing Anyway? Tradition and Modernity in Amharic Literature.* In Project Muse, Callaaloo, v.33#1, Winter 2010

Democracia, EPRP's publication, various issues.

Desse, Ayalew. *On Opposition Unity Formation.* With particular emphasis on COEDF and UEDF, and serialized at www.ethiomedia.com, 2010.

Ethiopian Ministry of Interior, Criminal Investigation Department (Forced Confessions): *Re: Tito Hiruy Tibebu et al, 1978*

Ethiopian Ministry of Interior, Criminal Investigation Department (Forced Confession): *Re: Ato Berhanemeskel Redda Wolde Rufael, 1979*

Fida, Haile. *Man and His Destiny.* UC Journal, Voices from the Past, AAUP, 2010.

International Crisis Group. *Eritrea: Scenarios for Future Transition,* March 2013.

Meison's Self-Criticism, July 1989.

Mekuria, Salem. *Deluge* (film video), 1997.

Redda, Berhanemeskel. *On the Mass Line, 1977*

——— *Gebre Aregawi's Hopes.* Something, Voices From the Past, AAUP, 2010.

Tareke Gebru. *The Red Terror in Ethiopia: An Historical Aberration?* www.ethiopiafirst.com, May 2004

Tekle, Amare. *A Response to Bahru Zewde, www.dehai.org/conflict/articles/bahru.html.*, January 22, 1999. Bahru's article appeared on the January 19, 1999 issue of the *Reporter*

Tegegne, Melaku. *EPRP: A Historical Background and a Critical Assessment of its Experience,* 1987.

Zega #7, Hamle/July 1995 edition.

Index

Aba Girmai, 102
Aba Takelle, 31
Ababiya Abajobir, 210
Abahoy, 136
Abate Kassa, 191
Abdalla Bahbari, 154
Abdi Abdulahi, xv
Abdissa Ayana, 139
Abdu, Captain, 34
Abduke Keffene, xi
Abdulmajid Hussein, 180
Abdul Mohammed, 49, 198
Abdulkadir Hirmooge, 216
Abdurahman Ahimed, 139
Abebe Beyene, 139, 140
Abebe Jember, 82, 83
Abebe Jemma, Lieutenant, 165

Abebe Worke, 177, 197
Abebech Bekele, xi, 77, 176, 178, 179, 180, 184, 185, 186, 187
Abebech (Mumina), 81
Abera (Key Zeb), 121
Abera Gemu, 181
Abera Wakjira, 163
Abera Yemane-ab, 48, 191, 196, 199
Aberash Berta/Maaza, 95, 115, 124, 125, 126, 136, 185
Abiyu Berle, 139, 169
Abiyu Ersamo, 164
Aboma Mitiku, 178
Abrham Engida, 203
Abrham Getu, 135
Abune Biru, xi, 203
Abyot, 8, 41, 159, 161, 228

EPRP

Adanech Nega, 184
Addis Alem, 168
Admassu Gebeyehu, 213, 214
Adolf Eichmann, 39
Adugna Mengistu, 79, 80, 81, 82, 139
Aelafseged Yohannes, King, 69
Afework Belay, 202
Afeworki Teklu, 51
Ahimed, xi, xii, 151
Aklilu Hiruy, 9
Aklilu Kebede, xi, 9
Aklog Nigatu, 2
Al Gemmer, Fitawrari, 114
Al Turk, 155
Alebachew, 77
Aleka Tesfai, 102
Alem Eshete, 107
Alemante Gebreselassie, 203, 204
Alemayehu Asfaw, Col., 14, 170
Alemayehu Deressa, 197, 198, 199
Alemayehu Egzeru, 6, 8
Alemayehu, 116, 141
Alemu Endale (Ermias), 202
Alemnesh, 185, 186
Alemtsehay Wodajo, 182

Ali Hussein, 63
Ali Mazrui, 59
Alula, 124
Aman Andom, Gen., 45
Amare Tekle, 52, 53
Amberbir, 125
Amha Abebe, Captain, 33
Amha Belete, 33, 122, 133, 152
Ammanuel, 8, 167
Amsale Tamrat, 182
Ana Gomes, 216
Andargatchew Assegid, 44, 46, 47, 52, 147
Andreas Eshete, 198
Andualem Mulaw, 209
Aregash Kidane, 188
Aregawi Berhe, 201
Arthur Koesler, 68
Asgedom, 81, 189
Askale Nega, 184
Asmamaw Hailu, xi, xv, 14, 49, 51, 168, 169, 184
Asmare, 104
Asnake Engida, Col., 209
Asrat, Maj. Gen., 108
Assefa Adefris, 190, 192
Assefa Chabo, 192, 194
Assefa Depaso, 209

INDEX

Assefa Dereso, 73
Assefa Endeshaw, 169
Assefa Mamo, 197
Assefa Negash, 203
Assefat Guba'e, 184, 185
Atnaf Yimam, 176, 182
Atnafu Abate, Col., 186
Aya Kurate, 150
Ayalew Kebede, 140
Ayalew Kibret, 164
Ayalew Mergia, 168
Ayalew Yimam, 168, 169
Ayalnesh, 122, 185
Ayalsew Desse, Lieutenant, 193, 199, 206, 209, 210, 213
Ayele Abaguade, Fitawrari, 94
Ayele Borejo/Gebreegzi, 14
Ayelech/Birkti, 125
Azeb Girma, 8, 178, 182

Bahru Zewde, 8, 42, 46, 49, 51, 52, 53, 170, 175, 176, 178, 230
Begashaw Atalay, Cap., 108
Beker, 30, 79, 80, 81, 100, 118, 121, 124, 125, 129, 130
Bekuretsion, 150
Belihu Wolde, Col., 165

Beljig Ali, xv
Bereket Habteselassie, 60
Bereket Simeon, 214
Berhane Andom, 181
Berhane Iyassu, 8, 33, 45, 173
Berhanemeskel Redda, viii, xviii, xxii, 28, 42, 45, 47, 49, 50, 62, 86, 140, 159, 160, 162, 166, 170, 173, 230
Berhaneselassie Assefa, 195, 203
Berhanu Abebe, 41
Berhanu Bayeh, 148
Berhanu Belay (Shaleka), xi
Berhanu Dibaba, 151
Berhanu Dinka, 148
Berhanu Dinke, 41
Berhanu Ejigu, 73
Berhanu Mulugeta, 37
Berhanu Nega, 14, 184, 212, 213
Berhanu Sertsu, xv
Berhanu Zerihun, 163
Berhe, 80, 100, 124
Berihun, Lt., 169
Bertukan Midekssa, 186
Beyene Gura'a, xi, 79, 131, 132, 133

Beyene Petros, 194, 195, 196, 197, 199, 200, 210, 214, 215

Beyene Solomon, 60, 62, 63, 181

Binyam Adane, 46, 139, 180

Binyam Bogale, 8

Bisrat, 95

CELU, xiii, 45, 59, 60, 61, 62, 63, 181

Chakle, 116, 141

Chanyalew Kassa, xv

Che Guevara, 70

Chekene Eshete, 204, 205

Cheru, 192

Christopher Clapham, 56, 57

Chuchuye, 6

COEDF, viii, xiii, 48, 96, 189, 191, 192, 193, 194, 195, 196, 197, 201, 206, 207, 210, 230

Critique-support, 44

Dagmawi Awoke, 207

Daniel Abebe, 202

Daniel Kiddu, 202

Daniel Kinde, 54

Daniel Tadesse, 43, 45

Daniel Tefera, 192

Daro Negash, 182

David Horowitz, 68

Dawit Assefa, 139

Dawit Siyum, 25

Dawit Tefera, 8

Dawit Yohannes, 198

Dawud Ibssa, 216

Demissie Hailemariam, 164

Democracia, 5, 8, 24, 32, 45, 65, 171, 230

Denbelo, 116, 141

Denekew, Captain, 207

Dereje, 122

Desta Damtew, 210

Desta Tadesse, 45

Dibekulu, 104

Dilay, 185

Dilu, 136, 208

Dirgue, xiii, xv, xvi, xvii, xxi, xxiii, 1, 2, 3, 4, 5, 6, 7, 9, 10, 11, 13, 15, 16, 17, 18, 19, 20, 21, 22, 23, 24, 26, 27, 28, 29, 30, 31, 32, 33, 34, 35, 36, 37, 38, 39, 40, 41, 45, 50, 52, 53, 54, 56, 57, 58, 62, 63, 65, 71, 77, 78, 79, 80, 81, 91, 94, 98, 99, 100, 101, 102, 103, 104, 105, 106, 107, 108, 109, 113, 114, 115, 116, 117, 126, 130, 131, 133, 139, 140, 145, 148, 149,

152, 153, 159, 160, 161, 162, 163, 164, 165, 166, 167, 172, 181, 182, 183, 186, 187, 193, 197, 207, 208, 224

Edmund Keller, 56

EDU, viii, xiii, 12, 15, 58, 82, 102, 103, 104, 107, 108, 161, 190, 191, 192, 206, 210

Edward Bernstein, 66

Efrem Dagne, 46

Efrem Yishaq, 190

Ejigayehu Debela, 6, 7

Ejigayehu Taye, 187

Eletai, 185

ELF, xiii, xxi, 13, 14, 15, 16, 17, 33, 46, 48, 49, 51, 52, 79, 153, 161, 169, 190

Elias, Abun, 211

Elizabeth Demissie, 187

Emaledh, 39

Endalkachew Yirgu (Chiqi), 202

EPLF, xiv, xvi, xxi, 13, 24, 26, 49, 50, 51, 52, 53, 56, 57, 95, 114, 120, 131, 145, 150, 153, 172, 184, 189, 190, 193

EPLO, xiv, 44, 46, 47, 49, 51, 68

EPRA, vii, viii, xi, xiv, xv, 2, 4, 11, 12, 13, 14, 15, 16, 17, 18, 19, 20, 21, 25, 26, 28, 29, 30, 31, 34, 49, 51, 77, 79, 80, 81, 82, 83, 84, 88, 89, 91, 93, 94, 95, 96, 101, 102, 103, 104, 105, 106, 107, 108, 109, 113, 114, 115, 116, 117, 118, 119, 120, 121, 122, 123, 124, 125, 126, 127, 129, 130, 132, 134, 135, 139, 140, 141, 142, 143, 144, 148, 152, 153, 167, 168, 169, 170, 171, 172, 180, 184, 185, 189, 203, 204, 206, 209, 228

EPRDF, xiv, 31, 42, 48, 53, 106, 108, 115, 135, 187, 190, 193, 194, 195, 196, 198, 200, 212, 214, 215, 216, 217, 218

EPRP, vii, viii, ix, xi, xiii, xiv, xv, xvi, xvii, xviii, xix, xxi, xxii, xxiii, 1, 2, 3, 4, 5, 6, 7, 8, 9, 11, 12, 13, 15, 16, 17, 18, 19, 21, 22, 23, 24, 25, 26, 27, 31, 32, 33, 34, 35, 36, 37, 38, 39, 40, 42, 43, 44, 45, 46, 47, 48, 49, 50, 51, 52, 54, 55, 56, 57, 58, 59, 62, 63, 64, 65, 68, 69, 71, 77, 78, 79, 82, 83, 85, 87, 89, 90, 91, 92, 93, 95, 96, 97, 98, 99, 101, 102, 103, 104, 106, 107, 111, 113, 114, 115, 116, 118, 120, 122, 126, 127, 129, 130, 131, 133, 134, 135, 139, 140, 145, 147, 148, 149, 150, 151, 152, 153, 154, 155, 157, 158, 159, 160, 161, 162, 163, 164, 165, 166, 167, 168, 169, 170, 172, 173, 176, 177, 181, 182, 183, 186, 188, 189,

190, 191, 192, 194, 195, 201,
202, 204, 206, 207, 208, 209,
210, 212, 217, 218, 219, 220,
229, 230

1st Congress, 8, 13, 149, 163

2nd Congress, viii, 95, 96,
100, 161, 198, 205

3rd Congress, 54

4th Congress, 23

5th Congress, 219

Esatu Tessema, 6

Eshetu Ararso, 45

Eskinder/Girmai, 8, 139

ESUE, xiv, xvii, 40, 41, 47, 48

ESUNA, xiv, xvii, 40, 41, 47, 48,
50, 71, 168, 178, 179

Faisel, 207

Fassika Belete, xii, 48, 83, 96,
129, 209, 210, 212

Ferdinand Markos, 224

Fikre Merid, 36

Fikreselassie Wogderess, 36

Fikrte Gebremariam, 6, 176,
179, 182, 185

Finote Democracy Radio, 100

Fisseha Desta, Col., 182

Fisseha Gebremariam, 151

Fisseha Manjus, 185

Fissehatsion Menghistu, 192

Fisuh Gebrai, 20

Fred Halliday, 66

Friedrich Engels, 66

GA, 95

Galfato Feqa, 216

Gashaw (Gurezaw), 120, 142

Gashaw Mengistu, 140

Gayyim, viii, 30, 50, 77, 78, 79,
93, 96, 100, 121, 124, 125,
129, 130, 134, 135, 136, 198

Gazu, 25

GB, 148

Gebeyehu Dagnew, 10

Gebreegziabher Hagos, 8

Gebrehiwot, 123, 144

Gebremichael, 125, 126

Gebrehiwot Gebregziabher,
Lieutenant, 19

Gebrekristos Desta, 7

Gebremeskel Azbtie, Brig. Gen.,
109

Gebremeskel, 141

Gebru Asrat, 133

Gebru Gebrewold, 203

Gebru Tareke, 38, 39, 182, 190

INDEX

Geleb Dafla, 14, 30, 95, 96, 100, 122, 170

George H. Bush, 131

Genenew Assefa, 43, 195, 197, 199

Genet Girma, 95, 176, 186, 189, 195, 197, 199, 205

Genet Tarekegne, xi

Genet Zewde, 176, 179, 198

Gerawork Gebreegziabher, 6, 182

Getachew Assefa, 197, 199

Getachew Begashaw, 178, 202, 203

Getachew Haile, 203

Getachew Maru, 3, 8, 28, 43, 159, 161, 163

Getachew Metaferia, 192

Getachew Midekssa, 152

Getachew Shibeshi, 34

Getachew Yerom, Maj., 209

Getahun Sisay, 168

Getahun Tessema, 61, 63

Gete, Corp., 131

Getnet, 13, 20

Gezahegne, 8, 10

Gezahegne Sime, 2

Ghelawdewos Araya, xi, 152, 159

Gideon Woldeammanuel, 8

Gigar, 81

Girma Woldegiorgis, Ex-President, 198

Girmachew Lemma, 33, 45, 63, 177

Girmay Abrha, xv, 139

Gomoraw (Hailu Gebreyohannes), 177, 189

Gondarit, 2

Goshu Wolde, Col., 192, 194

Grum, 170

GT, 23, 29, 39, 184

Gugsa, 81

Gurmu, 50

Habteselassie, 10

Habtegiorgis Churnet, 203

Habtom, 168

Haddis Bitew, 171

Hadish Beyene, 83

Hagos Gebreeyesus, 41

Haile Abay, 100, 113, 118, 124, 170

Haileeyesus Woldesenbet, 139, 140

Haile Fida, xviii, 42, 44, 45, 167

Haile Gebreselassie, 151

Hailemariam, 54, 101, 104, 148, 159, 161, 164, 167, 186, 207, 228

Hailu Gerbaba, 45, 151

Hailu Shawul, 213

Hailu Woldegiorgis, 140

Haimanot Lakew, 195

Hamrawit Tesfa, 220

Hannah Arendt, 39

Hanna Gobeze, 176

Hareka Hareyo, xv

Harold G. Marcus, 58

Harry Johnston, 192, 200

Hibret radio, 118

Hirut Abebe, 187

Hiruy, 7, 77, 230

Hiwot Teffera, xv, xxii, 9, 23, 27, 159, 178, 182

Humphrey Bogart, 70

Ibssa Gutema, 177

Imiru Haileselassie, Leul Ras, 63

Indrias, 170

Isayas Afeworki, 50

Ishmael, 150

Iyassu Alemayehu, 3, 23, 30, 78, 81, 83, 107, 152, 203, 204, 206

Iyassu Ayalkbet, Major, 210

Iyassu Mengesha, Gen., 62

Jabbir, 79, 96, 100, 125, 129, 135

Jamilla, 17, 185

Jemal, 141

Joe Slovo, 68

John Markakis, 57, 58

John Stuart Mill, 66

John W. Harbeson, 58

John Young, 16, 55

Jonathan Dimbleby, 180

Josef Stalin, 67, 70

Kahsay, 95, 189, 190, 205

Kahsay Abrha, xv, 20

Kalifah Kerar, Gen., 152

Karl Marx, 66

Kassahun Bisrat, 73, 190

Kebede Gebrai, 197

Kebede Mengesha, 44, 45

Kebede Tessema, Dejach, 62

Kedir Mohammed, 45, 151, 209, 210

Kelbesa Negewo, 187

Kibebe, 73

Kibrom Dafla, 95

INDEX

Kidane, Maj., 82

Kifle Ergetu, Dej., 62

Kifle Tigneh, 201

Kifle Wodajo, 198

Kiflu Tadesse, xi, xv, xxi, 1, 17, 22, 40, 44, 45, 46, 47, 49, 50, 51, 63, 147, 149, 159, 163, 164, 170, 171, 177, 183, 203

Kiflu Tefera, 3, 27, 45, 160

Kinfe Adefrsew, xi

Kinfe Gebremedhin, 197

Kjetil Tronvoll, 57

Konjit Berhan, xv

Lemma Siyum, 63

Lencho Letta, 199

Leszek Kolawokski, 68

Lidetu Ayalew, 213

Mahmood Mahfuz, 136

Mamo Muche, 203

Mamo Yihune, 201

Maoism, 55, 70, 96, 147

Marina & David Ottaway, 57

Markos Hagos, 6, 45, 181

Marta Mengistu, xii

Martha Mebrhatu, 176, 178, 179

Masresha, 185

Matewos, 96, 124, 125

Mebrat Haile, 19

Mekonnen Araya, xv, 88, 90, 91

Mekonnen Bayissa, 151

Mekonnen Belay, 74

Mekonnen Bishaw, 177, 213

Mekuanint Ejigu, 73

Melaku Markos, 58

Melaku Tefera, 19

Melaku Tegegne, 43, 47, 71, 96, 170, 177

Meles Ayalew, 41

Meles Tekle, 178

Meles Zenawi, 105, 148, 214

Melikte Yohannes, 165

Mengesha Siyum, Ras, 191, 192

Mengiste Defar, 165

Mengistu Hailemariam, 34, 38, 55, 64, 108, 145, 148, 160, 161, 166, 182, 186

Merera Gudina, 210, 214

Merid, Leftenant, 33

Meritsa, 185

Meron Assefa, 8, 9

Mersaehazen Woldekirkos, Blatta, 69

Mersha, xi, 30, 48, 77, 78, 79, 80, 81, 83, 94, 95, 96, 107, 129, 135, 148, 152, 189, 191, 195, 196, 197, 203, 205, 206, 209, 212

Mesfin Gelaneh, 73

Mesfin Medhine, xii

Mesfin Shiferaw, 160

Mesfin Tefera, xi, 118, 195, 196, 197, 200

Mesfin Woldemariam, 60, 213

Meskerem (Chakaw), 8, 104, 124, 125, 216

Meskerem Atalay, 216

Messay Kebede, 59, 71

Messelu, 141

Mewail Mebrhatu, 61

Mezgebnesh Abayu, 176, 182, 183, 185, 186

Michael Imiru, Lij, 211

Michael Gorbachev, 72, 97

Michael Teferi, 6

Minga Negash, 204

MM, 2

Mogus Woldemichael, 148, 164

Mohammed Ahimed Jemil, xi, xii, 96, 107, 129, 135, 151, 206

Mohammed Ali, Lt., 2

Mohammed and Ahimed, 151

Muhidin Mohammed, 2

Mulu Hadera, 6, 182, 185

Mulu Mejja, 198, 214

Mulualem Wassihun, 170

Mulugeta, 126

Mulugeta Alemu, 202

Mulugeta Hailu, 196, 209

Mulugeta Kebede, 151

Mulugeta Siyum, 196, 203

Muluken Muche, 195

Nash, 181

Nebiyu Aynalem, 160

Nega Ayele, 57, 58, 229

Negash Hailemariam, Maj., 207

Negede Gobeze, 148, 179, 196, 201

Netsanet Mengistu, 151, 176

Ngugi, 110

Nigist Adane, 45, 48, 176, 179, 182, 184

Nigist Tefera, 176, 182, 183

Nigusse, xi

Nigusse Tadesse, 7

Nimieri, 155

Nishan, 9

NM, 14

INDEX

Nolawi Abebe, 74

Olana Lemu, 212

OLF, xiv, xxi, 56, 65, 121, 153, 190, 194, 196, 199, 201, 207, 210, 211, 216, 217

Omar Tayyib, 155

Original Woldegiorgis, 175

Othman Saleh Sabeh, 48

Oumer, 81, 96

Paul Henze, 55

Paulos, 150

Paulos Milkias, 203

POMOA, xiv, 2, 18, 19, 26, 32, 34, 56, 148, 164

PPG, 44

Rahel, 9

Ramadan Mohammed Nur, 51

Randi Balsivik, 63, 71, 177

Raul Valdes Vivo, 54

Rectification Movement, 160, 165, 168, 170

Red Terror, xv, xvii, xxii, 3, 6, 21, 32, 36, 38, 39, 45, 48, 55, 56, 57, 151, 183, 184, 187, 227, 230

Reda'e, 20

Rick Mechar, 206

Roba, 25, 50, 78

Rosa Luxemburg, 67

Saba Kidanemariam, 8

Salem Mekuria, 48

Samuel Alemayehu, 1, 27, 30, 63, 78, 83, 95, 127, 130, 135, 180

Seamus Heaney, 225

Seifu Zewde, Lij., 192

Selamawit Dawit, 6, 167, 176, 182, 184

Semere-Ab, 139

Senay Likke, 41, 47, 148

Shumet Sishagne, 73, 203, 204

Siber, 80

Sileshi Belachew, 61

Simegne Lemma, 9

Sintayehu Gedda, 61

Sirak Tefera, 9

Sitotaw Hussein, 115, 122, 133

Siye Abrha, 133

Siyum Kebede, 139

Siyum Mesfin, 153

Siyum Wolde, 160, 180

Siyum Zenebe, 197

Solomon Gashaw, 203, 204

Solomon Workneh, xi, 151

TA, 22, 29, 148, 150

Tadelech Hailemichael, 166, 180

Tadelech Kidanemariam, 176, 178

Tadelle, 6, 23, 77, 122, 133

Tadesse Eba, 153

Taemeselassie Beyene, 51

Tafa Daba, Lt., 2

Tafere Abera, xi

Tafesse Woubshet, 202

Tahrir Guba, 126

Takelle Tsega, xii

Tamene Galore, Lt., 2

Tamrat, 207

Tamiru Feyissa, 177

Tariku Debretsion, xi, 151

Tariq Aziz, 50

Tasew Desta, Commander, 191

Taye Tilahun, Gen., 192

Taye Tola, 20

Taye Woldesemayat, 197

Tedla Samuel, Shambelbasha, 131

Tefera Deguefe, 11

Teferi Berhane, 139, 172

Tegegne Aboye, 212

Teka Tulu, Col., 34, 35

Terefe Woldetsdaik, 45

Tesfatsion Medhane, 54

Tesfaye Debessay, xviii, 3, 24, 26, 33, 44, 45, 50, 140, 163, 164, 170, 172, 220

Tesfaye, 136

Tesfaye Demmelash, 71

Tesfaye Eju, 129

Tesfaye Gebrekidan, 148

Tesfaye Habtemariam, Gen., 41

Tesfaye Mekonnen, xxi, 139, 140

Tesfaye Riste, xxii

Tesfaye Tadesse, 36, 151

Tesfu Kidane, 51

Teshome Gebremariam, 197

Teshome Tsegaye, 209

Tessema Deressa, 181

Tewodros (Atsie), 101, 110, 157, 208

Theodore Vestal, 203

Thomas Eskinder, 8

Thomas Jefferson, 157

Tilahun Gizaw, 42, 63, 151, 177

Tilahun Takelle, 41, 47, 62

Tirefi, Gen., 153, 154

INDEX

Tirsit/Konjit Teklu, 115, 184, 185

Tiruneh, 95

Tiruwork Waqeyo, 184

Tito Hiruy, 7, 8, 9, 10, 11, 230

Tohat Paul, 209

Tolossa, 150

TPLF, vii, viii, xiv, xvi, xvii, xxi, xxiii, 11, 12, 13, 14, 15, 16, 17, 18, 19, 20, 21, 22, 28, 29, 30, 31, 42, 49, 51, 53, 55, 65, 71, 78, 79, 80, 81, 83, 88, 91, 95, 96, 98, 100, 105, 106, 113, 114, 115, 116, 117, 118, 119, 120, 121, 122, 123, 124, 125, 126, 127, 128, 129, 130, 131, 132, 133, 134, 135, 136, 141, 142, 143, 144, 145, 150, 152, 153, 154, 155, 168, 169, 170, 184, 186, 187, 189, 190, 191, 192, 193, 194, 195, 197, 198, 201, 204, 206, 208, 209, 214, 217, 218, 229

Tsegaye Debteraw, 23, 30, 50, 77, 78, 83, 122, 133, 136, 173, 204, 209, 211, 229

Tsegaye Gebremedhin, 211

Tsegaye Tegenu, 204

Tsehay Birhanesellasie, 192, 203

Tsehay Solomon, 184

Tsehay Yeshitila, 176, 179

Tsehaye (MGE), xi, 23, 50, 53, 77, 78, 139

Tselote Hizkyas, 24, 163

Tsigereda Tadelle, 7

UF, xiv, 65, 161, 190, 191

USUAA, 23, 40, 42, 60, 61, 63, 169, 176, 177, 178

V.I. Lenin, 71

Wagshum Newete, 82

Waleligne Mekonnen, 177

Wassihun, 130

Whittaker Chambers, 68

William Hastings Morton, 58

Wilson Moses, 65

Woldeleul Kassa (Kesete), 169

Wondayehu Kassa, 213

Wondwossen, 2

Worku, 151

Wosenyelesh Debela, xi, 6, 7

Woubshet Retta, 172

WWESF, xiv, 151

Yacob Hailemariam, 53, 190

Ya'ebiyo, 20

Yemane, 25

Yemane Jamaica, 153
Yeshi, 181
Yeshi Mihretu, 179
Yeshi Wondimeneh, 190
Yewubmar Asfaw, 187, 227
Yifru, 8
Yilkal, 150
Yilma Kebede, 177
Yirga Tessema, 151, 170
Yishaq Debretsion (Abebe Bariaw), 30, 115, 122, 133
Yishaq Teshome, 8
Yoftahe Nigusse, 26
Yohannes (Atse), 69, 157
Yohannes Admassu, 177
Yohannes Berhane, 3, 5, 8, 45, 58, 73, 177
Yohannes Kassahun, 151
Yohannes Kifle, 151
Yohannes Sibhatu, 51
Yonas Admassu, 42, 77, 175

Yosef Adane, 3, 33, 163
Yosef Asferi, xii
Yosef Tesfaye, 198
Yosef Yazew, Maj., 216

ZB, 161
Zekaryas Mohammed, 139
Zeleke Alemu, xii
Zeleke Jember, 83
Zemecha, 45
Zemete Beyene, 103
Zenebe Feleke, 108
Zenebework Tadesse, 176, 179
Zer'abruk Abebe, 139, 172
Zergaw, 104
Zer'u Khishen, 3, 22, 24, 33, 149, 162, 163, 170
Zewalle Zegeye, 19
Zewdu Desta, 6
Zewdu Hailu, 176
Zewdu Mersha, 202